BROWNING AND THE TWENTIETH CENTURY

BROWNING AND THE TWENTIETH CENTURY

A STUDY OF ROBERT BROWNING'S
INFLUENCE AND REPUTATION

By A. ALLEN BROCKINGTON

New York
RUSSELL & RUSSELL
1963

FIRST PUBLISHED IN 1932
REISSUED, 1963, BY RUSSELL & RUSSELL, INC.
L. C. CATALOG CARD NO: 63—14501

PRINTED IN THE UNITED STATES OF AMERICA

To
H. V. ROUTH

PREFACE

THIS book was written at the suggestion of Dr. H. V. Routh, the University Reader in English Language and Literature, London. It was written to be submitted as a thesis for a doctor's degree of London University.

The suggestion was made because I have been a student and lover of Browning since I was a boy, and because I have also paid attention, in my capacity as lecturer, to the poets of a later time, and because, in another capacity, I have produced poems myself. I ought to know more than I do about poets and poetry. I have forgotten much through the tiresome effects of the War. Nevertheless, though the work of writing this book has been laborious, it has also been enjoyable and even exciting. Critics have often remarked on the influence of Browning; I have attempted to trace his influence in some detail. Every step I have taken is challengeable, but I have taken it in the hope that I was nearing the goal of truth. If I have failed, I can still say that I have made some fresh remarks about Browning and that to some readers my book may serve as an introduction to modern poetry.

There are two chapters definitely concerned with Browning's reputation. The bibliographical note—which, by the way, *is* a note and not a complete bibliography—also shows that Browning has not perished. I am not able to judge of his reputation in America, but I have gathered hints that indicate a greater esteem in that country than in ours.

I have to thank Mr. John Murray for permission to

use his copyright edition for all my quotations from Browning's poetry, as well as for permission to quote from the *Letters of Robert Browning and Elizabeth Barrett Barrett, 1845–6*, and from Mrs. Browning's *Letters to her Sister, 1846–59*.

I beg to acknowledge with thanks a grant made by the Senate of the University of London towards the publication of this book.

I have been helped and encouraged by my friend, the Rev. Dr. M. W. Myres, who has added to his other kindnesses by reading the proof-sheets. Mr. Fredk. Page has exercised his ripe scholarship and indefatigable care on my behalf in seeing this book through the Press.

I am also indebted to the officials of the British Museum Reading Room, the University Library of Cambridge, the Library of the Department of Education of Liverpool University, the Athenaeum, Picton and Hornby Libraries of Liverpool, and, especially, to Mr. R. Paden, the Hornby Librarian.

A. A. B.

CONTENTS

	Page
I. SOME NOTES ON BROWNING AND HIS ART	1
II. COMMON HUMANITY IN BROWNING AND SOME TWENTIETH-CENTURY POETS	35
III. THE REALISTIC MANNER OF BROWNING AND OF TWENTIETH-CENTURY POETS	75
IV. BROWNING THE PSYCHOLOGIST AND HIS INVENTION OF THE DRAMATIC LYRIC	111
V. THE CONVERSATIONAL METHOD IN THE TWENTIETH CENTURY	134
VI. BROWNING'S OPTIMISM	169
VII. OPTIMISM AND REACTION AGAINST OPTIMISM IN THE TWENTIETH CENTURY	197
VIII. BROWNING'S REPUTATION AS A LOVER	228
IX. BROWNING'S REPUTATION AS A MYSTIC	253
BIBLIOGRAPHICAL NOTE OF BROWNING LITERATURE IN THE TWENTIETH CENTURY	279
INDEX	287

1
SOME NOTES ON BROWNING AND HIS ART

INFLUENCE is not easy to trace. Events that loom large in a life may produce little reaction. A sunset touch, a fancy from a flower-bell, a chorus-ending from Euripides, or a single line from Browning may be more decisive than some one's death. Effects, also, may be long delayed. There cannot be effects without causes, but the train of causation may be so hidden, so impalpable, that the effect when it comes seems catastrophic. I am concerned in this study with the influence and reputation of Robert Browning the poet. Reputation is some guide to influence. But it is not by any means an infallible guide, even in the case of a soldier. The well-known commander's battles may be planned by a chief of staff who is comparatively unknown. The little poor man may save the city.

In the case of a writer one would be inclined to say that his writings must be read, for him to exercise any influence. But he may be well-reputed without being read. He may become a legend, like 'G.B.S.' Or he may exercise an influence through his life. Dr. Samuel Johnson is chiefly influential through James Boswell's *Life of Samuel Johnson*. His spontaneous talk, which the devoted and industrious Boswell recorded, and his letters, which Boswell collected, have produced a greater effect than all his works. Conversation is a chief part of life, and letters are a kind of conversation. If some contemporary Boswell had written a 'Life of William Shakespeare', recording his talk and giving selections from his letters, it is possible that it would have produced a greater effect than his plays. In Shakespeare's case, however, his poetry is his influence. And the influence continues and enlarges and penetrates in an incalculable manner. Men use his words and are most subtly influenced by his ideas without recognizing their source. It is altogether probable, too, that the poetry of Shakespeare has not yet attained its real effect, and the real effect may be delayed for many generations.

Another poet whose effect is almost wholly in his poetry is William Blake. His wide influence has been long delayed. He died in 1827, and it was not until a century later that part of his long poem, *Milton*, became a second English national anthem. But to how many of those who sing the anthem is Blake anything more than a name, even if they know it? And is there one in ten thousand who has read *Milton*? Perhaps the influence of the poem may be attributed to the fact that it was as spontaneous as talk and written down without premeditation or immediate labour of mind.

There is a curious parallel to the influence of Boswell's *Life of Samuel Johnson* just now making itself evident in the case of Robert Browning. His love-story, as recorded in letters, is being popularized. The central theme of *The Brownings*[1] (1928) and of *Andromeda in Wimpole Street*[2] (1929) is the courtship of Robert Browning and Elizabeth, *née* Moulton Barrett. This love-story[3] has already exercised some influence, but now the influence is become wide, and may eventually prove to be wider

[1] *The Brownings*, by Osbert Burdett (Constable).
[2] *Andromeda in Wimpole Street*, by Miss Dormer Creston (Thornton Butterworth).
[3] For further discussion see Chapter VIII: 'Browning's Reputation as a Lover.'

as well as deeper than that of Browning's poetical writings.

I wish to confine myself mainly in this study to the more or less calculable influence of the poetry of Browning upon the writing of succeeding poets. Yet I would crave to be allowed to glance at decisions in his life which have produced effects not calculable at all, or of which the effect may be long delayed. I remember predicting to Cecil Sharp, when a folk-song he had just collected reminded us both of a poem of Browning's, that the love-story of the Brownings would eventually endear the two poets to hundreds of people who did not read their poems. That prediction seems to be in course of fulfilment.

But, first, I must try to express my conception of the *essential* Browning, and, in so doing, to indicate all those aspects of my subject that I wish to discuss in the subsequent chapters.

I

I hesitate to state my chief conviction about Robert Browning, because it seems to conflict with the usual estimate of the poet and his work. I borrow the necessary words from Count Hermann Keyserling's description of the English: 'It is not intelligence but instinct—rising at the highest to intuition—which determines the course of their lives.' [1]

In the spring of 1829 Robert Browning announced to his father his intention to become a poet.[2] He said that

---

[1] *Europe*, by Hermann Keyserling, p. 19. I avoid the word 'mystic' for the present. I intend to come to grips later on with the subject of mysticism, with a view to establishing Browning's reputation as a mystic (see Chapter IX).

[2] *Life of Robert Browning*, by W. Hall Griffin and H. C. Minchin, p. 54.

he wished to see life in its best sense and to cultivate the powers of his mind rather than shackle himself in the very outset of his career by a laborious training foreign to that aim. Five years before, he had produced a volume of poems called *Incondita*, for which his father had made serious efforts to find a publisher. He had come under the influence of Byron, and then, more completely and enthusiastically, under the influence of Shelley. He was writing 'merely musically', when *Queen Mab* supplied him with a 'key to a new world'. On his sixteenth birthday (May 7th, 1828) his mother made him a present of Shelley's poems and henceforth he was 'vowed to liberty'. His father was one of the first subscribers to the new University of London in Gower Street. He paid for five sessions for Robert, but in his new-found freedom the aspiring disciple of Shelley declined to attend classes in the course of his second term, and made his momentous appeal to his father before the academical year ended.

One may imagine the reception of such an appeal by a 'sensible' father. He has paid for five sessions at the University. The boy is just beginning his real education. If this training at the University is foreign to that aim of becoming a poet, what is the training cognate to it? And can he by becoming a poet make a living? Is it a career at all? Seeing life? Who is to pay for this seeing of life? And how is he going to see it? And what does he mean by cultivating the powers of his mind? Has not the University been founded for just that cultivation? A boy of seventeen comes in, say, from a walk in Dulwich Wood and throws up his college course and announces that he is not going to learn anything in the ordinary way—'shackling himself', he calls it—but to train himself for the career of a poet in his own way, his own self-appointed, intuitively determined way. It was as if he had said: 'I walked in the wood, and I heard a voice telling me to be a poet. Please set me free to obey the voice.'

The boy was father to the man. At the age of thirty-three he found 'a bird in a cage'.[1] The cage was the house of her father, who would not let his bird out. The father counted the bird as his very own, and had therefore decided that she was not fit to be let out, and as for mating. . . .! So Robert Browning opened the cage. Another voice: 'Take the bird out.' Really, this was a more rash adventure than the other. If becoming a poet meant disaster, the disaster happened to himself, but by marrying and eloping with Elizabeth Barrett he ran the imminent risk of causing her death.

When he had read through the letters that passed between Robert Browning and Elizabeth Barrett (January 1845 to September 1846), George Meredith wrote to a friend:[2] 'I return the second volume of the antecedent Browning letters. They were a noble couple. Of him it will be remembered that he gave a woman fifteen years of unanticipated happy life with womanhood and maternity —plucked her from the graveside to do that. In truth, a miracle surpassing all previous tales and all fiction of the power of love.' But when Browning set out on September 19th, 1846 (he had been married on September 12th), he could have had no reasoned hope that any years of happy life would follow. The events reinforced his decision. That is what happens with intuitive

[1] This is Elizabeth Barrett's description of herself. Osbert Burdett uses the phrase as the title of the first chapter of *The Brownings*.
[2] Quoted from a correspondent to *The Times*, Feb. 11th, 1928, 12d.

persons: they decide on impulse and wait for events to justify the decision.

Turn from these crucial determinations to the subjects of his two greatest poems—*Pippa Passes* and *The Ring and the Book*.[1]

[1] As showing the recent interest in these poems one may notice that separate editions, with accompanying essays, of *Pippa Passes* were issued: by Arthur Symons in 1906, by J. Kasprowicz in 1910, by A. L. Irvine in 1924, and Edward A. Parker in 1927; and editions without essays: in 1905 (Broadway Booklets), in 1912 (Arden Books), in 1913 (King's Treasury Series), and in 1924 (Holerth Library); while between 1909 and 1924 there were at least six separate essays in book form on *The Ring and the Book*: by F. B. Hornbrooke in 1909, by C. W. Hodell in 1911, by N. Bogholm in 1918, by A. K. Cook in 1920, by Alexander Haddon (as a connected narrative) in 1924, and a paraphrase published by Blackwell in 1924.

In the theatrical season of 1926–7 Walter Hampden produced at his theatre in New York a dramatic version of *The Ring and the Book* called *Caponsacchi*. The play was published in 1928 by D. Appleton as *Caponsacchi, A Play in Three Acts, Prologue and Epilogue, based upon Robert Browning's poem, The Ring and the Book, with a foreword by William Lyon Phelps and an afterword by Clayton Hamilton*. Mr. Phelps writes: 'I regard this play as the chief event of the dramatic season in New York, and it is my hope that it will become a permanent feature on the American stage.' Mr. Phelps quotes one of the 'motion picture magnates' as saying: 'Robert Browning is the greatest writer for the movies who ever lived.' As a matter of fact, *The Ring and the Book* has been put on the screen, but, according to Mr. Phelps, who had the misfortune to see the motion picture version, the result was crude caricature.

Mr. Goodrich's play—Miss Rose Palmer is named as joint author with Arthur Goodrich, because she suggested the idea of making Caponsacchi the central figure of a stage-play—is far from being crude caricature. No play is for the study only. This play, therefore, ought to be seen. But judging by the book, the student of Browning will be disappointed. I can imagine that the poet himself would not choose to be popularized at such a price. His own words are occasionally used. They are torn from their context. Mr. Goodrich's verses are supposed by Mr. Hamilton to be indistinguishable from Browning's. The English poet wrote many bad verses, but in his worst hour he could not have been guilty of any of Mr. Goodrich's 'poetry'. Mr. Goodrich seems to think that because Browning is often rough and difficult he can be reproduced 'indistinguishably' by missing out words from commonplace sentences and forcing all

Mrs. Sutherland Orr in her *Handbook to the Works of Robert Browning* gives an account of the origin of *Pippa Passes*. One wishes one had Browning's own words. But in default of them Mrs. Orr is a good authority. She knew Browning so well that, in 1883, George Smith, the publisher, and Mrs. Procter (wife of 'Barry Cornwall') declared that there was 'something tender' between Mrs. Orr and Browning, and Thomas Hardy recorded in his diary Mrs. Procter's impatient remark: 'Why don't they settle it?' Mrs. Orr says: 'Browning was taking one of his solitary walks in Dulwich Wood when the image flashed upon him of one walking thus alone through life; one apparently too obscure to leave a trace of his or her passage, yet exercising a lasting though unconscious influence at every step of it; and the image shaped itself into the little silk-winder of Asolo, Felippa or Pippa.'

The opening of *Pippa Passes* reflects its origin. It comes upon us like a sudden burst of sunshine. It has

the characters to split their infinitives. He has not perceived that Browning is a dramatic writer. The idiom of *Giuseppe Caponsacchi*, of *Pompilia*, of *The Pope* is Browning's idiom. One is able to recognize the poetry of all these three poems as Browning's poetry. But the mode of speech of each of the characters is, nevertheless, congruous to the speaker. It may be said that Pompilia could not have spoken as Browning makes her speak. No one speaks in blank verse except by accident. Granted the accident, and granted the situation, and granted the fact that the writer is Browning—and all these things must in the nature of the case be granted—not only her thoughts but the mode of expressing her thoughts may be said to reveal Pompilia. And *Giuseppe Caponsacchi* reveals Caponsacchi and *The Pope* the Pope. In Mr. Goodrich's play all the characters speak garbled Browningesque without distinction of persons.

Another play on *The Ring and the Book*, called *Pompilia*, was issued by David Graham in 1928. In addition, one ought to name the essay and notes on *The Old Yellow Book* by C. W. Hodell in 1908 and Sir Frederick Treves's fascinating volume, *The Country of The 'Ring and the Book'*, in 1913, of which a cheap edition has lately been published.

the rapture of a new dawn. Something fresh and
original has happened to the poet's mind. He has seen
the light; and we recognize the sublime quality of high
instinctive poetry.

Pippa Passes contains the 'suggestions of experience
wrought up into new combinations'. He embodies in
the poem the impressions of his visit to Italy. He had
both seen and listened to the girls talking on the steps
of the Duomo; he had marked a man and a woman who
had afterwards stood for Sebald and Ottima; a Luigi
came into his mind when he wanted him; the Bishop
and the Intendant were public characters.

Browning tells us himself [1] that on a fierce windy June
day (in 1860) he was walking in the streets of Florence
when a 'Hand, always above his shoulder,' pushed him
to an open-air stall on the steps of the Riccardi Palace,
where he saw exposed for sale six books, of which one
was an old volume bound in yellow vellum—part print,
part manuscript. This he bought for a lira. On the
fly-leaf of it he wrote long afterwards: 'But for me the
Muse in her strength prepares her mightiest arrow.' [2]

The resultant poem was *The Ring and the Book*. Here
again we have the suggestions of experience. Browning
perceived in *The Old Yellow Book* a vehicle for the disclosure of his own most intimate history. Just as he had
snatched the bird from the cage, so Caponsacchi
snatched Pompilia from her living death at Arezzo.
And what Caponsacchi says of Pompilia is a reflexion
of what Browning thought of his wife, Elizabeth. And

[1] *The Ring and the Book:* 'The Ring and the Book', ll. 33 ff. Browning's
description of the market wares is a marvel of observation. His mind
was evidently keyed up to a pitch of extreme sensitiveness so that he
noticed everything. See Chapter IX: 'Browning's Reputation as a
Mystic'.   [2] ἐμοὶ μὲν ὦν Μοῖσα καρτερώτατον Βέλος ἀλκᾷ τρέφει.

what Pompilia said of Caponsacchi is a reflexion—almost a recollection—of what Elizabeth had actually said of her lover. It is interesting to compare Pompilia's praise of Caponsacchi in the poem that bears her name with *The Sonnets from the Portuguese*, Elizabeth Barrett Browning's most intense and enduring work. One can perceive that Browning could hardly have written *Pompilia* without the intimate outpourings of his wife's love for him.[1]

An earlier poem already alluded to, *The Flight of the Duchess*, originated in a curiously similar way to *The Ring and the Book*. We are told that Browning as a boy heard a woman singing in the street and was haunted by the refrain of the song: 'Following the Queen of the Gipsies, O!' and long afterwards fashioned his poem out of this refrain. I think it likely that he heard the whole song. I heard a woman sing it in a cottage of Combe Florey village in Somerset.

> There were three gipsies a-came to my door,
>   And downstairs ran this a lady, O!
> One sang high and another sang low,
>   And the other sang bonny bonny Biscay, O!
>
> Then she pulled off her silk finished gown
>   And put on hose of leather, O!
> The ragged ragged rags about our door—
>   She's gone with the wraggle taggle gipsies, O!
>
> It was late last night when my lord came home,
>   Enquiring for his lady, O!
> The servants said on every hand:
>   She's gone with the wraggle taggle gipsies, O!

[1] Sonnet XLI, beginning: 'I thank all who have loved me in their hearts', and Sonnet XLIII, beginning: 'How do I love thee? Let me count the ways,' give an indication of the material Browning had for the thoughts of Pompilia about Caponsacchi.

Then her husband goes in search of her. In Browning's poem he does not seek. But the things she says she is missing are the things which the old gipsy queen encourages the little duchess to sacrifice for the sake of love—house and land and money and a newly wedded lord, and last, but not least, a comfortable sleeping-place.

> Last night you slept on a goose-feather bed,
>   With the sheet turned down so bravely, O!
> And to-night you'll sleep in a cold open field,
>   Along with the wraggle taggle gipsies, O!
>
> What care I for a goose-feather bed,
>   With the sheet turned down so bravely, O!
> For to-night I shall sleep in a cold open field,
>   Along with the wraggle taggle gipsies, O!

Browning found the theme of his poem in this chance-heard folk-song, just as he afterwards found the theme of *The Ring and the Book* in the chance-found volume on the stall. But he says that a Hand 'pushed' him towards the stall. Would he have said that a Hand pushed him into the street to hear the woman? In both cases he obeyed the impulse.

These examples of crucial determinations for his career and for his marriage and for the subjects of his poems indicate that Browning felt free to follow the suggestions that came into his mind. As a poet, he did not listen to 'the seven watchmen that sit aloft on a high tower',[1] and dictate to poets what they shall write about and how they shall write.

I am inclined to connect his freedom of subject and the allied freedom of treatment (often styled Realism) not only with his temperament but also with his education—which, after all, was largely the result of his

[1] Ecclesiasticus xxxvii. 14.

temperament. He could exercise his intense interest in men and women without those limitations of sympathy that are sometimes imposed by cultural establishments. He was free, too, from the narrower conventions of poetical expression. In these respects he showed the way to succeeding poets, especially to those who, like himself, had not been 'shackled' at the outset of their careers by a formal education of the orthodox kind.[1]

II

Browning's interest in men and women was in what is called the 'soul'.

He wrote to J. Milsand, of Dijon, a letter which should serve as a Preface to the 1863 edition of *Sordello*. A sentence of the letter has been quoted more often than any part of the poem itself: 'My stress lay on the incidents in the development of the soul: little else is worth study.' That this referred to his poetical work in general is evident from the next sentence: 'I, at least, always thought so. You, with many known and unknown to me, think so—others may one day think so: and whether my attempt remain for them or not, I trust, though away and past it, to continue ever yours.'

Thomas Hardy evidently thought that this was the *essence* of Browning, for he wrote in his diary the day after Browning died: 'Dec. 13. 1889. Read in the papers that Browning died in Venice yesterday.... "Incidents in the development of a soul! little else is worth study"—Browning.'[2]

Browning's closest friend before his marriage was

[1] See Chapter II: 'Common Humanity in Browning and some Twentieth-Century Poets'.
[2] *Early Life of Thomas Hardy 1840–1891*, p. 292.

Alfred Domett, who is the original of 'Waring'. Domett called Browning a 'subtle-souled psychologist'[1] in days before psychology was much regarded. The description may stand—Browning is the man who, first and last, sees into and understands his fellow men. Hermann Keyserling says that this is the result of instinct in the Englishman. Browning seems to dwell on the necessity of study.

Browning looked upon men and women from the point of view of one who wishes to be fair to them. He invited them to talk, to say what they could for themselves. Men look upon events from different angles, and the difference of view may throw light upon the events, but, most of all, the differences of view reveal what the men are in themselves. Men and women show themselves in their reaction to events. They do not wholly show themselves in their actions. That one man has killed another tells us little about him. Let us hear him expound, defend, justify, extol his deed. So with all crucial deeds and determinations. They are incidents in development. Accidents may acquire significance which occur in the direction of development. You may study these incidents and accidents from the outside. But if you can get inside, if you can let the man tell his own tale or sing his own song, you will know him much better.

Browning comes near to realizing Keats's notion of the poetical nature: 'The poetical nature has no self—it is everything and nothing; it has no character—a poet has no identity—he is continually in for and filling some other body.'

[1] For fuller discussion see Chapter IV: 'Browning the Psychologist and his Invention of the Dramatic Lyric'.

For the purpose of this study of incidents in the development of a soul Browning invented and gradually perfected the Dramatic Lyric, to which I shall return for fuller exposition and discussion in a later chapter. The dramatic lyric has had, and will go on having, a great influence on the writing of poetry by all poets whose concern is with men and women.

Wordsworth defined poetry as the 'spontaneous overflow of powerful feelings'. How can study go along with spontaneity of utterance? To lead the way to an answer, regard for a moment the activities of a great soldier, Marshal Foch. His extraordinarily close study of the art of war is well known. His *Des Principes de la Guerre* is a text-book for military students. Yet an observer [1] has written of him: 'I noticed that when first one addressed Marshal Foch he seemed most inclined to listen. His manner was courteous and quiet, his look grave; his mind seemed patient, receptive, unresponsive —but this at least was misleading, for in fact every question received an answer. Sometimes an interval elapsed; sometimes the retort was instantaneous. Instinct seemed to be at work as much as intellect, and when he spoke one occasionally had the feeling that a power outside and greater than himself was working through him.' Foch said that the plan of the battle of July 18th, 1918, 'came' to him. He had only to receive it. He could not have received it unless he had been a student of the art of war. His obedience to his instinct or to the 'power outside and greater than himself' was conditioned by his previous training and experience.

We turn to the poet. We are familiar in this genera-

[1] 'Ten Years Ago: A Talk with Marshal Foch', from *The Times*, July 7th, 1928, 15 f.

tion with 'automatic writing'. No writing is, strictly speaking, automatic, but some writing seems so much the result of a power outside working through the writer that the word has been adopted to describe it. The poet Blake said of *Milton*: 'I have written this poem from immediate dictation, twelve or sometimes twenty or thirty lines at a time, without premeditation and even against my will. The time it has taken in writing was thus rendered non-existent, and an immense poem exists which seems to be the labour of a long life, all produced without labour or study.'

One may get a feeling of this spontaneity in separate passages or even single words. Take the best-known stanza of *Milton*:

> I will not cease from mental fight,
>   Nor shall my sword sleep in my hand,
> Till we have built Jerusalem
>   In England's green and pleasant land.

Some stanzas have the air of careful calculation. But this one! Take the word 'sleep'. We can almost see it leap out of the page to startle the writer. And it is the final and necessary word: it has magic.

There is a similar magic in the following:

> But the best is when I glide from out them,
> Cross a step or two of dubious twilight,
> Come out on the other side, the novel
> Silent silver lights and darks undreamed of,
> Where I hush and bless myself with silence.[1]

And in:

> Never conclude, but raising hand and head
> Thither where eyes, that cannot reach, yet yearn
> For all hope, all sustainment, all reward,

[1] *One Word More.*

Their utmost up and on,—so blessing back
In those thy realms of help, that heaven thy home,
Some whiteness which, I judge, thy face makes proud,
Some wanness where, I think, thy foot may fall!¹

The lines are the overflow of powerful feelings and, if one may trust one's impression, they are spontaneous—they were written down without labour or hesitation. Nevertheless, they enshrine the experience of many years and the closest and most intimate study by Robert Browning of incidents in the development of a soul—viz. the soul of his own wife.

An indication that Browning wrote spontaneously is that he forgot what he had written. 'I remember with what amused gusto he related one day how a lady friend had been reading him out certain verses, and how he had slapped his thigh (a very characteristic action, by the way) and said, "By Jove, that's fine"; how then she had asked him who wrote them and he could not say; and how surprised he was when she told him they were his own.' ²

Browning never speaks, as Blake does, of 'immediate dictation'. But he indicates quite clearly that he was helped by the spirit of his wife in the writing of *The Ring and the Book*. How the help came he does not specify, except that it came naturally. On December 19th, 1864, he wrote to Miss Isa Blagden: ³ 'Yes, dearest Isa, it is three Christmases ago *fully* now: I sometimes see a light at the end of the dark tunnel of life, which was

---
¹ *The Ring and the Book:* 'The Ring and the Book', ll. 1410 and ff.
² *The Colvins and their Friends*, by E. V. Lucas.
³ *Letters of Robert Browning to Miss Isa Blagden*, arranged for publication by A. J. Armstrong, printed at Baylor University Press, Waco, Texas, 1923, p. 105. The italics of the sentence beginning 'The difference . . .' are mine.

one blackness at the beginning. It won't last for ever. In many ways I can see with my human eyes why this has been right & good for me, as I never doubted it was for Her, and if we do but re-join any day, the break will be better than forgotten, remembered for its uses. *The difference between me and the stupid people who have "communications" is probably nothing more than that I don't confound the results of the natural working of what is in my mind, with vulgar external appearances.* . . . Well, for myself, I am certainly not unhappy, any more than I ever was: I am, if the phrase were now to be coined first, *resigned*, but I look on everything in this world with altered eyes, and can take no more interest in anything I see there but the proof of certain great principles, strewn in the booths at a fair: I could no more take root in life again than learn some new dancing step. On the other hand, I feel such comfort and delight in doing the best I can with my own object of life, poetry, which I think I never *could* have seen the good of before, that it shows I have taken the root I *did* take *well*. I hope to do much more yet: and the flower of it will be put into Her hand somehow.'

The 'flower' was *The Ring and the Book.* This also he forgot. Twelve years after its publication, he said he had not looked at it since it appeared in print. 'At present I have the faintest memory concerning any particular part or passage in it.'[1] His biographer finds this attitude surprising, but it is not surprising if Browning wrote as he hints that he wrote.

Spontaneity, though it would seem superficially to have to do with the manner of an Art, is really associated

[1] *The Life of Robert Browning,* by W. Hall Griffin and H. C. Minchin, p. 241.

with the matter at least as much as with the manner. The objection that the matter of *The Ring and the Book*, for example, was present to Browning's hand in the form of *The Old Yellow Book* will not carry weight with those who have thought themselves back into the position of the poet. The matter of his own experiences was also present to Browning. The matter of the poem itself is a new thing and may have 'come' to him as spontaneously as *Milton* came to Blake or the plan of a battle to Foch.

III

With regard to Browning's message—much derided word!—or 'central meaning', as he himself calls it, of his poetry, I may quote another passage from Hermann Keyserling's estimate of the English:

'Yet sometimes, within the limits of this innocent existence, we encounter a soul endowed with natural depth, and then its happiness is like the happiness of the blest. Then it means being anchored in that serenity which out of its strength can accept in joy all the world's pain. Then it means being lifted for ever beyond the plane of the tragic....'[1]

Pippa, in *Pippa Passes*, is lifted beyond the plane of the tragic; or, rather, the poet interprets life in that sense. It is not fair to a dramatic writer to credit him with the sentiments of his characters. It is not fair to Shakespeare to credit him with Macbeth's

> To-morrow, and to-morrow, and to-morrow,
> Creeps in this petty pace from day to day,
> To the last syllable of recorded time;
> And all our yesterdays have lighted fools
> The way to dusty death....

[1] *Europe*, by Hermann Keyserling, p. 37.

It would not be fair to Browning to credit him with Pippa's
> God's in His heaven—
> All's right with the world!

Yet, taking this poem with others, we may say that Browning was lifted beyond the plane of the tragic. He did accept in joy all the world's pain. He surveyed life from the higher plane, and the survey constitutes the meaning of his poetry. It is usual to contend that his 'Optimism' (so called) had to do with such things as the sympathetic atmosphere of his home life and the robust state of his body. That may be so, but the connexion is not of necessity. Keyserling seems to me to speak more decisively: 'Sometimes . . . we encounter a soul endowed with natural depth.' My son, Lieut. Conrad Clive Brockington of the 2nd Welch Regiment, fell in the First Battle of the Somme at the age of 18. I met him on the Albert–Amiens road less than a month before he was killed, and we had a talk. An Exeter lady had sent him a copy of *Shakespeare*, and he had been reading it.

'I think', he said, 'the tragedy is a mistake.'

'A mistake?'

'Yes,' he said, 'there is no tragedy in life.'

He had just come through the sharpest phase of what was, up to then, the greatest battle of the War. His closest friend had been killed by a 'pip-squeak' in the face. And yet he said, calmly and without defence or explanation, as if the conclusion were self-evident to him and did not admit of question or argument: 'There is no tragedy in life.'[1]

Sir Arthur Quiller Couch, in a little book called *Poetry*,[2] says that 'in the beginning Poetry and Music

[1] See Chapter VI: 'Browning's Optimism'.   [2] p. 23.

did their business together (with the Dance conjoined as third partner); and that, by practice, men have tended to trust Poetry, for an interpreter, more and more above Music, while Dancing has dropped out of the competition'.

'"Meaning" actually is the primary thing everywhere. Grand music is wonderfully meaningful, but its meaning cannot be defined in intellectual terms. Programme music is a mistake; if Richard Strauss is said to bear a musical correspondence to all pictures and impressions, this is caused by a special and untransferable correspondence within his brain and spirit, which has no supra-individual background. A purely chromatic composition may be full of deep meaning in its way—but this meaning cannot be expressed in any other language than in just that of colour.'[1]

In the same way Dancing is often wonderfully meaningful, but its meaning cannot be expressed in any other language than in just that of bodily motion. I quote from a modern poem that does indeed attempt to correlate the meaning of Dancing to another meaning, but only as all significances are related to the one unseizable significance, which is the ultimate unseizable spiritual reality.

> As at the end of an old country dance
> The dancers 'make a knee' to one another,
> And the musician plays a final note
> Delayed beyond expectancy—a note
> That rounds off the impression of the dance.
> And he who hears and watches has the sense
> Of something pleasant that can never end—
> A Gospel of the eternal in man's life.

[1] *Creative Understanding*, by Hermann Keyserling, pp. 58-60.

The real reason why men have tended to trust Poetry for an interpreter more and more above Music is that language is the direct expression of significance. The trust has nothing to do with Poetry as such, but with Poetry as the highest use of language. 'Language is the greatest work of genius the human mind has achieved up to now, because the spiritual expresses itself in it with the direct ingenuousness of the blossoming plant.'[1] The final test of greatness in Poetry concerns, of course, the use of language, and may be simply stated as the ability to express the spiritual, that is to say, to indicate in words the ultimate reality.[2]

Browning appraised meaning as the primary thing, at any rate in poetry so far as he himself practised it. In another letter[3] to Miss Blagden he wrote: 'That critique was fair in giving the right key to my poetry, in as much as it *is* meant to have "one central meaning seen only by reflexion in details"; "our principle" says the Critic: "mine and good" say I.' If the central meaning is seen only by reflection, it may be impossible to express it in a single phrase. But I would suggest 'a testament of hope' as conveying the impression Browning leaves upon the mind. In this sense, the substance of things hoped for is the ultimate spiritual reality.

IV

We come to the consideration of form. What constitutes poetry? What is the distinction between poetry and prose?

The modern tendency is to obscure the distinction. In a recent article J. Middleton Murry has set out the

[1] *Creative Understanding*, by Hermann Keyserling, p. 57.
[2] See also Chapter III: 'The Realistic Manner of Browning and of Twentieth-Century Poets.' [3] *Ut supra*, p. 101.

parable of the Prodigal Son in a stichometrical arrangement and examined it in the light of Keats's definition of Poetry in order to show that the story, as it stands, is a poem and completely satisfies Keats's demands. The tendency is modern. In the past, poetry has been associated with verse. In speaking of poetry the underlying assumption has been that poetry was written in verse, even though verse or rhythmical speech was said to be 'no cause to poetry'.[1] J. S. Mill boldly claims as a poet 'whosoever writes out truly any human feeling', but when he quotes poetry it is always verse that he quotes. The fifty-two English poets, whose 'lives' were written by Dr. Samuel Johnson, wrote in verse. Dr. Johnson [2] himself draws a distinction between poetry and verse. He treated as poets only those writers who wrote in verse, but he was emphatic in denying the name of poetry to some verse.

'I related a dispute between Goldsmith and Mr. Robert Dodsley, one day when they and I were dining at Tom Davies's, in 1762. Goldsmith asserted, that there was no poetry produced in this age. Dodsley appealed to his own *Collection*, and maintained that, though you could not find a palace like Dryden's *Ode on St. Cecilia's Day*, you had villages composed of very pretty houses; and he mentioned particularly *The Spleen.' Johnson.* 'I think Dodsley gave up the question. He and Goldsmith said the same thing; only he said it in a softer manner than Goldsmith did; for he acknowledged

---

[1] 'Verse being but an ornament but no cause to poetry.' *An Apologie for Poetrie*, by Sir Philip Sidney (Arber's reprint of the first edition, 1595, p. 28).

[2] Boswell's *Johnson* ('Oxford Standard Authors'), ii. 26. I quote this passage in full, in view of the numerous attempts to define Poetry. For further discussion, see Chapter V: 'The Conversational Method in the Twentieth Century'.

that there was no poetry, nothing that towered above the common mark. You may find wit and humour in verse, and yet no poetry. *Hudibras* has a profusion of these; yet it is not to be reckoned as a poem. *The Spleen* in Dodsley's *Collection*, on which you say he chiefly rested, is not poetry.' *Boswell.* 'Does not Gray's poetry, Sir, tower above the common mark?' *Johnson.* 'Yes, Sir; but we must attend to the difference between what men in general cannot do if they would, and what every man may do if he would. Sixteen-string Jack towered above the common mark.' *Boswell.* 'Then, Sir, what is poetry?' *Johnson.* 'Why, Sir, it is much easier to say what it is not. We all *know* what light is; but it is not easy to *tell* what it is.'

Poetry, then, should tower above the common mark; and this, having regard to the difference between what men in general cannot do if they would, and what every man may do if he would. Sixteen-string Jack was a noted highwayman who towered above the common mark in his foppish dress and particularly in wearing a bunch of sixteen strings at the knees of his breeches. Every man may imitate Sixteen-string Jack. The poet is in a different category. And when Johnson says with reference to poetry that 'we all *know* what light is; but it is not easy to tell what it is', he does not mean that we all know what Poetry is, but that those of us who do know what Poetry is do not find it easy to tell what it is. And it is here a question not of the indefinable content of poetry but of the expression, because the content of the poem as such has no existence apart from the expression. The expression must tower above the common mark, which in the case of poetry is the mark of verse.

When Robert Browning spoke of poetry as his one

BROWNING AND HIS ART

object in life, he meant by poetry, writing in verse. He kept within the traditional limits of prosody. The change in the matter and manner of his art, which has had a marked influence on succeeding poets, did not extend to what is called free verse. Though Arthur Compton-Rickett regards him as the 'father of modern experimental verse',[1] his experiments were made in recognizable metres. He was continually finding fresh tunes,[2] and his method of speech resisted the fashion of his own day, yet his inventions and innovations were in verse that was accepted in his own day as the form of poetry. If he was responsible for the 'modernist' movement, it was only indirectly. There is no obvious connexion between his poetry and the following:

> *Sunset.*
>
> stinging
> gold swarms
> upon the spires
> silver
>
> chants the litanies the
> great bells are ringing with rose. . . .[3]

Or, with the following:

> *Here we go round the prickly pear*
> *Prickly pear prickly pear*
> *Here we go round the prickly pear*
> *At five o'clock in the morning.*

---

[1] *Robert Browning: Humanist* (1924).

[2] e.g. *Rudel to the Lady of Tripoli* or *White Witchcraft*:
'If you and I could change to beasts what beasts should either be?
Shall you and I play Jove for once? Turn fox then, I decree.
Shy wild sweet stealer of the grapes! Now do your worst on me.'

[3] For the whole poem (by E. E. Cummings) I would refer the reader to *A Survey of Modernist Poetry*, by Laura Riding and Robert Graves, where it is explained and defended.

> Between the idea
> And the reality
> Between the motion
> And the act
> Falls the Shadow
>
> *For Thine is the Kingdom*
>
> . . . . . .
>
> For Thine is
> Life is
> For Thine is the
>
> *This is the way the world ends*
> *This is the way the world ends*
> *This is the way the world ends*
> *Not with a bang but a whimper.*[1]

These may be accepted in our day as poems. Browning may have opened up the avenue that leads to them. But the ordinary student of poetry will be inclined to connect them with Walt Whitman rather than with Browning, though Walt Whitman was born in 1822 and was therefore contemporary with Browning and in his *Song of the Exposition* demands the same freedom to deal with the facts of everyday life as Browning exer-

---

[1] From *The Hollow Men: A Penny for the Old Guy* by T. S. Eliot (1925). Unless the following be held responsible:

> When earth held one so ready
> As he to step forth, stand steady
> In the middle of God's creation
> And prove to demonstration
> What the dark is, what the light is,
> What the wrong is, what the right is,
> What the ugly, what the beautiful,
> What the restive, what the dutiful,
> In Mankind profuse around him? . . .'
>
> *Of Pacchiarotto.*

See for further discussion, Chapters III and V.

cised. Walt Whitman was avowedly an experimentalist, searching for new words, new potentialities of speech. 'The new times, the new people need a tongue according, yes, and what is more, they will have such a tongue—will not be satisfied until it is evolved.'

As a matter of fact, the modernists and the apologists for modernism are often scornful of Browning, even credit him with affectation and, what is stranger still, with pandering to the public. Nevertheless, they may have received a powerful initial impulse from his poetry. And it is curious that the charge brought against them of being eccentric and chaotic was the charge brought at first against Browning,[1] though, as it is necessary to insist, Browning's experiments were within the range of accepted verse-forms.

V

Those persons who have been influenced by Browning's poetry have felt that influence through the reading or hearing of his poetry, but chiefly through reading.

Is sound the key to the effects of poetry?[2] If it is, the effects may be sharper through the hearing of poetry. Yet the sound may be heard in the mind. And the reader has the advantage of paying more attention to the poem. Poetry demands more attention than prose. Rhythm, through which sound comes to its full power, and metre, which may be said to be 'time heard',[3] help to focus the reader's attention or, in other words, to circumscribe the area of consciousness, so that within

[1] The charge is brought, in respect of subject, by Walter Bagehot (*Literary Studies*, vol. ii, p. 374).
[2] For this paragraph see *On Relation of Poetry to Verse*, by Sir Philip Hartog (1926), and *The Principles of Literary Criticism*, by Ivor Armstrong.
[3] T. S. Omond.

this area the reader's mind may be more alert and aware of the poet's experience of high *vigilance*.[1]

Reading Browning demands more attention than reading other poetry, partly because of the dependence of the syntactical construction upon the context. As Shadworth Hodgson wrote as long ago as 1870: 'This dependence of the syntactical construction . . . is what compels the reader to be constantly interpreting the parts by the whole instead of the whole by the parts, and constitutes, as it seems to me, at once the peculiar difficulty and the peculiar beauty of Mr. Browning's style.'[2]

Few poets have suffered more through misreading than Browning. And lest it should be thought that this misreading is confined to those whose intellects cannot bear any unusual strain, I will illustrate by two examples, one from Sir Oliver Lodge, and the other from Mr. G. K. Chesterton.

Sir Oliver Lodge,[3] in support of the statement that 'a remarkable face, casually encountered, or even a word from a stranger, has been known occasionally to call up thoughts akin to worship in the most unritualistic follower of George Fox', quotes the famous lines from *Bishop Blougram's Apology*:

> Just when we are safest, there's a sunset-touch,
> A fancy from a flower-bell, some one's death,
> A chorus-ending from Euripides,—
> And that's enough for fifty hopes and fears
> As old and new at once as nature's self,
> To rap and knock and enter in our soul.

The followers of George Fox are notoriously eager for

[1] Dr. Head's word.
[2] Quoted by Mr. Oliver Elton in *The Brownings* (1924), p. 68, from *The Theory of Practice*, ii. 272.   [3] *Man and the Universe*, Section II, chap. 6.

signs of the Spirit; they trust them far more than others; they are men disposed to worship. But the person contemplated by Browning is the *unbeliever*, and the argument is that the most stubborn unbeliever may be suddenly betrayed into belief by any of these things: the sunset touch, the fancy from a flower-bell . . .; that any of these things may cause him to doubt his unbelief, and set up on its base again the 'grand Perhaps'. Browning's passage does not fit Lodge's suggestion. Lodge's suggestion is that religiously minded people find all kinds of objects and events sacramental. Browning's suggestion is that the sceptic is as open to doubt of his scepticism as, it is alleged, the religious man is to doubt of his faith. The suggestion is a *tu quoque*. Gigadibs, the Bishop's sceptical guest, had said, just as Lodge says in regard to the two great sacraments and the Athanasian Creed, that a man cannot be a fixed believer. Blougram retorts, 'Can we be fixed unbelievers? No. Just when we are safest (i.e. in our unbelief) there's a sunset touch. . .'

Mr. Chesterton, writing of Browning in *The Victorian Age in Literature,* says: 'The two or three great and true things he really had to say he generally managed to say quite simply. Thus he really did want to say that God had indeed made man and woman one flesh; that the sex-relation was religious in this real sense that even in our sin and despair we take it for granted and expect a sort of virtue in it. The feelings of the bad husband about the good wife, for instance, are about as subtle and entangled as any matter on this earth; and Browning really had something to say about them. But he said it in some of the plainest and most unmistakable words in all literature; as lucid as a flash of lightning. "Pompilia, will you let them murder me?" Or again, he did really want to say that death and such moral terrors were best taken in a military spirit; he could not have said it more simply than: "I was ever a fighter; one fight more, the best and the last." He did really wish to say that human life was unworkable unless immortality were implied in it every other moment; he could not have said it more simply: "leave now to dogs and apes; Man has for ever". The obscurities were not merely superficial, but often covered quite superficial ideas. He was as likely as not to be most unintelligible of all in writing a compliment in a lady's album. I remember in my boyhood (when Browning kept us awake like coffee) a friend reading out the poem about the portrait to which I have already referred, reading in that dramatic way in which this poet must be read. And I was profoundly puzzled at the passage where it seems to say that the cousin disparaged the picture, "while John scorns ale". I could not think what this sudden teetotalism on the part of John had to do with the affair, but I forgot to ask at the time and it was only years afterwards that, looking at the book, I found it was "John's corns ail", a very Browningesque way of saying that he winced.'

Mr. Chesterton's first quotation is from *Guido* (*The Ring and the Book*). Westcott [1] praises the passage.

[1] *On some Points in Browning's View of Life* (Nov. 1882) to the Cambridge Browning Society by B. F. Westcott. Westcott was much esteemed as a commentator by Browning himself. Miss Vernon, daughter of the late Prebendary John Vernon, of the Rectory, St. Audries, Bridgwater, has allowed me to copy out the subjoined letter, which was sent by Browning to her father (July 16, 1886): 'In reply to your kind letter and request, I can only say that when you have read Mrs. Orr's handbook (published by Bell) and—at all events—picked and chosen among the essays collected in the various annual reports of the Society that bears my name —you will exclaim only too probably '*satis superque novi*'. Most of these

Westcott does not isolate the line. Isolation robs it of its force, even of its meaning. Guido [1] was a bad husband, and Pompilia a good woman. Pompilia, however, had never pretended to love Guido ('I could not love him, but his mother did'). He had come into contact with her, just as he had come into contact with his mistress, Margherita. What Guido came to recognize was the goodness of Pompilia—her 'love' in another sense than any he had acknowledged. And so it is, after he has appealed to other helpers, in whom he does not really believe and in whom he has never believed, that he appeals to the woman, now dead, who was called his wife.[2] The comment of Westcott is as follows:

'Thus in the midst of strenuous endeavour or of patient suffering, the lesson of life, the lesson of love, is brought within man's reach. It is finally taught perhaps by a sudden appeal of distress (*Caponsacchi*); or by human companionship (*By the Fireside*); or by a message felt to be divine (*Easter Day*).

'There are also sharper ways of enforcing the lesson. One illustration I cannot forbear quoting, for it brings

have done me too much honour—but the painstaking examination of what I have tried to do by such men as Canon Westcott, Mr. Nettleship, Mr. Birrell and many others, has been indeed a surprise to me.'

Browning's own translation of *satis superque novi* is given in *The Ring and the Book* (*Dominus Hyacinthus de Archangelis*, l. 682): '*Satis superque novi*, both enough and to spare.'

[1] For a short account of the story of *The Ring and the Book* see Chapter II.

[2] Notice that Guido makes an appeal to Pompilia as the poet himself had made an appeal to his dead wife for help ('O Lyric Love . . .'). There may be here some faint unconscious echo of Browning's own need of his wife to tread out the evil which protruded into his mind ('Some wanness where I think thy foot may fall!'). The parallel between Guido and Robert Browning himself is difficult to follow without offence. See Chapter IV.

out the basis of Browning's hopefulness, and combines two passages which in different ways, for grandeur of imagery and for spiritual insight, are unsurpassed in Browning—I will venture to say in literature.

'I need not recall the character of Guido, which Browning has analysed with exceptional power and evidently with the deepest interest. This, at last, is the judgement which the Pope pronounces on him:

> For the main criminal I have no hope
> Except in such a suddenness of fate.
> I stood at Naples once, a night so dark
> I could have scarce conjectured there was earth
> Anywhere, sky, or sea, or world at all;
> But the night's black was burst through by a blaze—
> Thunder struck blow on blow, earth groaned and bore,
> Through her whole length of mountain visible:
> There lay the city thick and plain with spires,
> And, like a ghost disshrouded, white the sea.
> So may the truth be flashed out by one blow,
> And Guido see, one instant, and be saved.

'Degraded and debased, Guido is seen to be not past hope by the true spiritual eye. And what is the issue? Up to the last, with fresh kindled passion, the great criminal reasserts his hate. He gathers his strength to repeat his crime in will. I grow, he says, one gorge

> To loathingly reject Pompilia's pale
> Poison my hasty hunger took for food.

So the end comes. The ministers of death claim him. In his agony he summons every helper whom he has known or heard of—

> Abate,—Cardinal,—Christ,—Maria,—God, . . .

and then the light breaks through the blackest gloom:

> Pompilia, will you let them murder me?

In this supreme moment he has known what love is, and knowing it, has begun to feel it. The cry, like the intercession of the rich man in Hades for his five brethren, is a promise of a far-off deliverance.'

I have quoted this passage in full, partly because it illustrates the quality of the best of the older commentators (side by side with that of the liveliest of the moderns), and partly because it does indicate a 'great thing' that Browning seems to have wanted to say.

Mr. Chesterton quotes, for another 'great thing', *Prospice*. He misquotes slightly. What Browning said was:

> I was ever a fighter, so—one fight more,
> The best and the last!

Prospice is one of the few personal utterances of Browning. He faces death in the hope of reunion with Her. 'If we do but rejoin any day, the break will be better than forgotten, remembered for its uses.'

The third quotation is from *A Grammarian's Funeral*. According to his disciples, who are carrying the grammarian's body to burial,

> He said, 'What's time? Leave Now for dogs and apes!
> Man has Forever.

The old scholar believed it was

> God's task to make the heavenly period
> Perfect the earthen.

So that in the case of *Prospice* the great thing Browning wanted to say was that death was not the end, but beyond the last fight of dying lay the happiness of reunion with his wife; and, in the case of *A Grammarian's Funeral*, the great thing was that the work, incomplete on earth, was only a stage in the heavenly period. Many men find human life workable without believing that 'immortality is implied in it every other moment' (why, 'every other moment'?) and, indeed, without believing in immortality at all. Browning's view of life was not that immortality is implied in it for men and not for animals, but that man can find this life good because it is a necessary part of what God intends. He did not contemn the Now—in fact, few poets have believed more in its possibilities—but the greater glory of the Now is the hope of the Forever. Sometimes the Forever seems uncertain, and yet he finds a use in uncertainty. His belief in immortality was liable to fluctuate; his belief in life was steady.[1]

The question of Browning's obscurities is not solved by saying that the obscurities are not merely superficial, but often cover quite superficial ideas. In prose—if one may diverge—he is often obscure and difficult when he is writing to Elizabeth Barrett. But the letters to Miss Isa Blagden present no difficulties. One may venture to say that on the whole he is clearer in poetry than prose, when we compare his earlier poems (except, of course, *Sordello*) with his earlier letters, and more difficult in poetry than prose when we compare his later poems with his later letters.[2]

Sir Sidney Colvin says: 'The mere act of writing seemed to have a peculiar effect upon him, for I have known him manage to be obscure even in a telegram.'

[1] For these conclusions, see also Chapter VI and Chapter IX. *Prospice* is personal, but *A Grammarian's Funeral* is dramatic. I admit the difficulty of drawing a distinction, and many critics of Browning's work ignore it. Even Sir Henry Jones in his *Browning as a Philosophical and Religious Teacher* seems to ignore it. But Sir Henry Jones's book is on the whole the best exposition of Browning's ideas, and every lover of Browning should consult this book for interpretation of Browning's philosophy.

[2] Though *Red Cotton Night-cap Country* is not difficult.

Obscurity in a telegram is not uncommon. C. H. Herford [1] is nearer the mark:

'Browning is confessedly a difficult poet, and his difficulty is by no means all of the kind which opposes unmistakable impediments to the reader's path. Some of it is of the more insidious kind, which may coexist with a delightful persuasion that the way is absolutely clear, and Browning's "obscurity" an invention of the invertebrate. The problems presented by his writing are merely tough, and will always yield to intelligent and patient scrutiny. But the problems presented by his mind are elusive, and it would be hard to resist the cogency of his interpreters, if it were not for their number.'

Browning himself emphasized the necessity of reading his poems with close attention. In a letter from which I have already quoted, he says of a critic: 'he is more than fair in praising one portion of my works at the expense of all the rest, unfair in saying I have never even *tried* to do, what I have done, well or ill, in long poems. He is pleased, not to call failures, but pass clean over: thus, I never describe ("Flight of the Duchess"), never delineate the quieter female character ("Colombe") and so on. The fact is, there is more in my works than a new comer can take in at once, or by next month, when the article ought to be ready.' [2]

My own feeling is that there are not enough 'peptic intervals' in Browning. His mind is so athletic and he speeds along at so great a pace that the reader is apt to suffer from mental, or even imaginative, indigestion.

Another cause of obscurity, which has not hitherto

---

[1] *Robert Browning*, by C. H. Herford. Modern English Writers Series, 1905, Preface.   [2] *Letters to Miss Blagden*, p. 101.

been noticed, may be indicated here, though a fuller discussion must be reserved for a later chapter. A certain obscurity seems to be inherent in the form that Browning invented and increasingly used, viz. the Dramatic Lyric.[1]

[1] See Chapter IV: 'Browning the Psychologist and his Invention of the Dramatic Lyric'.

II

COMMON HUMANITY IN BROWNING AND SOME TWENTIETH-CENTURY POETS

ONE of the threads left hanging loose in the first chapter was the alleged influence of Browning's freedom of subject upon the succeeding poets, especially those who, like him, had not been 'shackled' (to use his own word) by a formal education of the orthodox kind. In this inquiry I must be content to follow up the threads one by one. For example it is obvious that freedom of subject is closely connected with freedom of treatment. Freedom of treatment is, in some cases, almost the same as freedom of subject. A poet may choose for his theme the stories of King Arthur and the Round Table. Tennyson chose that theme in *The Idylls of the King*. In his book, *Midsummer Night*, John Masefield has chosen the same theme. But the mode of treatment by Masefield has the effect of making the subject different. Arthur seen through the eyes of his bastard son Modred is not the same person as the King Arthur of Tennyson's *Idylls*. The separation of subject from treatment may seem arbitrary. But I hope the reader will allow me to concentrate in this chapter upon one aspect of what is generally called *Realism*—I mean an interest in common humanity and an expectation from unsophisticated, uncultured persons of the highest qualities of our nature. Browning had this interest and this expectation and may be held responsible for the awakening or fostering of both in some of the twentieth-century poets.

Wordsworth declared as long ago as 1798: 'They (i.e.

the Lyrical Ballads) were written chiefly with a view to ascertain how far the language of conversation in the middle and lower classes of society is adapted to the purposes of poetic pleasure.'[1] Wordsworth and Coleridge, who with Wordsworth was responsible for *Lyrical Ballads*, were interested in the uncultured. But the interest is not quite the same interest that we find in the poetry of Browning, and following him, of John Davidson, Rudyard Kipling, John Masefield, and W. H. Davies.

Browning's great contemporary, Tennyson, was, like Wordsworth and Coleridge, engrossed in the 'purposes of poetic pleasure'. If he chose to write about the uncultured he was careful in his treatment to cover up or to avoid the crude and unpleasant. Their 'language of conversation' does not go so near to reality as the diction of Wordsworth's peasants. The things Enoch Arden is said to think about when he is cast away on a tropical island are not so convincing as the thoughts Wordsworth put into the mind of Michael or his 'Waggoner'. One can judge how far we have travelled by comparing *Enoch Arden* with John Masefield's *Dauber*. The distance is between poetic interest for the purposes of poetic pleasure and a serious interest for the purposes of truth.

I think the change to seriousness may be traced to Browning. From the time of *Pippa Passes* Browning is content to take his men and women on the ground of their common humanity. He expects to find in the uncultured the great qualities of our nature. He expects great effects from common, everyday experiences—experiences which all men may share. There is no

[1] Advertisement to *Lyrical Ballads*.

barrier of education that has to be leaped before a human being can range freely all the country of noble achievement.

I have spoken of his own lack of formal education. He was brought up outside the cultural stream. His father, also named Robert, was a dissenter, and it was not until June 1871 that an Act was passed to admit students to the Universities of Oxford, Cambridge, and Durham without religious tests.[1] The elder Robert Browning was a man of a 'strange sweetness of soul', a 'good, unworldly, kind-hearted religious man, whose powers natural and acquired would have so easily made him a notable man, had he known what vanity or ambition or the love of money or social influence meant'.[2] But he was capable of resolute decisions. When he was twenty he had given up a lucrative position on his late mother's sugar plantation, because he conceived a hatred of the slave system. The consequent quarrel with his father 'induced him to go at once and consume his life after a fashion he always detested'.[3] This fashion was to become a clerk in the Bank of England.

One may note the strength of conviction implied by this decision to leave the sugar plantation. It was the same conscientiousness that caused him to become a 'proprietor' of the new University of London in Gower Street, where the education was to be unsectarian. Robert Browning the younger, at the time of the opening of the new University (1828), was just coming under

---

[1] See vol. xii of the *Statutes* (second revised edition, 1896). The vital clauses are Nos. 3 and 7.
[2] See *Letters to Miss Blagdon*, June 20th, 1866.
[3] Vol. ii, p. 479, *Letters of Robert Browning and Elizabeth Barrett*.

the influence of Shelley and was so indifferent to the ministrations at the Congregational Chapel in York Street, Walworth, which he attended with his parents, that he once brought upon himself the rebuke of the pastor in open church. Robert Browning, the father, had been a member of the Church of England until 1820. He might so easily have strained a point and entered his son at an Oxford or Cambridge college. The education at Gower Street was cheaper. But cost was not an insuperable difficulty. The real difficulty was the strength of his own convictions as a dissenter.

The poet's school was his father's library. He left Gower Street in his second term. His father's library was large and contained many unusual books. He found there the material for *Paracelsus* and *Sordello*. He also found many subjects for poems in Nathanael Wanley's *Wonders of the Little World*.[1] His reading was prodigious. He mastered the dictionary and read through fifty volumes of the *Biographie Universelle*. He uses in his writings an enormous vocabulary. Quite early in his life he was an accomplished classical scholar, and it would be hard to name a man of wider knowledge or one who moved with greater ease in many languages. But he had no 'tiedness' of culture. I mean that the influence of cultural establishments is often in the direction of limiting their alumni. We speak, for example, of the 'Public School spirit'. The Public School

[1] His use of this large and curious collection of stories, historical instances, and strange pieces of information, made by a parish priest in the eighteenth century, is elusive. I have read Wanley (new ed. 1806) with reasonable attention. But I should be unwilling to affirm that Browning really used this or that passage as material for this or that poem or part of a poem. One can only say there is a presumption that he did.

man may think that this spirit is confined to the Public Schools. A son of Eton and Oxford may expect a certain 'form' from similar sons but not from any son of man.[1] Newman said of a university course that it shows a man 'how to accommodate himself to others, how to throw himself into their state of mind, how to bring before them his own, how to influence them, how to come to an understanding with them, how to bear with them'.[2] It may, however, show him all this and yet exercise a subtle limiting influence. It may limit his sense of respect and expectation. He does not respect the uncultured, as he respects his own class, and he does not expect from them the same qualities. I remember the immense surprise with which a brilliant young soldier of my acquaintance spoke of the fine qualities of some Lancashire miners. He was given command of a battery, and the miners were the rank and file. He tested them —and, I suppose, they tested him—in the tense days of March 1918. He was convinced by the test. But he was immensely surprised. He had not *expected* what he saw. His education had shown him 'how to accommodate himself to others', but it had limited his sense of respect and expectation.

[1] Mary Gladstone, in a letter of 9 March, 1877, wrote: 'R. Browning, whom I liked less than ever. He talks everybody down with his dreadful voice, and always places his person in such disagreeable proximity with yours and puffs and blows and spits in your face. I tried to think of *Abt Vogler* but it was no use—he couldn't ever have written it.' Mary Drew afterwards 'went Browning-mad'. Somewhere about 1885 she held a much more favourable opinion of him. 'Sitting next him at dinner, he talked to me about *La Saisiaz*, and, later, dining with the Bensons at Lambeth he talked again about his poems', and in 1889 she speaks of his death as 'an ungetoverable personal loss'. (*Mary Gladstone: Diaries and Letters*, ed. by Lucy Masterman, 1930, pp. 116, 411, 454.)

[2] *The Idea of a University*, by J. H. Newman, p. 178 (1921 ed.).

I

Robert Browning's championship of the ordinary is disguised by the apparent remoteness and unusualness of his subjects. It was his habit to veil his own passionate interests. He admired his wife's poetry because, he said, she spoke directly and he only spoke dramatically. He might almost have substituted 'indirectly' for 'dramatically'. If we look a little closely at his earlier work we find an intense interest in lowly persons. We also find that they are credited with high qualities and shown to exert a great influence on the lives of others.

The championship begins with *Pippa Passes*. This was the poem Elizabeth Barrett admired above all others at the time when their courtship was progressing. I have spoken of the origin of *Pippa Passes* as described by Mrs. Sutherland Orr. One person influencing unconsciously the lives of others might be any kind of person. The idea of Mr. A. A. Milne's Play, *Mr. Pim Passes By*, is taken straight from *Pippa Passes*, but Mr. Pim is a polite and kindly old gentleman. Pippa is a poor uncultured little silk-weaver. It is she who utters great truths and by her artless singing affects instantly the lives of all who hear her. Perhaps she is regarded by many readers as a 'voice', a spirit like Ariel in *The Tempest*, but she has a distinct individuality and is as real as Sebald and Ottima or the girls on the steps of the Duomo. With Pippa, Browning made a beginning of those 'studies' of artless, ingenuous, uncultured persons of which the chief example is Pompilia in *The Ring and the Book*.

Akin to Pippa is David in *Saul*. This is not the place to speak particularly of the consummate workmanship

(Elizabeth Barrett contributed by her criticisms to the finish of it),[1] the splendid vividness, the prophetic fire of this sublime poem. But one may note that there is here nothing crabbed, nothing harsh, nothing obscure. And the greatest energy of expression is reserved for the climax of the thought. As the ministry of the minstrel becomes more and more effective, so the appeal of the poem becomes more and more urgent.

David is a shepherd lad. At once we have the joyfullest contrast: the great man, overwhelmed, gloomy, black, agonizing, and the lad, manifestly God's child, fresh, beautiful, eager, alert, heedless of heavy things— —'as if no wild heat were now raging to torture the desert'—clear-eyed and unafraid in the king's presence. He is the hope of all the warriors; there lives in his winsome gladness of heart more force than in their ripe wisdom and soldierly prowess and long experience of men.

Since the King, O my friend, for thy countenance sent,
Neither drunken nor eaten have we.

He is the king's hope and their hope. If this gold-haired, laughing boy, radiant in the health of his body, radiant in the sweetness of his mind—if he cannot lead Saul out of the heart of his dull agony, then they feel that no one can. He is called to be the minister of life, the verve of Spring, to the deadness of his master.

David rouses Saul by singing of the ordinary human experiences of ordinary human people. He begins indeed with the infra-human, the wholly instinctive life.

---

[1] Browning submitted the first part (nine sections) for her criticism before they were married. See *New Poems by Robert and Mrs. Browning*, ed. Sir Frederic Kenyon (1914), pp. 155-9.

David bears his witness to the unity of man with the other animals. Has he not led the sheep home with his voice and made the free-flying quails follow him, and set the crickets in conflict, and caused that wonder, the jerboa, the restless, quick-moving wonder, to sit musing outside his sand house?

He passes to something higher—man in his sympathetic grief, in his sympathetic gladness, in his sympathetic boldness, in the mystic fellowship of worship.

When he turns to Saul's own experience, it is an experience that he might have shared in essentials with any one, the abounding joy of his physical vigour, his father and mother and their witness, the friends of his boyhood. He speaks, of course, of his anointing, and the gifts of God and of the immortality of good, of the everlasting fame of his great deeds. But the love that David felt for Saul, when the man took the boy between his knees and laid his hand, soft and grave, on his brow, and pushed his fingers through his hair and scrutinized his face, is the love that any boy might feel for any man; and it is in the light of this love that David interpreted the 'ineffablest crown' of God's love for us.

Any Wife to Any Husband is the title of the poem that Browning wrote about the marriage relationship. In his two short, almost entirely monosyllabic, poems about friendship, *Before* and *After*—the two friends have quarrelled and *Before* is before the duel they fight and *After*, after one has fallen—the central line is,

How he lies in his rights of a man!

and what the survivor remembers is his boyhood's companionship with the dead friend.

Memorabilia begins with a reference to Shelley, but the experiences of stanzas III and IV might happen to any one.

> I crossed a moor, with a name of its own
> And a certain use in the world no doubt,
> Yet a hand's-breadth of it shines alone
> 'Mid the blank miles round about:
>
> For there I picked up on the heather
> And there I put inside my breast
> A moulted feather, an eagle-feather! . . .

The duchess in *My Last Duchess* is also of the family of Pippa. It is true that the villain is a duke—just as he is, though a weaker villain, in *The Flight of the Duchess*—but the commonplace situation is disguised by the setting. A jealous labourer, if he had had the opportunity, might have treated his wife in the same way as Ferrara treated his duchess. Browning, however, does not as a rule make villains out of labourers.

The boy of *The Boy and the Angel* became the new Pope, Theocrite. He is bidden

> Resume the craftsman and the boy!

His voice's praise, when he was a boy, seemed weak, yet when it dropped, 'Creation's chorus stopped'.

Instans Tyrannus gives account of the influence of the entirely obscure, apparently friendless person—a person as starved and mean in his humanity as the landscape of *Childe Roland* is in its natural features. His influence is due to the fact that he 'caught at God's skirts and prayed'—which any one might do.

In the fine poem, called *The Italian in England,* the central figure is a splendid peasant woman. The exile's chief desire is to see her again:

>I think then, I should wish to stand
>This evening in that dear, lost land,
>Over the sea the thousand miles,
>And know if yet that woman smiles
>With the calm smile; some little farm
>She lives in there, no doubt: what harm
>If I sat on the door-side bench,
>And, while her spindle made a trench
>Fantastically in the dust,
>Inquired of all her fortunes—just
>Her children's ages and their names,
>And what may be her husband's aims
>For each of them. I'd talk this out,
>And sit there, for an hour about,
>Then kiss her hand once more, and lay
>Mine on her head, and go my way.

The Flight of the Duchess is founded on a folk-song. The little duchess of the poem—a similar character to the duchess of *My Last Duchess*—is offered the prize of love in the primitive life by an old gipsy and gives up everything to take it. The spokesman is a rough retainer, and it is as much his devotion to his little mistress as her brave choice that makes the attraction of the poem. He looks upon the duke as a poor sad fellow, but just because he is in his service he is going to see him through.

Christmas Eve, the first of the visionary poems about religion, begins with a picture, almost a contemptuous picture, of the congregation in a chapel on the edge of a common, into which the narrator strayed to escape the rain on Christmas Eve.

> In came the flock: the fat weary woman,
> Panting and bewildered, down-clapping
>   Her umbrella with a mighty report,
> Grounded it by me, wry and flapping,
>   A wreck of whalebones; then, with a snort,
> Like a startled horse, at the interloper
> (Who humbly knew himself improper,
> But could not shrink up small enough)
> —Round to the door, and in,—the gruff
> Hinge's invariable scold
> Making my very blood run cold.
> Prompt in the wake of her, up-pattered
> On broken clogs, the many-tattered
> Little old-faced peaking sister-turned-mother
> Of the sickly babe she tried to smother
> Somehow up, with its spotted face,
> From the cold, on her breast, the one warm place;
> She too must stop, wring the poor ends dry
> Of a draggled shawl, and add thereby
> Her tribute to the door-mat, sopping
> Already from my own clothes' dropping,
> Which yet she seemed to grudge I should stand on:
>   Then, stooping down to take off her pattens,
> She bore them defiantly, in each hand one,
> Planted together before her breast
> And its babe, as good as a lance in rest. . . .

But the visionary having made the round of many places of worship or religious inquiry, comes back to the chapel.

> Meantime, in the still recurring fear
>   Lest myself, at unawares, be found,
>   While attacking the choice of my neighbours round,
> With none of my own made—I choose here!

The giving out of the hymn reclaims me;
I have done: and if any blames me,
Thinking that merely to touch in brevity
    The topics I dwell on, were unlawful,—
Or worse, that I trench, with undue levity,
    On the bounds of the holy and the awful,—
I praise the heart, and pity the head of him,
And refer myself to Thee, instead of him,
Who head and heart alike discernest,
    Looking below light speech we utter,
    When frothy spume and frequent splutter
Prove that the soul's depths boil in earnest!

In *Cleon*—another of the religious poems—there is a positive distrust and contempt for culture.

I, Cleon, have effected all those things
Thou wonderingly dost enumerate.
That epos on thy hundred plates of gold
Is mine,—and also mine the little chant,
So sure to rise from every fishing-bark
When, lights at prow, the seamen haul their net.
The image of a sun-god on the phare,
Men turn from the sun's self to see, is mine;
The Poecile, o'er-storied its whole length,
As thou didst hear, with painting, is mine too.
I know the true proportions of a man
And woman also, not observed before;
And I have written three books on the soul,
Proving absurd all written hitherto,
And putting us to ignorance again.
For music,—why, I have combined the moods,
Inventing one. In brief, all arts are mine; . . .

Cleon, for all his culture, has been led to an expectation that life does not satisfy. He deprecates making inquiry of a mere barbarian Jew like Paulus, but it is the Barbarian who holds the secret.

A word or two may be permitted concerning the poems on music.[1] Of all the poets who have written much on music, Browning's are the least about music as such. One could almost affirm that he was not interested in music for its own sake.[2] He is interested in common humanity. In *A Toccata of Galuppi's* he uses the piece called a toccata (or overture, a touch piece) to condemn the artificial, sophisticated life of Venice. In *Master Hugues of Saxe Gotha* we weary of his One, Two, Three, Four, Five, and we are glad when they are bidden clear the arena—though we suspect he is not doing justice to the fugue—and we can come to the grotesque picture of the sacristan showing the organist a light down the rotten-runged, rat-ridden stairs, and especially to the violent image of the last line:

> Do I carry the moon in my pocket?

Abt Vogler voices Browning's philosophy of hope, to which we shall come in due course. It concerns life, not music. He finds his resting place in the 'C Major of this life'—the common chord: a significant end. ' 'Tis we musicians know', and 'God has a few of us whom he whispers in the ear' might seem to claim some peculiar power of revelation through music. But Browning really made no such claim. A woman artist, Eleanor Fortescue Brickdale, has illustrated the line: 'God has a few of us. . . .' She gives us a picture of a scullery-maid carrying a bucket, the other arm being stretched and

---

[1] Even W. H. Davies has written more convincingly on music than Browning.

[2] I mean, from the witness of the poems.

crooked to balance its weight. It is the look in the maid's eyes that tells us she is, like Pompilia, catching the accents of a message. It was of Pompilia that the Pope said, praising her obedience to the inward motion to resist her husband—

> It was authentic to the experienced ear
> O' the good and faithful servant.

Eleanor Brickdale has caught Browning's spirit.

But it is *The Ring and the Book* that brings out most fully and elaborately Browning's belief in the common man. *The Ring and the Book* was a new kind of epic, the 'epic of common-place humanity', as it has been called. In it Browning 'elaborated into praise' the character of Pompilia. He said he found Pompilia just as she is in the *Old Yellow Book*, the volume, part print, part manuscript, giving account of a forgotten Roman murder case of the end of the seventeenth century. In the *Old Yellow Book* she is Francesca Pompilia, the reputed daughter of Pietro and Violante Comparini. She is married secretly to Count Guido Franceschini and goes to live with him at his castle in Arezzo. She is really the daughter of a harlot, and she cannot read or write. She endures a tortured existence with her husband, and then, for the sake of her unborn child, appeals to Giuseppe Caponsacchi, a canon of Arezzo, to rescue her. They flee together, hoping to reach Rome. They are, however, overtaken by Guido at Castelnuovo and arrested. At the subsequent trial Caponsacchi is relegated for three years to Civita Vecchia and Pompilia is placed in the care of some nuns, and afterwards allowed to go with her little son to the home of her foster-parents, the Comparini. At their home, Guido, with the help of four rustic associates, attacks and slays Pietro and Violante and mortally wounds Pompilia. His son has, however, been transferred to the care of a nurse. Pompilia lives long enough to tell the story of the murder. The *Old Yellow Book* contains the documents of pleadings and evidence and some pamphlets and descriptive letters connected with the trial and condemnation of Guido and his accomplices. The final condemnation came from the Pope, to whom Guido appealed against the sentence of the Court.

Browning's use of this material was severely criticized both then and afterwards. Carlyle spoke of an 'Old Bailey case'. Stopford Brooke says that the characters are not great and the fates concerned are not important. Pompilia is an unlettered girl, the 'daughter of God knows who'. Caponsacchi is a priest who frivols away his time until the advent of Pompilia. He is a cultured, artistic dilettante, who becomes a soldier saint when he sets aside all other considerations and yields to the impulses of pity and love and acts as any man might act. Guido the murderer, and Paolo, his brother who plans the dreadful sequence of villainies, are the products of a decadent and aristocratic society, vile in motive, self-indulgent, and unscrupulous. The Pope, the other great figure in the drama, is set as judge of the actors of it. In his review of events and persons he first regards himself as the supreme governor, but when he comes to pronounce judgement he divests himself of his popedom and takes his stand as Antonio Pignatelli, the ordinary man, looking at his fellow men from the standpoint of the ordinary man.

At the beginning of *Balaustion's Adventure* (Balaustion is one of his most alluring women characters) Browning quotes,[1] with reference to the transcript from Euripides included in the poem:

> Our Euripides, the human,
> With his droppings of warm tears,
> And his touches of things common
> Till they rose to touch the spheres.

The description may well apply to himself, especially as the author of *The Ring and the Book*.

II

We pass to a poet whose passion for the common man was almost morbid—JOHN DAVIDSON. His last written words were: 'Men are the universe become conscious; the simplest man should consider himself too great to be called after any name.' These words give the key to his poetry, and they suggest the consuming zeal for man as man which perhaps caused James Elroy Flecker to speak of him as the 'first realist that has appeared in English poetry'. He is not the 'first realist' in any other sense, but he does seem to take his place alone by reason of this interest, which is not only forth-right and sincere but, as I have said, passionate even to the pitch of morbidity. He might have exclaimed with the Latin poet, 'I count nothing human alien from me', or indeed, more embracingly, 'the common concerns of common men are my concern—my very own'.

John Davidson was born at Barrhead in the county of Renfrew on April 11th, 1857. He was the son of a minister of the Evangelical Union, and his first formal education at the Highlanders' Academy, Greenock, was interrupted at the age of 13, when he was sent to the chemical laboratory of Walker's Sugar House in the

[1] From *Wine of Cyprus*, by Elizabeth Barrett.

same town. In the following year (1871) he became assistant to the town analyst there.

The publication in January 1930 of a play called *The Devil and the Lady*, written by Alfred Tennyson at the age of 14, opened up possibilities of discussion. *The Times* [1] asked, 'What is the best school for genius? May not a genius be kept too long at school? Should he indeed be sent there at all?' It is probable that in the case of John Davidson there was no recognition on the part of his parents of any special quality in him. He was sent away to earn his living. A more pertinent question is: 'How far is it good for a poet to abandon any other employment and to try to earn his living by poetry?' Trying to earn his living by writing was fatal to John Davidson. He produced a very considerable amount of work and obtained some recognition. In 1906 he was helped by a grant of a Civil List pension of £100 a year. In 1908 he went to live at Penzance. But he was plagued by poverty and on March 23rd, 1909, he disappeared from his house. He had drowned himself in a fit of depression.

His Will contains the following clauses:

'No word except of my writing is ever to appear in any book of mine as long as the copyright endures.'

'No one is to write my life now or at any time; but let all men study and discuss in private and in public my poems and plays, especially my Testaments and Tragedies.'

His Testaments are: *The Testament of a Vivisector, The Testament of a Man Forbid, The Testament of an Empire Builder, The Testament of a Prime Minister, Testament of John Davidson.* The best known of his poems are: *Fleet*

[1] Jan. 28th, 1930, third article.

Street Eclogues, Fleet Street Eclogues (Second Series), *Ballads and Songs, New Ballads, The Last Ballad and Other Poems, Fleet Street and Other Poems.* But none of them is well known. Even *Fleet Street Eclogues* is out of print.

As will be seen from the quoted clauses of his Will he took himself very seriously as a poet. He wrote *A Ballad in Blank Verse of the Making of a Poet.* He suggests that a poet is 'a martyr for all mundane moods to tear' and describes his function as

>   to catch
> The mutterings of the Spirit of the Hour
> And make them known, and of the lowliest
> To be the minister: and therefore reign
> Prince of the powers of the air, lord of the world
> And master of the sea.

He has an intense sympathy with the courageous lowly people who are perpetually struggling with poverty and other adversities. Witness *Thirty Bob a Week*:

> But the difficultest go to understand,
>   And the difficultest job a man can do,
> Is to come it brave and meek with thirty bob a week,
>   And feel that that's the proper thing for you.
>
> It's a naked child against a hungry wolf;
>   It's playing bowls upon a splitting wreck;
> It's walking on a string across a gulf
>   With millstones fore-and-aft about your neck;
> But the thing is daily done by many and many a one;
>   And we fall, face forward, fighting on the deck.

or *A Northern Suburb*:

> The lowly folk who scarcely dare
>   Conceive themselves perhaps misplaced,
> Whose prize for unremitting care
>   Is only not to be disgraced.

SOME TWENTIETH-CENTURY POETS

Even when he is writing a happy poem called *Autumn* he suddenly thinks of them:

> More than would for all suffice
> From the earth's broad bosom pours;
> Yet in cities wolfish eyes
> Haunt the windows and the doors.
> Mighty One in Heaven who carvest
> The sparrows' meat,
> Bid the hunger and the harvest
> Come together, we entreat!

And when in *A Highway Pimpernel* he has described with vividness the little flower, he links it up with the life of the lowly—

> But not a petal now will budge—
> Fast asleep since the stroke of noon!
> And weary beggar and hawker trudge
> Grazing its leaves with their mouldy shoon,
> And wheels and hoofs go by with a grudge
> To think that a flower should rest so soon.

John Davidson has moments when he is convinced of the far-reaching influence of lowly people who set themselves to do their 'chares' and 'keep their useless tears till night'. This is the theme of *A Ballad of an Artist's Wife*. She it is who works out an eternal peace for her husband.

Davidson's moods vary. Sometimes he contemplates the future with hope, as in *Spring*—a poem that inevitably recalls one of Browning's most famous lines:

> Oh foolish fancy, feebly strong!
> To England shall we ever bring
> The old mirth back? Yes, yes; nor long
> It shall be till that greater Spring;
> And some one yet may make a song
> The birds would like to sing.

His hope reaches far in *A Ballad of Heaven*, which is an echo of the spirit of *Abt Vogler*:

> He doubted; but God said 'Even so;
> Nothing is lost that's wrought with tears;
> The music that you made below
> Is now the music of the spheres.'

or

> And out of Time's obscure distress
> The conquering scherzo thundered Day.

If he cannot always rise to such certainty in his contemplation of what lies beyond death, he has, as a rule, a kind of faith in life. In *A Song of the Road* he sings:

> Soon he came where men abode
> And loved, and wrought, and died;
> And straight the Broad and Narrow ways,
> Heaven fair and Hell obscene,
> For ever vanished out of space,
> Spectres that ne'er had been.

And in *Piper Play!*

> We are of the humblest grade;
> Yet we dare to dance our fill:
> Male and female were we made—
> Fathers, mothers, lovers still!
> Piper, softly; soft and low;
> Pipe of love in mellow notes,
> Till the tears begin to flow,
> And our hearts are in our throats!
>
> Nameless as the stars of night
> Far in galaxies unfurled,
> Yet we wield unrivalled might,
> Joints and hinges of the world!
> Night and day! Night and day!
> Sound the song the hours rehearse!
> Work and play! Work and play!
> The order of the universe!

The Testament of a Man Forbid in the end glorifies the human;

> With mud bespattered, bruised with staves and stoned—
> 'You called us dung!'—me from their midst they drove.
> Alone I went in darkness and in light,
> Colour and sound attending on my steps,
> And life and death the ministers of men,
> My constant company. But in my heart
> Of hearts I longed for human neighbourhood,
> And bent my pride to win men back again.

At the close of a sentence, many stanzas long, in *St. Valentine's Eve*, we have this:

> If one man and one woman, heart and brain
>   Entranced above all fear, above all doubt,
>   Might wring the essence out,
> The groaning of the universe in pain
>   Were as an undersong in love's refrain.
>
> Then in a vision holy Time I see
>   As one sweet bridal night, Earth softly spread
>   One fragrant bridal bed,
> And all my unrest leaves me utterly:
>   I sometimes feel almost that God may be.

The speakers of his *Eclogues*, however, give their differing views and perhaps one is not justified in treating the utterance of any one of them as the speech of John Davidson. Menzies, on *All Hallows' Eve* (*Fleet Street Eclogues*, Second Series), speaks as A. E. Housman or Thomas Hardy might speak:

> We must play the game with a careless smile,
>   Though there's nothing in the hand;
> We must toil as if it were worth our while
>   Spinning our ropes of sand;
> And laugh and cry and live and die
>   At the waft of an unseen wand.

But in *The Testament of John Davidson* we have the poet's own voice:

> Farewell to hope that mocked, farewell despair
> That went before me still and made the pace.
> The earth is full of graves, and mine was there
> Before my life began, my resting-place;
> And I shall find it out and with the dead
> Lie down for ever, all my sayings said—
> Deeds all done and songs all sung,
> While others chant in sun and rain,
> 'Heel and toe from dawn to dusk,
> Round the world and home again.'

Yet, perhaps in the end

> out of Time's obscure distress
> The conquering scherzo thundered Day.

Man, the ordinary toiling, suffering, often inarticulate man, wields unrivalled might. Out of him it is 'Cathedrals rise and Heaven blossoms fair'. His toil and suffering also have a redemptive value. Nothing is lost that is wrought through his tears. And the beauty and sweetness of his home life bring great ease and are a strong persuasion that God's in his heaven. We may read all this in Davidson.

III

There is no need to quote much from RUDYARD KIPLING. Those who read no other poetry are often acquainted with his. Unlike Davidson, he early found the secret of a widespread and (so far) enduring popularity. His *Barrack Room Ballads* was first published in April 1892 and the fifty-ninth edition was issued in 1926. The other books of poems, *Departmental Ditties, The Seven Seas, The Five*

Nations, and *The Years Between*, have been nearly as successful, while the songs interspersed with his short stories have been a regular feature of his work and have contributed not a little to its appeal. This early popularity is a strange contrast not only to the work of John Davidson but to that of Browning. A letter to Isa Blagden, dated April 23rd, 1867, contains the following reference to *The Ring and the Book*:[1] 'I want to get done with my Poem, sixteen thousand lines! Booksellers are making me pretty offers for it. One sent to propose, last week, to publish it at his own risk, give me *all* the profits, and pay me the whole *in advance*. "For the incidental advantage of my name." Oh. R. B. who for six months once did not sell one copy of the poems! I ask £200 for the sheets to America and shall get it, or rather Pen[2] will.'

Rudyard Kipling was born in Bombay on December 30th, 1865. He was the son of J. Lockwood Kipling, C.I.E., and Alice Macdonald. His mother was one of a band of sisters who all married famous men. He was educated at the United Services College, Westward Ho!, Bideford, North Devon. He left school to become the assistant editor in India of *The Civil and Military Gazette* and *The Pioneer* when he was 17. His education comes nearer to the orthodox than that of any of the group we are considering, but the United Services College was a 'limited liability company, paying four per cent.', and 'the school lacked the steadying influence of tradition; and men accustomed to the ordered routine of ancient foundations found it occasionally insubordinate'.

In Rudyard Kipling's case one can show more or less

[1] *The Ring and the Book* eventually exceeded twenty thousand lines.
[2] Pen, of course, is his son.

direct acknowledgement of the influence of Browning. United Services College is the school of *Stalky and Co.* Some years ago I ventured to ask Kipling if Beetle in *Stalky and Co.* was a portrait of himself. He answered: 'Beetle is not altogether myself by any means.' I thought of George Eliot's saying that her early novels were not transcripts from life but the suggestions of experience wrought up into new combinations. In his case, as in hers, the suggestions were very strong and the combinations not very new. At any rate we may take it that Beetle's enthusiasm for Browning was altogether Kipling's, especially as in a later letter Kipling was free to confess that 'Browning was one of his poets'.

Here is a reference to Browning: 'The book was a fat, brown-backed volume of the later Sixties, which King [1] had once thrown at Beetle's head that Beetle might see whence the name Gigadibs came. Beetle had quietly annexed the book, and had seen—several things. The quarter-comprehended verses lived and ate with him, as the be-dropped pages showed. He removed himself from all that world, drifting at large with wondrous Men and Women [2] till McTurk hammered the pilchard spoon on his head and he snarled.'

Another reference is typical of the 'effect' of Browning, if we take Stalky as representing one section of the public, McTurk another, and Beetle a small minority.

[1] King is a housemaster. Gigadibs is the name of the journalist who was Bishop Blougram's guest (*Bishop Blougram's Apology*).
[2] *Men and Women* is the title of the book (published in two volumes in 1855) which contains many of the most famous of Browning's poems, including *Evelyn Hope, Fra Lippo Lippi*, '*Childe Roland to the Dark Tower Came*', *The Patriot, Andrea del Sarto*, the completed *Saul, Holy Cross Day, Cleon, A Grammarian's Funeral* and, at the end, *One Word More*. It had been published *before* the six-monthly return referred to in Browning's letter.

SOME TWENTIETH-CENTURY POETS

Beetle opened the book on the table, ran his finger down a page and began at random:

> Or who in Moscow toward the Czar
> With the demurest of footfalls,
> Over the Kremlin's pavement white
> With serpentine and syenite
> Steps with five other generals—

'That's no good. Try another,' said Stalky.
'Hold on a shake; I know what's coming.'
McTurk was reading over Beetle's shoulder—

> 'That simultaneously take snuff
> For each to have pretext enough
> And kerchief-wise unfold his sash
> Which—softness self—is yet the stuff

(Gummy! What a sentence!)

> To hold fast where a steel chain snaps
> And leave the grand white neck no gash.' [1]

(Full stop)
"Don't understand a word of it,' said Stalky.
'More fool you! Construe!' said McTurk. 'Those six bargees scragged the Czar and left no evidence. *Actum est* with King.'[2]
'He gave me that book [3] too,' said Beetle licking his lips:

> 'There's a great text in Galatians,
>   Once you trip on it entails
> Twenty-nine distinct damnations,
>   One sure if another fails.' [4]

Then irrelevantly:

> 'Setebos! Setebos! and Setebos!
> 'Thinketh he liveth in the cold of the moon.' [5]

---

[1] *Waring.*
[2] The poem gives them a hint for 'scragging' King without leaving any 'evidence'.   [3] Evidently *Dramatic Romances and Lyrics.*
[4] *Soliloquy of the Spanish Cloister.*
[5] *Caliban upon Setebos* (*Dramatis Personae*). The accurate quotation is 'Setebos, Setebos, and Setebos! 'Thinketh, He dwelleth i' the cold o' the moon.' Beetle is not really irrelevant. This may well refer to King.

Tommy Atkins, the private soldier, is the hero of *Barrack Room Ballads* as he is of *Soldiers Three*. The book of ballads is dedicated to T. A.:

> I have made for you a song,
>   And it may be right or wrong,
> But only you can tell me if it's true;
>   I have tried for to explain
>   Both your pleasure and your pain,
> And, Thomas, here's my best respects to you!

It may not be true. Kipling was handicapped through lack of real experience. He has not occupied a bed in a barrack room. He has not known what it is to be a real Tommy. But it is his attempt to tell the truth. He does not cover anything up. And the song is full of respect for Tommy, and Kipling expects to find in him the qualities he thinks of as great—thoroughness in doing his job, a humorous acceptance of hardship, sincerity in the common relationships, and a sanguine temper of mind. For an example we may take one of his early efforts: *Mandalay*. He describes Mandalay from the point of view of a common soldier who has 'carried on' with a native girl in those parts, just as Browning describes the country of the folk-song in *The Flight of the Duchess* from the point of view of an old retainer who is in love with the duchess's maid. When Tennyson wrote *The Northern Farmer* he was exercising himself in dialect for the benefit of his numerous readers. They thought how 'funny' the farmer was and how clever it was of the poet to hit him off so well. When Tennyson wrote an avowedly serious poem about a fisherman who was also a fishmonger he covered up the crudities. Fish in a fish-basket becomes 'ocean spoil in ocean-smelling osier'. When he tells us Enoch Arden's impressions of the tropical island in which he was marooned we hear of the scarlet shafts of sunrise and the long convolvuluses —a gorgeous account of great splendours—and nothing else. *Mandalay* is a serious poem. The soldier gives the impressions of a soldier. Kipling no longer thought it necessary to cover up things because he was writing about a 'low' person ('Ow I 'ate anyfink wot's low!).

These early poems are much more live and instant than his conscious efforts at edification—such as *The White Man's Burden* and *The Recessional*.[1] And they are live because he is sympathetic with individual men and women. Tennyson thought of the northern farmer as a curious type to be studied. He felt seriously about the situation of Enoch Arden, but he tried to 'drape' Enoch Arden, because he did not think that the readers of poetry would be interested in the man himself (perhaps he never *saw* the man himself) or credit him, being a fisherman, with the right kind of piety. So *Enoch Arden*, in spite of all the conscious artist could do, remains ridiculous—something to jeer at, as even Walter Bagehot jeers —while *Mandalay* almost rises to nobility, the love of the soldier for the girl being so consuming and enlightening.

Every reader will recall other poems of Kipling in which he shows his belief in the common man, the ordinary uncultured man, not excluding the heathen and the savage: *Danny Deever, Fuzzy Wuzzy, With Scindia*

---

[1] But these 'preaching' poems have certainly contributed to his prodigious popularity. I had some acquaintance with Lady Burne-Jones. I remember her saying, 'My nephew gave his great call to the nation in *The Recessional*.' It may have been true. Kipling has created the points of view and attitudes and moods of most Englishmen possessing what used to be called the sanguine temperament, and he speaks to them as his own people. Nevertheless, though the appeal may be wide, the ground of the appeal is narrow.

to *Delhi*, *Kitchener's School*, *The Broken Men*, *The Wage Slaves*, *Buddha at Kamakura*, *Pharaoh and the Sergeant*, where the representative of England is Sergeant Whatisname, *The Instructor*, *The Married Man*, *Piet*, *Chant Pagan*, *The Benefactors*, *Epitaphs*.

Kipling is a careful craftsman, not ignorant of metrical devices, but most often he has the magic of the necessary words when he is dealing with machines or animals or children. These seem to move him to a real enthusiasm, and even in his poetry (which is on a lower level than his prose) when he is writing of these, the words seem to grow into their places. I would instance *The Camp Song of the Baggage Animals* and the lovely little elegy in *Just-So Stories*, beginning 'Of all the Tribe of Tegumai'. The elegy has a personal note, and the last stanza is the most beautiful Kipling has yet written:

> For far—oh, very far behind,
> So far she cannot call to him,
> Comes Tegumai alone to find
> The daughter that was all to him.

This is worthy to be placed beside Robert Bridges's poem *On a Dead Child* or Richard Middleton's. I cannot forbear to quote the end of Richard Middleton's, because he was a true lover of Beauty, who has not yet been assigned his proper rank, and once wrote in a letter: 'I feel drawn towards young children and people who are simple and kindly and not too clever. They give me a glimpse of the life I have missed in my passionate search for enjoyment.'

> God knows, and in His proper time disposes,
>   And so I smiled and gently called your name,
> Added my rose to your sweet heap of roses,
>   And left you to your game.

IV

JOHN MASEFIELD and W. H. DAVIES were two of the contributors to *Georgian Poetry*.

As the Georgians were supposed [1] to have written under the leadership of Browning and Walt Whitman, some remarks upon the origin and success of Georgianism may be permitted. Rupert Brooke [2] suggested in the hearing of Edward Marsh that he might write a book of poetry and publish it as a selection from the works of twelve different authors. It occurred to Edward Marsh that as there were at least twelve flesh-and-blood poets whose work, if properly thrust under the public's nose, had a good chance of producing the effect desired, it would be simpler to use the material that was ready to hand. The book was successful beyond expectation. In fact the two poetic phenomena of the years immediately preceding the War were the vogue of Masefield's narrative poems, especially *The Everlasting Mercy* (first printed in 1911 in *The English Review*) and the astonishing sale of *Georgian Poetry*. It is customary to say that Georgianism is a dead movement, and that the five volumes—for Georgian poetry books continued to appear at intervals up to 1922—'have now a sepulchral air, like five chambers of a mausoleum where faded chaplets hang round a company of the embalmed'. Edward Marsh hoped that the collection would help the lover of poetry 'to realize that we are at the beginning of another "Georgian Period" which may rank in due time with the several great poetic ages of the past'. If this hope has not been fulfilled, an indication of the service done by the first

[1] See *The Realistic Revolt in Modern Poetry*, by A. M. Clark (Blackwell).
[2] See Memoir of Rupert Brooke prefixed to his *Collected Poems*.

of the little books will be found in a letter of Charles H. Sorley.[1] He writes under date March 2nd, 1913: 'I have newly squandered 3*s.* 6*d.* on another new toy. It is called *Georgian Poetry* and is an anthology of the best poetry—short poetry, of course—of the last two years. There is little in it that is bad and the vast majority is quite inconsequent. But there are two poets with strange names—Lascelles Abercrombie and Walter de la Mare—whom I am very glad indeed to have met: very striking, both of them.'

I wonder he did not remark that John Masefield, whose *Everlasting Mercy* and *The Widow in the Bye Street* had greatly excited him, is here represented by one of his best short poems, *Biography*. This poem, written in heroic couplets, without any of those strange and forced rhymes and bathetic lapses that mark (or even mar) much of Masefield's work, indicates a life of adventure and wandering in other lands—he mentions his first sight of the Cordilleras and 'wild days in a pampero off the Plate'—and emphasizes his happiness in the 'water trampling ships' and the company of two friends who were also sea-followers, sea-wrestlers, and sea-peers,

> Whose feet with mine wore many a bolt-head bright,
> Treading the decks beneath the riding light.

When this poem appeared, John Masefield was 38 (born June 1st, 1878). He had left his Herefordshire home (of which memories may be found in *London Town* and *Broadways*) and, after spending some years on the *Conway*, had gone to sea, as the 'Dauber' of his finest narrative poem did. He worked as a sailor and then—to quote from *The Daily News* of May 3rd, 1913—

[1] Author of *Marlborough and Other Poems.*

'he took the road to America, living a free and vagrant life, sleeping in barns, working here and there on farms, finally turning up in New York where he got a job at ten dollars a month in the Colonial Hotel.... At about two or two-thirty a.m. he went to his garret, where he read *Morte D'Arthur*,[1] his only book, until he fell asleep.'

He also worked as a gardener [2] before returning to England. There he obtained a post as editor of the Miscellany column of the *Manchester Guardian*. Eventually he came to London and settled in Bloomsbury. His chief friend was J. M. Synge,[3] the Irish dramatist. His walks and talks with Synge are also dwelt on in *Biography* as well as the symposia of a larger company.

John Masefield sounds the note of his interest in the uncultured in the poem prefaced to his first book of poetry, *Salt Water Ballads*:

> Others may sing of the wine and the wealth and the mirth,
> The portly presence of potentates goodly in girth:—
> Mine be the dirt and the dross, the dust and the scum of the earth.

But Masefield is not (to adopt a phrase of Henry James's) 'simply recording his saturation'. We nearly always have the application he is inspired to make of the advantage of the saturation. Even Max Beerbohm's verse-tag implies that. The tag is appended to a caricature of Masefield looking over the roof of a row of slum-dwellings into the street below, at a number of unkempt,

[1] He returned to Malory's book in *Midsummer Night*.
[2] This work is also mentioned in *Biography*.
[3] It was Synge who propounded the judgement: 'It may be said that before verse can be human again it must learn to be brutal.'

coarse, quarrelsome men and women with two or three ragged, admiring children. The verse-tag runs:

> A swear-word in a rustic slum
> A simple swear-word is to some,
> To Masefield something more.

It is the 'something more' that really excuses the swear word. Masefield was confessedly the disciple of Kipling in *Salt Water Ballads*, but there, as in the later narrative poems, he has a more intimate knowledge of the life he chronicles than Kipling had of his 'particular acquainted state', and he is more passionately disposed to reveal its essential nobility.

Masefield's poems of his middle period—if we may call it that—are shamelessly undodgy. He is in clear revolt against some of the bright practitioners of the Victorian age. He wishes to be close and fresh and authentic. In *The Widow in the Bye Street* the facts are there in dense if not unconfused array—even the exact appearance of Anna's overlaid child, the horrible courting talk and acts, and the exact words of Jimmy when he has struck down Ern with the spudder, the exact comments of the people in the court. But in the last account of her, the mother's unchanged love for Jimmy provides us with a point of reconciliation, so that the loathsome landscape of evil human passions is irradiated by the sunshine of her crazed affection.

And in *Dauber* we see in the ship's painter a creature full of power and beauty with none to understand, or teach or save him. There is the making in him of miracles, and all cast away, lost. We can only cling to his own high faith, not knowing his meaning perhaps, but realizing the intenseness of his fading soul and counting the last utterance of it inspired, prophetic, 'It will go on'.

Charles H. Sorley voiced the feeling of many of the younger generation at the advent of Masefield:[1]

'Masefield has founded a new school of poetry and given a strange example to future poets; and this is wherein his greatness and originality lies: that he is a man of action not imagination.[2] For he has one of the fundamental qualities of a great poet—a thorough enjoyment of life. He has it in a more pre-eminent degree than even Browning, perhaps the stock instance of a poet who was great because he liked life. Everyone has read the latter's lines about "the wild joys of living, the leaping from rock up to rock". These are splendid lines: but one somehow does not feel that Browning ever leapt from rock up to rock himself. He saw other people doing it, doubtless, and thought it fine. But I don't think he did it himself ever....[3]

'[Masefield] is the first of a multitude of coming poets (so I trust and pray) who are men of action before they are men of speech and men of speech because they are men of action. Those whom, because they do not live in our narrow painted groove, we call the Lower Classes, it is they who truly know what life is: so to them let us look for the true expression of life. One has already arisen, and his name is Masefield. We await the coming of others in his train.'

Masefield is perhaps unwilling to be identified with the lower classes. He begins to draw away towards what may be called 'the English scene'—a change

---

[1] *Essay on Masefield*, 3 *November* 1912.
[2] He is using the word in a narrow sense.
[3] He wrote *La Saisiaz* about a climb.

comparable to Kipling's new departure in *Puck of Pook's Hill*. It is easy to see that *Reynard the Fox* is a better poem from the point of view of technique than *The Everlasting Mercy*, but from the point of view of subject that first breath-taking poem has a far deeper appeal. The conversion of a profligate is a greater theme than a foxhunt. Masefield is deeply interested in fox-hunting and horse-racing (*Right Royal*). He has written appealing poems on both subjects. Yet the human process that obviously moves him more than the emotions and experiences of those who ride horses—or than the imagined emotions and experiences of the animals themselves—is the spiritual phenomenon of conversion. And this process he traces best in Saul Kane and the blind beggar in *Good Friday*. When they are converted both men rise to heights of real poetic utterance.

If one applies Matthew Arnold's test of the 'total impression of the piece' I think it will be agreed that the impression of any of this first group of narrative poems is profounder and more enduring than that of the later narratives. Probably they were written on a more genuine impulse, and took shape out of a more genuine instinctive sympathy. In them he is true to his original 'consecration'. Even in *Reynard the Fox* the most impressive of his thumbnail sketches is that of Bun who was converted by 'sweet Polly Conway': unless it be Belle, the daughter of Bill and Sal Ridden, who reminds one inevitably of the little duchess in *The Flight of the Duchess*.

A later poem, *King Cole*, is the story of a kind of conversion. It comes alive when the members of the circus troupe are described.

I have an unsupported conviction that the secret of

the success of John Masefield is his spontaneity. This may also be the secret of his strange and sudden failures —those failures that induced one critic to say that his art always seemed to be trying to commit suicide. He does not seem to know when he is an artist and when he is not. Nevertheless, spontaneity may bring one nearer to the greatest effects than conscious artistry. And all very great poets have written much bad verse—except Milton, and how many readers are there of Milton?

One indication, indeed, tends to support my conviction. John Masefield writes: 'I do not know how to answer your inquiry; but should say that, on the whole, when I have written a thing, I do not think of it again.'

V

Our last advance to illustrate the theme of this chapter is the Welsh poet, WILLIAM H. DAVIES. He was born at Newport, Monmouth, on April 20th, 1871. He has written a remarkable prose book called *Autobiography of a Tramp*, which he himself has conveniently summarized for us:

'Picked up knowledge among tramps in America, on cattle boats, and in the common lodging-houses in England. Apprenticed to the picture-frame making; left England when apprenticeship closed and became a tramp in America; during tramp days, which lasted six years, picked fruit occasionally and made eight or nine trips with cattle to England; came back to England and settled in common lodging-houses in London; made several walking tours as a pedlar of laces, pins, and needles; sometimes varied this life by singing hymns in the streets; after eight years of this, published his first book of poems; became a poet at 34 years of age; been one ever since.'[1]

There is no need to apologize for Davies's artistry. He is really a much more accomplished and careful artist than Masefield. He says of himself in a poem called *Evil*:

> Call me a nature poet, nothing more,
>   Who writes of simple things, not human evil;
> And hear my grief when I confess that friends
>   Have tried their best to make a cunning devil!

But he is more than a nature poet.

> But, Lord in Heaven, had I the power
>   To show my inward spirit there,
> Then what a pack of human hounds
>   Had hunted me to strip me bare.
>
> A human pack, ten thousand strong,
>   All in full cry to bring me down;
> All greedy for my magic robe,
>   All crazy for my burning crown.

In *A Song of Life* he says that 'a quiet life with Nature is my choice', and reviews in memory his travels, sailing the great Atlantic, going up North, seeing again in dreams,

> the full-rigged Ship
> Wearing the Moon as a silver ring at night
> On her main finger,

the iceberg, Colorado's rushing stream; but in the end,

> I'll place my hope in some few simple deeds
> That sacrificed a part of my own needs
> All for the love of poor humanity—
> Without a single thought, O Lord, of thee.

[1] *Who's Who*, 1932.

His most moving poems concern this 'poor humanity'. He confesses that he has no knowledge in detail of Nature, though he claims her 'heart's fulness through the face of things';[1] his observation of the human detail is close and intensely sympathetic. A poem entitled *Catherine* concerns the talk of two little boys, one called Dave, who are waiting for Catherine at the garden gate to go along with her to the village school. They outvie one another in extravagant projects of what they will do for Catherine. The one is going to find a coral isle and give it to her, if he sees it first. Dave says that 'some ruler in a far countree' will build a shining throne for her and then every one will listen to her and adore her face and form. He is just going on eagerly to the next development,

> When came a man there pale and wan,
> Whose face was dark and wet though kind,
> He, coming there, seemed like a wind
> Whose breath is rain, yet will not stop
> To give the parchèd flowers a drop:
> 'Go, children, to your school,' he said—
> 'And tell the master Catherine's dead.'

He speaks of the presence of a blind child in a green garden (*A Blind Child*):

> I see them all: flowers of all kind,
>   The sheep and cattle on the leas;
>   The houses up the hills, the trees—
> But I am dumb, for she is blind.

W. H. Davies has the gift of curiosity. Browning's curiosity was almost sublime in its freedom, as, I think, Henry James remarks; Davies's curiosity is more anxious

[1] *The Soul's Destroyer.*

and not so hopeful. He has come closer to the life of homely people; his sympathy with them is more natural, not so much an effort of the imagination, but, when he is face to face with defects and disabilities in human beings or with death, he is not looking deeper and farther, as Browning invariably did. Contrast *A Blind Child* with Browning's *Deaf and Dumb*:

> Only the prism's obstruction shows aright
> The secret of a sunbeam, breaks the light
> Into the jewelled bow from blankest white;
> So may a glory from defect arise:
> Only by Deafness may the vexed love wreak
> Its insuppressive sense on brow and cheek,
> Only by Dumbness adequately speak
> As favoured mouth could never, through the eyes.

In *Jenny* Davies describes lovingly her appearance and allurement, but the last stanza is merely an expression of grief:

> Ah, Jenny's gone, I know not where;
> Her face I cannot hope to see;
> And every time I think of her
> The world seems one big grave to me.

Contrast this with *Prospice*.

Yet none has ever before noted in poetry with so sure a touch the intimate thoughts of the humble. In *One Thing Wanting* he is speaking to an old charwoman and telling her that she can rest now because her children are so good. She laughs for joy,

> And still her voice, with all her years,
> Could make a song-bird wonder if
> A rival sweetness challenged him.

Then her face becomes full of trouble. There is one

thing wanting. She wished she could tear her sister Alice out of her grave—her sister who taunted her when she was poor—and make her understand these words:

> 'See, I have everything I want,
> My children, Alice, are so good'—
> If I could only once do that,
> There's nothing else I want on earth.

And in *A Chant* he appreciates the serenity of Martha, whose work is to lay out the dead and to help the midwife to 'give strength and breath to babes'.

On a different level is *Wondering Brown* (which, by the way, it would be interesting to compare with Matthew Arnold's *The Strayed Reveller*). Riley notices a strayed reveller who has come to sell his shirt. He tells Brown that he knew this man in better days when he made as much as three shillings a day at picking peas. Brown says he can scarcely believe it, though as a matter of fact he himself knows a man, once an inmate of the lodging-house, who now owns a fish-shop:

> 'He was a civil sort of cove,
>   But did queer things, for one low down:
> Oft have I watched him clean his teeth—
>   As true as Heaven's above!' cried Brown.

He can feel for 'Australian Bill' who came out of a hospital cured to find his wife, Liz, and her child gone. Liz would be sure to send the child to school, and so Bill spends his time between the alehouse and a school, for he drinks to drown his grief, and watches a strange school every day in the hope of seeing his child.

He voices an unusual sense of the beautiful. There are three things 'more beautiful than any man could wish to see': a full-rigged ship, the wind and sun playing in a field of corn,

> The third, a woman, young and fair,
> Showing her child before it is born.

Other poems cognate to the present theme are: *A Song of Love,* especially XXXV, LII, LIII, LVIII–LX; *In a Lodging House; Facts; Money; Impudence; Christ, the Man.*

III

THE REALISTIC MANNER OF BROWNING AND OF TWENTIETH-CENTURY POETS

A CONTEMPORARY critic, Walter Bagehot,[1] said of Browning: 'He is the most of a realist and the least of an idealist of any poet we know.' Bishop Westcott was at pains to show that Browning was an idealist, or, rather, that he valued all those things of which Bagehot said he had not appreciation. But Westcott would have accepted the description, 'realist'. Bagehot quotes from *Caliban upon Setebos* and *Holy Cross Day* to illustrate and enforce his judgement. These poems, he says, are examples of the grotesque art. So that, in his view, the characteristic art of the realist is the grotesque art. Mr. G. K. Chesterton has followed him in his book on Browning in the 'English Men of Letters' series by treating Browning's art as the grotesque art.

The word 'realist' may perhaps be held to convey its own meaning sufficiently. Emphasis, however, has been laid upon the disagreeable side of realism. What Bagehot seems to mean is that Browning chooses unpleasant subjects and dwells upon the unpleasant aspects of subjects. Caliban is an unpleasant creature, who has nasty thoughts. Browning dwelt unduly upon the nastiness of his thoughts, having begun by making him a more unpleasant creature than Shakespeare's Caliban. On Holy Cross Day the Jews were brought together to hear a Christian sermon, with a view to their conversion,

[1] *Literary Studies*, vol. ii: Wordsworth, Tennyson, and Browning; or Pure, Ornate, and Grotesque Art in English Poetry.

and Browning tells us what they really said as they went to church:

> Fee, faw, fum! bubble and squeak!
> Blessedest Thursday's the fat of the week.
> Rumble and tumble, sleek and rough,
> Stinking and savoury, smug and gruff,
> Take the church-road, for the bell's due chime
> Gives us the summons—'tis sermon-time!

One can imagine the shock to those whose ears were accustomed to another kind of chime:

> Thou seëst all things, thou wilt see my grave:
> Thou wilt renew thy beauty morn by morn;
> I earth in earth forget these empty courts,
> And thee returning on thy silver wheels.[1]

But a little way farther on in the same poem of *Holy Cross Day* Browning has a passionate stanza—neither realistic nor grotesque—full of a personal apprehension of the reality of Christ's advent:

> Thou! if thou wast He, who at mid-watch came,
> By the starlight, naming a dubious name!
> And if, too heavy with sleep—too rash
> With fear—O Thou, if that martyr-gash
> Fell on Thee coming to take thine own,
> And we gave the Cross, when we owed the Throne—
> Thou art the Judge....

Bagehot was so preoccupied with the 'Fee, faw, fum!' that he seems not to have noticed this stanza.

A dictionary[2] defines Realism[3] as the 'representation of what is real in fact; the effort to exhibit the

---

[1] *Tithonus.*   [2] *Century Dictionary.*
[3] H. V. Routh thinks the whole problem of Realism most complicated. He suggests that there are two kinds: (*a*) A revolt not against the avoid-

literal reality and unvarnished truth of things; treatment of characters, objects, scenes, events, circumstances, &c., according to actual truth or appearance, or to intrinsic probability, without selection or preference over the ugly of what is beautiful or admirable; opposed to idealism and romanticism'. To take another attempt, 'By Realism I mean simply the observation of things as they are, the familiarity with their aspect, physical and intellectual, and the consequent faculty of reproducing them with approximate fidelity'.

The second attempt at definition lays no emphasis upon the unpleasant, and the first only says that the realist does not reject the ugly in favour of the beautiful. The realist is not said to *choose* the ugly rather than the beautiful. Bagehot's conclusion that the grotesque art is characteristic of the realist presupposes that the realist 'takes the type, so to say, in *difficulties*. The grotesque art, to use the language of science, deals not with normal types but with abnormal specimens; to use the language of old philosophy, not with what Nature is striving to be, but with what by some lapse she has happened to become'.

The fact is that the realist avoids types. But he does not therefore deal with abnormal specimens. The Jews on Holy Cross Day were not abnormal specimens. Caliban *is* an abnormal specimen. Shakespeare's Caliban is abnormal; so is Shakespeare's Ariel. But it has never been held to be characteristic of Shakespeare that

ance of reality but against the melodramatizing of reality. Or, if you prefer the phrase, an attempt at *honesty* of statement. Perhaps Robert Browning belongs to this class. (*b*) A definite examination and exposure of the new evils which arise out of the triumphs of civilization. Gissing, Zola, Goncourt belong to this class. They are simply facing the enemies of modern life.

he dealt with abnormal specimens. Nor is it characteristic of Browning. He tells us what the Jews really said. He is out for the presentation of the truth. He tells us what the girls on the steps of the Duomo really said. He tells us what Pippa really sang about. He tells us how David really charmed Saul out of his black mood. He gives us the homely, comic, true picture of the *bourgeoisie* of Hamelin. He makes us see John of the Temple and the men who put him to death. The people in the Chapel of *Christmas Eve* are real individuals. None of these is an abnormal specimen. There is not an abnormal specimen in the whole of *The Ring and the Book*, unless Guido be held to be abnormal in his villainy. He is not more abnormal than Iago. And, as for Nature, we can but dimly guess what Nature is striving to be. Browning is a realist, yet no poet has 'guessed' more nobly about that human nature which the Word did not disdain to take. He treats the lapses without shrinking or shirking. He 'has dared to look on the darkest and meanest forms of action and passion, from which we commonly and rightly turn our eyes, and he has brought back for us from this universal survey a conviction of hope. He has laid bare what there is in man of sordid, selfish, impure, corrupt, brutish, and he proclaims in spite of every disappointment and every wound, that he still finds a spiritual power in him, answering to a spiritual power without him, which restores assurance as to the destiny of creation.'[1]

As for Nature, in the narrower sense, he is concerned with the reproduction of vivid impressions. I suppose he did really feel that the sound could take care of itself.

[1] Bishop Westcott, *ut supra*.

Does this imply that when he was describing natural objects he preferred sense to sound? Sense and sound cannot be divorced thus. The sense suggested the sound and the sound, thereafter, conveyed the sense. One can imagine a charm from a series of unintelligible sounds. A listener, who knew no Greek, might be charmed by hearing a passage from Homer. He might say that the mere sound pleased him. But the essence of language is meaning. And meaning in the description of a natural object is the impression of the object.

I

The Nature aspect of Realism has not been sufficiently noticed. Browning applied the same method of curiosity to all natural appearances as he applied to human nature. He asked himself, to put the matter objectively, 'What do I really see?' The answer to the question determined the statement. The method was in revolt against the Tennysonian manner. The Tennysonian 'statement' was not in answer to the question, 'What do I really see?' Tennyson was a close observer of natural appearances, but he ruled out certain appearances or certain accounts of appearances from his statement. There are rough, abrupt, even violent things in Nature, and these could not be made subject to the Tennysonian manner, which was smooth, musical, and elegant. Smoothness, musicalness, and elegance were the marks of poetic beauty. Bagehot calls the art of Tennyson the 'ornate art'. The ornate art calls off the stress of fancy from real life. And this was what the art of Tennyson tended more and more to do. On the one hand it took refuge from a tense situation or a disagreeable or indelicate subject in pretty accessories; on the other hand—and this is now my special point of emphasis—he called off the stress of fancy from actual appearances. Browning had a different conception. He says in a letter to Miss Isa Blagden, dated January 19th, 1870: 'We [Tennyson and I] look at the object of art in poetry so differently! Here is an Idyll about a knight being untrue to his friend and yielding to the temptation of that friend's mistress after having engaged to assist him in his suit. I should judge the conflict in the knight's soul the proper subject to describe. Tennyson thinks he should describe the castle, and the effect of the moon on its towers, and anything *but* the soul.'

We must leave the important sentence about the 'conflict in the knight's soul' for further comment. Notice now that Tennyson uses natural appearances as a refuge. He refuses to regard closely the difficult and delicate matter of the seduction of the woman, and draws away to a description of the castle and the effect of the moon on the towers. And the appearances he describes are a dream, just as *Enoch Arden* is a dream. They are not actual appearances any more than Enoch Arden is an actual sailor.

Here is the realist's manner: [1]

Well, now, look at our villa! *stuck like the horn of a bull* [2]
Just on a mountain-edge as bare as the creature's skull,
Save a mere shag of a bush with hardly a leaf to pull!
—I scratch my own sometimes to see if the hair's turned wool.

. . . .

[1] *Up at a Villa—Down in the City.*
[2] The italics in these 'Nature Realism' quotations from Browning, Meredith, and Housman are, of course, mine.

Some think fireflies pretty, when they mix i' the corn
    and mingle,
Or thrid the stinking hemp till the stalks of it seem
    a-tingle.
Late August or early September, the stunning cicala is
    shrill,
*And the bees keep their tiresome whine round the resinous firs on
    the hill.*
Enough of the seasons—I spare you the months of the
    fever and chill.

Or this, from *Old Pictures in Florence*:

> —With the chapter-room, the cloister-porch,
>   The church's apsis, aisle or nave,
> Its crypt, one fingers along with a torch,
>   *Its face set full for the sun to shave.*

The natural features in *By the Fire-side* are intensely described:

> On our other side is the straight-up rock;
>   And a path is kept 'twixt the gorge and it
> By boulder-stones where lichens mock
>   The marks on a moth, and *small ferns fit
> Their teeth to the polished block.*
>
> Oh, the sense of the yellow mountain-flowers,
>   And thorny balls, each three in one,
> The chestnuts throw on our path in showers!
>   For the drop of the woodland's fruit's begun,
> These early November hours,
>
> *That crimson the creeper's leaf across
>   Like a splash of blood, intense, abrupt,
> O'er a shield else gold from rim to boss,
>   And lay it for show on the fairy-cupped
> Elf-needled mat of moss,* . . .

A Serenade at a Villa begins:

> That was I, you heard last night,
>   When there rose no moon at all,
> Nor, *to pierce the strained and tight
>   Tent of heaven*, a planet small:
> Life was dead and so was light.

There is a new comparison for Solomon in *Popularity*:

> Enough to furnish Solomon
>   Such hangings for his cedar-house,
> That when, gold-robed, he took the throne
>   In that abyss of blue, the Spouse
> Might swear his presence shone
>
> Most like the centre-spike of gold
>   Which burns deep in the bluebell's womb,
> What time, with ardours manifold,
>   The bee goes singing to her groom,
> Drunken and overbold. . . .

The description of the duke's country in *The Flight of the Duchess* is crammed into one sentence and befits the character of the retainer who describes it. 'The vast red drear burnt-up plain' prepares the way for the mean and starved landscape of *Childe Roland to the Dark Tower Came*. In that poem, Browning tells of Roland's encounter with an old horse. Browning loved horses. His most popular poem, *How They brought the good News from Ghent to Aix*, has a horse for its hero, and he has also written the finest of all animal poems, *Muléykeh*, about a horse. But he does not shrink from describing the dreadful creature of the Roland quest:

> As for the grass it grew as scant as hair
>   In leprosy; thin dry blades pricked the mud
> Which underneath looked kneaded up with blood.

One stiff blind horse, his every bone a-stare,
Stood stupefied, however he came there:
  Thrust out past service from the devil's stud!
Alive? He might be dead for aught I know,
  With that red gaunt and colloped neck a-strain,
  And shut eyes underneath the rusty mane;
Seldom went such grotesqueness with such woe;
I never saw a brute I hated so;
  He must be wicked to deserve such pain.[1]

Continuity demands that the poetical work of GEORGE MEREDITH (b. Feb. 12th, 1828; d. May 18th, 1909) should be considered, though nearly all his poetry had been published before the close of the nineteenth century. The main subject of that poetry is the Earth as it is, man being Earth's child and chief product. The titles of two of his books are *Poems and Lyrics of the Joy of Earth* and *A Reading of Earth*, and there are several separate poems with 'Earth' in the title. In *Earth and Man* Earth's cherishing of her best-endowed is defended. An early poem, *The South-West Wind in the Woodland*, is elaborated into *The Spirit of Earth in Autumn*. In *Earth and a Wedded Woman* the splendour of Earth's elemental forces is revealed to her, and this revelation works a salutary change. In *Earth's Preference* Meredith again defends the evolutionary process. The poet's faith is in the ultimate attainment to God through Earth. In *A Faith on Trial* a vision of a wild white cherry in bloom causes him to pass beyond observation to feeling and renews his faith. Whatever mystical convictions he has take their origin from his feeling for the Earth. Perhaps his finest poem is *The Wood of Westermain*. Only the man who enters the Woods of Nature with courage and love

[1] Note how Düreresque this is.

can interpret her spirit. In this poem he touches on the main subject of his novels and seeks to show that through the interpretation of Nature's spirit the rampant dragon of egoism may be changed and stamped for service to others.

Meredith's manner is nearest of all to that of Browning. His later poems are so difficult, involved, and allusive as to make Browning seem easy by comparison. It may even be that obscurity became an affectation with him. Nevertheless, his mode of expression grew out of the character of his mind, and his mind was not unlike Browning's. He was probably encouraged to write poetry by the example of Browning. I do not mean that he would not have written at all if it had not been for Browning, but that having written, say up to the time of the first version of his loveliest poem, *Love in the Valley*, he was prompted by the example of Browning to express in verse the intricate arguments that shaped themselves in his mind. His historical commentaries in the form of odes on Napoleon and French history are the kind of discussion that Browning's later work would stimulate such a writer as Meredith to cast into verse. But while Browning never or hardly ever ceases to be a poet, Meredith causes one to review the innumerable definitions of poetry to see if some of his poems can possibly satisfy any of them.

One or two passages must suffice to illustrate his close observation of Nature and the vividness with which he reproduces his impressions.

> The aspens, *laughers at a breath*,
> In showering spray-falls mixed their cries,
> Or raked a savage ocean-strand
> *With one incessant drowning screech.*

Here stood a solitary beech,
That gave its gold with open hand,
And all its branches, toning chill,
Did seem to shut their teeth right fast,
To shriek more mercilessly shrill,
And match the fierceness of the blast.[1]

Doves of the fir-wood walling high our red roof
  Through the long noon coo, crooning through the coo.
Loose droop the leaves and down the sleepy roadway
  Sometimes pipes a chaffinch; *loose droops the blue.*
Cows flap a slow tail, knee deep in the river,
  Breathless, given up to sun and gnat and fly.
Nowhere is she seen; and if I see her nowhere,
  Lightning may come, *straight rains and tiger sky.*[2]

The following crowded passage from *Alsace-Lorraine* eems the very echo of Browning:

Sack-like droop bronze pears on the nailed branch-frontage of huts,
To greet those wedded toilers from acres where sweat is a shower.
Snake, cicada, lizard on lavender slopes up South,
Pant for joy of a sunlight driving the fielders to bower.
Sharpened in silver by one chance breeze is the olive's grey;
A royal-mantle floats, a red fritillary hies;
The bee, for whom no flower of garden or wild has nay,
Noises, heard if but named, so hot is the trade he plies.
Processions beneath green arches of herbage, the long colonnades;
Laboured mounds that a foot or a wanton stick may subvert;
Homely are they for a lowly look on bedewed grass-blades,
On citied fir-droppings, on twisted wreaths of the worm in dirt.

[1] *The Spirit of Earth in Autumn.*   [2] *Love in a Valley.*

THOMAS HARDY (b. 1840; d. 1928), who began writing novels in 1871, did not publish a book of poems until his career as a novelist ended. His great poem, the drama of *The Dynasts*, falls wholly within the twentieth century. Nevertheless, his first love was poetry. As a young man (1866-7), he prepared himself for the writing of poetry by reading nothing but verse for two years. He conceived the idea of *The Dynasts* as early as 1875. His diary for the month of June 1875 has this entry:[1] 'Mem: A Ballad of the Hundred Days. Then another of Moscow. Others of earlier campaigns—forming altogether an Iliad of Europe from 1789 to 1815.' In 1876 he explored the field of Waterloo and spent some time in investigating the problem of the actual scene of the Duchess of Richmond's ball. He also paid another visit to Chelsea and talked with the pensioners about the battle. And in June 1877 we have this note: 'Consider a grand drama, based on the wars with Napoleon, or some one campaign (but not as Shakespeare's historical dramas). It might be called "Napoleon" or "Josephine", or by some other person's name.'

I shall have another opportunity of considering Thomas Hardy's work from a different point of view, but if I may diverge for a moment from the immediate theme of this chapter, I should like to make a suggestion that is not unimportant. When we try to track out the influence of a poet we have to take into account not merely the characteristics of his poetry but his poetic achievements generally. In 1875 Browning's most magnificent work, *The Ring and the Book*, had been in circulation for seven years. What more natural than that Thomas Hardy should contemplate the feat of writing

[1] *The Early Life of Thomas Hardy* (1840-91).

such a work and ask himself, 'Why should not I write a great poem?' Especially when the subject of the Napoleonic wars occurred to his mind. And, moreover, Browning had looked at the same series of events from a dozen points of view. The Napoleonic wars could be looked at from many different points of view. One might take the national points of view: English, French, Austrian, Prussian, Russian. One might take the national view on several sides: the statesman, the sailor, the soldier, the king, the aristocrat, the merchant, the townsman, the rustic.

One way, then, of estimating the influence of Browning is to regard the impression of his poetic achievement. This applies to any vocation. A man sees what another man in the same walk of life as himself has achieved, and he is stimulated to attempt something similar—'If he could do that, why should not I?' James Elroy Flecker was stimulated to write *Don Juan* by regarding Browning's work. In a letter to Mr. Frank Savery from the Cotswold Sanatorium in November 1910 he writes: 'I am sick of writing little pretty lyrics. When I read immortal stuff like Browning I am miserable, thinking of the poverty of my language and ideas.'[1] He straightway began writing his play of *Don Juan*—which was one of Browning's subjects.[2] So I suggest that the stimulus to Thomas Hardy for his greatest work,[3] *The Dynasts*, was Browning's greatest work, *The Ring and the Book*.

[1] Preface to *Don Juan*.
[2] *Fifine at the Fair*. *Don Juan* was followed by *Hassan*.
[3] 'Greatest work' is the description of the *Dynasts* by Joseph Conrad. Mr. Lawrence Holt (Lord Mayor of Liverpool, 1929–30) told me that when Joseph Conrad was his guest he asked him who was the greatest writer of our time. Joseph Conrad said that Thomas Hardy was, in his opinion, the greatest writer and *The Dynasts* his greatest work.

To resume: The first fresh interest of Thomas Hardy's writings is in what he *sees*. His business as an artist is to give an account of his vision. He is not careless, as Browning was alleged to be, of lyrical phrases; but he is sometimes content to be rough and even ugly because the lyrical phrase is subordinated to the vision. To take example from two or three stanzas of an attractive personal poem in which the lyrical phrase would not on the whole displease a Tennysonian we may still notice the fidelity of his statement. The poem is called *Afterwards*. It has a threefold interest: it brings out his qualities, lets us into his aims, and indicates his judgement of himself.

>   When the Present has latched its postern behind my tremulous stay,
>   And the May month flaps its glad green leaves like wings,
>   Delicate-filmed as new-spun silk, will the neighbours say,
>   'He was a man who used to notice such things'.
>
>   If it be in the dusk, when like an eyelid's soundless blink,
>   The dew-fall hawk comes crossing the shades to alight
>   Upon the wind-warped upland thorn, a gazer may think,
>   'To him this must have been a familiar sight'.
>
>   If I pass during some nocturnal blackness, mothy and warm,
>   When the hedgehog travels furtively over the lawn,
>   One may say, 'He strove that such innocent creatures should come to no harm,
>   But he could do little for them; and now he is gone'.

The lilt of the verse is perhaps carefully contrived—one cannot tell—but it seems to be natural to the expression of the thought, because the talk of the neighbours is exact:

'He was a man who used to notice such things.'
'To him this must have been a familiar sight.'

(This inversion is often used in prose for the sake of emphasis. Compare, 'A very interesting man—that'.)

'He strove that such innocent creatures should come to no harm, but he could do little for them; and now he is gone.'

The metaphor of the first line strikes the poetical note. He leaves the house of life in which his stay, or the last of it, has been tremulous, and the wooden latch is heard to fall in the socket—the house is an old Wessex cottage—and, outside, the green leaves of May are flapping. The unexpected word for this poet to use is 'glad'.

Notice the exactitude of the simile for the silence of the hawk's movement, and the epithet 'dew-fall' for the hawk, and for the thorn, 'wind-warped upland'. The hawk is in movement and 'dew-fall' indicates the time when one is likeliest to see him flying low, as also the time of the year, and he passes so quickly that one can only note (or guess from the silence of his passage) that he is a hawk—a gazer less familiar with the countryside might have confused him with an owl—and, therefore, nothing else is said about him. But the thorn is stationary, and its position is stated and also the look of it in the dusk.

'If I pass during some nocturnal blackness' is ugly, and 'nocturnal blackness' is a bloated phrase for a dark night. The excuse for 'nocturnal blackness' is that 'black' is better than 'dark' for the poet's purpose and he wishes to describe the blackness of the night. The sound of the end-words in the two following lines, 'warm' and 'lawn', is almost the same, especially if one slurs the final consonants, and 'harm' does not really rhyme with 'warm'; and one has to say, 'Now he is gawn', like a Cockney, to get the last rhyme-ending right. But he gives the very character of the night air and also makes one *feel* the hedgehog, even though one cannot see him.

On another plane, imagine the effect of a moth that brushes your face in the blackness and a hedgehog that you can just hear travelling furtively over the lawn. Would you think of either as an innocent creature which you were anxious not to injure? Well, he did.

The work of A. E. HOUSMAN consists of *A Shropshire Lad*, first printed in 1896, and *Last Poems*, first printed in October 1922—two tiny books. Housman is Professor of Latin in the University of Cambridge. He said, in answer to an inquiry: 'I have a great admiration for some of the poetry which Browning wrote between 1835 and 1869, especially in the period of *Bells and Pomegranates*; but on my own writing he has had no influence at all, except that the phrase "to rest or roam" [1] in one of my poems is probably a reminiscence of "to roam or rest" in one of his.'

After this, one cannot without discourtesy bring A. E. Housman into the line of succession. Housman has a claim to be called the 'faultless poet', even as Andrea del Sarto in his time was called the 'faultless painter'. The *Shropshire Lad* and *Last Poems* are technically perfect. They are both marked by the strictest economy in the use of language, and they have a Greek brevity and clarity which perhaps might be expected. But I am

[1] 'To rest or roam' occurs in the first poem, *The West*, of *Last Poems*.

tempted, in spite of his disclaimer, to adduce some examples of his language-making for comparison with the passages quoted from Browning. I do so because I believe that Browning's clearness of vision, sharpness of apprehension, and fidelity to appearances became part of the poetic atmosphere.

> The ship of sunrise burning
> Strands upon the eastern rims.
>
> Wake: the vaulted shadow shatters
> Trampled to the floor it spanned,
> And the tent of night in tatters
> Straws the sky-pavilioned land.[1]

This reminds one of Browning's 'strained and tight tent of heaven'. In Housman the tent has been torn.[2]

> The vanquished eve, as night prevails,
> *Bleeds* upon the road to Wales.
>
> 'Tis the old wind in the old *anger*.
>
> And like a sky-lit water stood
> The blue-bells in the azured wood.

---

[1] 'Réveille' in *A Shropshire Lad*.

[2] The attempt to make the impression vivid to the reader involves the use of metaphor. A poet is known by the use of metaphor, and the use for metaphor releases a word and gives it a place in the poetic vocabulary. 'Sleep' has been the occasion for the release of many words, e.g.—

> Sleep that knits up the ravelled sleeve of care;
> That midnight-stealing high-pooped galliass,
>   Sleep!

Lascelles Abercrombie considers the word 'bicycle' an unpoetic word. I saw three riders of bicyles come round a corner of a street, and I also just heard them: the faint rush through the air and the almost imperceptible pressure of the rubber on the hard smooth surface of the road, the riders themselves gracefully poised and silent. Here is another metaphor to hand for the dreaming of a summer night, if a poet arises to use it. And then 'bicycle' will be released.

> He stood and heard the steeple
> > Sprinkle the quarters on the morning town,
> > One, two, three, four, to market-place and people
> > It *tossed* them down.
>
> Now to *smother* noise and light,
> Is stolen abroad the wildering night.
> The half-moon westers low, my love,
> > And the wind *brings up* the rain.
>
> On russet floors, by waters idle,
> > The pine lets fall its cone,
> The cuckoo *shouts all day at nothing*
> > In leafy dells alone;
> And traveller's joy beguiles in Autumn
> > Hearts that have lost their own.

Whatever may have been the influence of Browning upon Housman, it is certain that Housman's *Shropshire Lad* has had a great influence on the poets of this century.

W. H. DAVIES, who is proud to be known as a Nature poet, uses realistic comparisons from human experiences more freely than any modern. A good example is *The Wind*:

> Sometimes he makes the childrens' happy sound
> When they play hide and seek, and one is found.
> Sometimes he whineth like a dog in sleep,
> Bit by the merciless small fleas; then deep
> And hollow sounds come from him, as starved men
> Oft hear rise from their empty parts; and then
> He'll hum a hollow groan, like one sick lain,
> Who fears a move will but increase his pain.
> And now he makes an awful wail, as when
> From dark coal-pits are brought up crushed, dead men
> To frantic wives.

KIPLING and MASEFIELD are just as much realists in their descriptions of Nature as they are in their presentation of human 'specimens'—now no longer accounted abnormal because they belong to the unimportant multitude. To judge the influence (for better or for worse) of the new realism, compare the presentation of the scene by the lake in Tennyson's *Morte d'Arthur* with Masefield's version: [1]

> So Lucan called, a hurt man's feeble cry.
> No answer followed save a stir of wings,
> That and the creeping water's whisperings
> Ant-like about the bodies of the dead.
>
> * * * * * *
>
> A curlew called: he fell upon his knees,
> And lo, his failing eyes beheld a ship
> Burning a path athwart the water-rip;
> The water gleamed about her like soft flame,
> Her gear creaked in the breeze;
> Towards him, nosing through the soaken sand,
> To rest her at his side, the vessel came.

Under the heading of this section may be included the human setting—streets, houses, towns—as well as the infra-human creation. I might even claim Robert Bridges's famous poem, *London Snow*, as an example of realism. But I will content myself with two passages from Flecker's 'first realist', JOHN DAVIDSON.

> Unthronged or crowded densely
> By people business-led
> The pavements, tuned intensely,
> Rang hollow to the tread.

[1] *Midsummer Night and Other Tales in Verse.*

The traffic hurled and hammered
  Down every ringing street;
Like gongs the causeys clamoured,
  Like drums the asphalt beat.

While ruling o'er the olden
  Abode of fog unclean,
In watchet weeds and golden
  The still air sparkled keen.[1]

And this, from *A Woman and her Son*:

Outside, a city-dweller's tipsy tread
Severed the silence with a jagged rent;
The tall lamps flickered through the sombre street,
With yellow light hiding the stainless stars:
In the next house a child awoke and cried;
Far off a clank and crash of shunting trains
Broke out and ceased, as if the fettered world
Started and shook its irons in the night;
Across the dreary common, citywards,
The moon among the chimneys sunk again,
Cast on the clouds a shade of smoky pearl.

The later realists seek out images that make Browning's grotesqueness seem mild. HUMBERT WOLFE has a poem on the house of the heart called *The End*.[2]

the sun comes in by the window
  at the broken window-pane,
till night with her blackened dish-cloth
  stops it up again.

. . . .

Downstairs in the cellar the darkness
  is deep enough to swim in,
and, there, washing back and forwards
  are pale men, and pale drowned women.

[1] *A Frosty Morning.*   [2] From *The Unknown Goddess.*

T. S. ELIOT has a new kind of 'moon' poem (*Rhapsody on a Windy Night*).

> Regard the moon,
> La lune ne garde aucune rancune,
> She winks a feeble eye,
> She smiles into corners,
> She smooths the hair of the grass.
> The moon has lost her memory.
> A washed-out smallpox cracks her face,
> Her hand twists a paper rose,
> That smells of dust and eau de Cologne,
> She is alone
> With all the old nocturnal smells
> That cross and cross across her brain.

Turning to the infra-human creation, we have already noticed Browning's love for animals. He is even said to have made a companion of a toad. His sympathy, like everything about him, was intense. You watch him watching the jerboa and he is as interested and pleased as if the jerboa were a boy. Hardy looked upon a moth and a hedgehog as innocent creatures he would keep from harm. Neither Browning nor he had any dislike—as Dr. A. C. Bradley thinks Shakespeare had—for a dog. Browning's *Tray* is a tract against vivisection, but its power is in his feeling for the dog. Hardy's most pathetic poem in *Winter Words* is about a mongrel. The tax-paying day was coming along and the mongrel had to be drowned.

I need only refer to Kipling's and Masefield's animal poems. *Reynard the Fox* and *Right Royal* give a real expression of the intensity of animal life. One may compare these poems with the pictures of Mr. Alfons Purtscher, lately exhibited in London.

Of the interesting juniors, RUPERT BROOKE had a genuine feeling for animals. Miss Sybil Pye [1] says of the poet himself: 'He often made one think of the qualities of animals. The line of his jaw when he laughed had the fine length and curve that are seen in lions on Assyrian friezes—or in the gentler type that lives with St. Jerome in his cave; and his gestures, too, had the quick flexible precision of creatures whose force can be concentrated and released again in one flashing moment. He lay, one day, on the floor, playing with a puppy which was still at that "loose" stage when, as he said, it seemed able to turn right round inside its skin; and the same gay, rapid elasticity appeared to mark both their movements, those of the darting puppy and of the hands which played a second to its game.'

Among his early poems is *The Song of the Beasts* (sung, one night, in the cities in the darkness).

> Keep close as we speed,
> Though mad whispers woo you, and hot hands cling,
> And the touch and the smell of bare flesh sting,
> Soft flank by your flank, and side brushing side—
> *Tonight* never heed!
> Unswerving and silent follow with me,
> Till the city ends sheer,
> And the crook'd lanes open wide,
> Out of the voices of night,
> Beyond lust and fear,
> To the level waters of moonlight,
> To the level waters, quiet and clear,
> To the black unresting plains of the calling sea.

This poem prepares us for another that has become famous, in which the poet exhibits an intimate knowledge

[1] *Life and Letters*, May 1929.

of, or at any rate a sympathy with, a still more remote form of life. *The Fish* has originality, unusual insight, and music:

>   And all's one,
> Gentle, embracing, quiet, dun,
> The world he rests in, world he knows,
> Perpetual curving. Only—grows
> An eddy in that ordered falling,
> A knowledge from the gloom, a calling
> Weed in the wave, gleam in the mud—
> The dark fire leaps along his blood;
> Dateless and deathless, blind and still,
> The intricate impulse works its will;
> His woven world drops back; and he,
> Sans providence, sans memory,
> Unconscious and directly driven,
> Fades to some dank sufficient heaven.

RALPH HODGSON's *The Bull* deserves to be placed alongside Browning's *Muléykeh*. The bull is old and unhappy, sick in soul and body, waiting for death. He has come bravely by his fall, and he dreams of his early life, of his mature powers, of his triumphs:

> Not a leopard bright as flame,
> Flashing fingerhooks of steel
> That a wooden tree might feel,
> Met his fury once and came
> For a second reprimand,
> Not a leopard in the land;
>
> Not a lion of them all,
> Not a lion of the hills,
> Hero of a thousand kills,
> Dared a second fight and fall,
> Dared that ram terrific twice,
> Paid a second time the price.

> Pity him, this dupe of dream,
> Leader of the herd again
> Only in his daft old brain,
> Once again the bull supreme
> And bull enough to bear the part
> Only in his tameless heart.

II

The realistic manner on its human side has become so much *the* manner of the twentieth-century writers that illustrative instances seem almost superfluous. Browning began it long before Walter Bagehot took notice. And yet the following passage might have been written yesterday. Some poor girls are talking together. One, called 3rd Girl, tells how she pleases her lovers, and then catches sight of a beetle and kills it.

> (See how that beetle burnishes in the path!—
> There sparkles he along the dust: and, there—
> Your journey to the maize-tuft spoilt at least!)
> *1st Girl.* When I was young they said if you killed one
> Of those sunshiny beetles, that his friend
> Up there, would shine no more that day nor next.
> *2nd Girl.* When you were young? Nor are you young, that's true!
> How your plump arms that were have dropped away!
> Why, I can span them! Cecco beats you still?
> No matter, so you keep your curious hair.
> I wish they'd find a way to dye our hair
> Your colour—any lighter tint, indeed,
> Than black—the men say they are sick of black,
> Black eyes, black hair!

4th Girl.	Sick of yours, like enough.
	Do you pretend you ever tasted lampreys
	And ortolans? Giovita, of the palace,
	Engaged (but there's no trusting him) to slice me
	Polenta with a knife that had cut up
	An ortolan.
2nd Girl.	Why there! Is not that Pippa
	We are to talk to, under the window,—quick,—
	Where the lights are?
1st Girl.	That she? No, or she would sing,
	For the Intendant said ...
3rd Girl.	Oh, you sing first!
	Then, if she listens and comes close. ... I'll tell you,
	Sing that song the young English noble made,
	Who took you for the purest of the pure,
	And meant to leave the world for you—what fun!

JOHN DAVIDSON treats in his more sombre fashion of the outcast life:

> I cannot see the stars and flowers,
> Nor hear the lark's soprano ring,
> Because a ruddy darkness lowers
> For ever and the tempests sing.
> I see the strong coerce the weak,
> And labour overwrought rebel;
> I hear the useless treadmill creak,
> The prisoner cursing in his cell;
> I see the loafer-burnished wall;
> I hear the rotting match-girl whine;
> I see the unslept switchman fall;
> I hear the explosion in the mine;
> I see along the heedless street
> The sandwich-men trudge through the mire;
> I hear the tired, quick, tripping feet
> Of sad, gay girls who ply for hire.

Even a writer like WALTER DE LA MARE, whose

delicate and elusive art is supposed to be *sui generis*, has been affected by this freedom to use the stark image or to paint the picture without blurring the disagreeable detail. In his book, *The Veil and Other Poems*, there is a group, from which I take the following passages:

In the Dock.

Pallid, mis-shapen he stands. The world's grimed thumb,
Now hooked securely in his matted hair,
Has haled him struggling from his poisonous slum
And flung him mute as fish close-netted there.
His bloodless hands entalon that iron rail.
He gloats in beastlike trance. . . .

The Wreck.

She sprawls sand-mounded, of sea-birds the mock.
Her sailors, drowned, forgotten, rot in mould,
Or hang in stagnant quiet of the deep;
The brave, the afraid, into one silence sold. . . .

Drugged.

Inert in his chair,
In a candle's guttering glow;
His bottle empty,
His fire sunk low;
With drug-sealed lids shut fast,
Unsated mouth ajar,
This darkened phantasm walks
Where nightmares are. . . .

This is realism with a difference. The stark realist would not have universalized the experienced policeman as the 'world's grimed thumb'. The policeman may even have grabbed his prisoner by the hair, but, as he stands in the dock, the thumb is only metaphorically hooked securely in it.

The sea-birds do not really 'mock' the wreck. The mockery is assigned to them by the observer. Nor were the sailors 'sold' into silence, though the word 'sold' is the true poet's word and reminds one of William Blake's 'Nor shall my sword *sleep* in my hand'.

The first lines of *Drugged* are realistic, but another element is introduced when the man is called a 'darkened phantasm' and said to 'walk'.

Whatever the subject, the realist's treatment must be actual. In the first poem of *Georgian Poetry* [1] LASCELLES ABERCROMBIE pictures Saint Thomas, the apostle of Jesus Christ, just about to embark for India. He engages in conversation with the Captain of the vessel, and the Captain tells him of the sadistic cruelty of the king of the country. Nothing is glossed in the interests of our mental comfort, and no conventional interpretation is accepted. A Stranger, who is Thomas's Master, appears and reveals the apostle's sin.

> Now, Thomas, know thy sin. It was not fear;
> Easily may a man crouch down for fear,
> And yet rise up on firmer knees and face
> The hailing storm of the world with graver courage.
> But prudence, prudence is the deadly sin. . . .

In the same book JAMES STEPHENS has a poem on the loneliness of God.

The work of Kipling and Masefield and W. H. Davies was called realistic—I dislike these tea-caddy definitions, but there is no help for it—because it dealt faithfully with the lower classes. The subject was supposed to constitute realism. Strange to say, Ruskin was among the first to revolt against the Tennysonian choice of

[1] *The Sale of Saint Thomas*, recently completed and published separately, 1931.

subject, without perceiving that Browning had flared across the path or that the Tennysonian subject might be treated in a manner very different from Tennyson's. Writing to Tennyson in September 1859, about *The Idylls of the King*, he said: 'As a description of various nobleness and tenderness the book is without price; but I shall always wish it had been nobleness independent of a romantic condition of externals in general.... And merely in the facts of modern life—not drawing-room, formal life, but the far-away and quite unknown growth of souls in and through any form of misery or servitude—there is an infinity of what men should be told, and what none but a poet can tell. I cannot but think that the intense, masterful, and unerring transcript of an actuality, and the relation of a story of any real human life as a poet would watch and analyse it, would make all men feel more or less what poetry was, as they felt what Life and Fate were in their instant workings.'

There is more in poetry than the transcript of an actuality. The realist, however, *qua* realist, is aiming at the transcript of an actuality, but the realistic manner —intense, masterful, unerring—may be applied to things that are not actual in the narrow sense. The poet may concern himself with the romantic aspect of externals and still be intense and masterful and, within limits, unerring. He may employ the realistic manner even in his search for significance.

The stuff of poetry is experience. The poet who looks at a garden has the experience of an onlooker, he will write about a garden from that point of view. The poet who works in a garden will write from a different point of view. The poet who looks on at war from a distance will write a war poem from that point of view; the poet who has engaged in battle and endured as a soldier cannot, if he would, write as an onlooker. But neither the gardener-poet nor the soldier-poet, write he never so intensely, masterfully, and unerringly, need concern himself with the transcript of an actuality only. Because he is a realist he need not therefore *not* be an idealist or a mystic. When I say that the realistic manner is the characteristic manner of the twentieth century I mean that the writers of our time are questioning all phenomena with a view to the elucidation of the truths of phenomena. I do not mean that they have no eye for the Truth, the ultimate Significance, if haply such Truth and Significance may emerge for recognition. But it will not emerge by neglecting the separate truths, even the least of them.

For example, let us take two war poems, one by LAURENCE BINYON, called *The Fallen*, and the other by ROBERT GRAVES, called *The Leveller*. The fallen are thus appraised by Binyon:

> They went with songs to the battle, they were young,
> Straight of limb, true of eye, steady and aglow.
> They were staunch to the end against odds uncounted,
> They fell with their faces to the foe.

Graves takes two of the fallen—two who were struck by the same shell near Martinpuich.

> One was a pale eighteen-year-old,
> Blue-eyed and thin and not too bold,
> Pressed for the war ten years too soon,
> The shame and pity of his platoon.

The other was a wild cut-throat who had known death and hell before in American countries. In his death the cut-throat groaned 'Mother! Mother!' like a child, and the poor innocent died cursing God. Old Sergeant Smith, kindest of men, wrote the same letter to cheer the womenfolk of each:

> He died a hero's death: and we
> His comrades of 'A' company
> Deeply regret his death; we shall
> All deeply miss so true a pal.

Sergeant Smith's letter is the same in substance as Binyon's poem, and Sergeant Smith wrote in the kindness of his heart to cheer the womenfolk—not to tell the truth. Sergeant Smith's method also saves time and trouble.

I am not discussing now the question: 'Is Graves's poem better than Binyon's?' I am seeking to show that Graves, by following the method of curiosity which is pre-eminently the method of Browning, has written, not a poem about anybody in any war, but a poem about somebody on the French Front in the Great War of 1914–18.

This method will not regard all soldiers as the same soldier nor a particular soldier as the same all the time. CHARLES SORLEY, one of the most sincere of war-poets, records his different moods even when they seem to conflict with his faith. He came by his faith through the rain,[1] just as George Meredith came by his through the sight of a wild cherry tree. If Sorley seems to shift from that faith it only means that he is truthful in

---

[1] There are fourteen or fifteen references to the effect of rain upon Sorley's mind in his little book, *Marlborough and Other Poems*. I am thinking here of *German Rain* (No. XXII):

> Then suddenly I saw what more to see
> I never thought: old things renewed, retrieved.
> The rain that fell in England fell on me,
>   And I believed.

revealing his moods. He can be joyously reminiscent and anticipatory in a verse-letter to his friend [1]—that is one mood—and he can be disheartened as in the sonnet beginning: 'When you see millions of the mouthless dead.'

This sonnet might have served as a warning of his death. It indicates a weariness for which there must be relief. I remember meeting in the early days of July 1916 an old pupil of mine who was a major of heavy artillery. We met in the ruined village of Carnoy. He was at that time as joyous as Sorley is in his home-poem. He said that I was taking the War too seriously, and that one ought not to take seriously anything for which one was not responsible. In December 1916 I received a letter from him expressing the same discouragement and apparent disbelief as Sorley's sonnet. He had died before the letter reached me. His weariness was a signal.

I mention this incident because it confirms the impression of Sorley's reality. He does not pretend. The true realist exercises his curiosity with the utmost freedom, and he does not pretend about the result in order to make it square with other results. He is content to be inconsistent. 'Just when we are safest, there's a sunset touch. . . .'

But may the artist be inconsistent? Ought not his work of art to be a living whole? A novel should have a beginning and a middle and an ending. The plot should hang together. A poem ought to have a similar consistency. Are there no canons of art? This is where the classical and the realistic art conflict. The classical art is like a creed—it imposes limits beyond which one

[1] No. XXXVI.

is not allowed to pass without the risk of exposing oneself to error. The realist always does pass the boundaries. Shakespeare was a realist who recognized his own tendencies. At the end of the magical singing—magical because so simple, so homely—about the Cotswold country in *Love's Labour's Lost,* Armado says: 'The words of Mercury are harsh after the songs of Apollo. You that way; we this way.' The words of Mercury have long become a classic; they have established themselves as a form of art. But when Shakespeare wrote he was open to the reproach of not being an artist at all. The songs of Apollo were art.

So that when we come to the latest development of realism—the realism that is best defined by Chehov—we ought not to be too hasty in rejecting the new products. 'I write things', said Chehov, 'in which there are a hundred persons, summer, autumn—and they do all sorts of inconsequential things; they become confused, forget.' 'There is in Chehov's works' (says Gerhardi) 'that fluid undercurrent by which we recognize existence, because we see that he at least did not simplify life in order to round off his picture of it (the loose-end nature of it being just the picture he has set out to portray).'

In this portrayal of the 'loose-end nature' of life Chehov is followed, in prose, by Katherine Mansfield. In poetry he seems to be followed by the Imagists and the Sitwells and the so-called Modernists. The Imagists proposed a 'creed' of poetry: to use the *exact* word; to create new rhythms as the expression of new moods; to allow absolute freedom in the choice of subject; to present an image; to produce poetry that is hard and clear. Most of them believed that 'concentration is the very essence of poetry'. But Chehov's 'all sorts of inconsequential things' is the impression their poetry produces.

> I must be mad, or very tired,
> When the curve of a blue bay beyond a railroad track
> Is shrill and sweet to me like the sudden springing of a tune,
> And the sight of a white church above thin trees in a city square
> Amazes my eyes as though it were the Parthenon. . . .[1]

And then we get 'images' of a mast and of a tea-clipper, and of a Chinese coolie leaning over a rail.
Or this:

> Through gilded trellises
> Of the heat, Dolores,
> Inez, Manuccia,
> Isabel, Lucia,
> Mock time that flies,
> 'Lovely bird, will you stay and sing,
> Flirting your sheenèd wing—
> Peck with your beak and cling
> To our balconies?'
> They flirt their fans, flaunting—
> 'O silence enchanting
> As music!' then slanting
> Their eyes,
> Like gilded or emerald grapes
> They take mantillas, capes,
> Hiding their simian shapes.[2]

We get 'all sorts of inconsequential things' in T. S. Eliot's *The Waste Land*. We get 'those are pearls that

[1] *Meeting House Hill*, by Amy Lowell.
[2] *Through Gilded Trellises*, by Edith Sitwell. Prof. Louis Cazamian calls the Sitwells a 'kind of literary cubists' (*Hist. Lit.* vol. ii).

were his eyes' from *The Tempest*; then a section beginning:

   When Lil's husband got demobbed;

then a line from Spenser's *Prothalamion*,

   Sweet Thames run softly till I end my song;

then the song of the Three Thames Daughters corresponding to Wagner's Rhine Daughters. There is a connexion—so one is almost led to believe—but it is hard to trace.

 Part V is called 'What the Thunder Said', and has (so we are told in an explanatory note) three themes: the Journey to Emmaus, the Approach to Chapel Perilous, and the Present Decay of Eastern Europe. We begin with the exciting line:

   Who is the third who walks always beside you?

This, surely, is the Emmaus theme? It is, but it refers mainly to Shackleton's Expedition.

 The suggestion has been made that *The Waste Land* is a poetic 'leg-pull'. *The Waste Land* is, to judge from an examination of the author's poems, a distinct and calculated break from his old manner, in order to get something expressed in poetry that he felt ought to be expressed. In his earlier days he wrote satirical and humorous verse:

> Upon the glazen shelves kept watch
> Matthew and Waldo, guardians of the faith,
> The army of unalterable law.[1]

> I shall not want Capital in Heaven
> For I shall meet Sir Alfred Mond:
> We two shall lie together, lapt
> In a five per cent. Exchequer Bond.

    [1] *Cousin Nancy.*

or
> Miss Helen Slingsby was my maiden aunt,
> And lived in a small house near a fashionable square
> Cared for by servants to the number of four.
> Now when she died there was silence in heaven
> And silence at her end of the street.

or
> I mount the steps and ring the bell, turning
> Wearily, as one would turn to nod good-bye to Rochefoucauld,
> If the street were time and he at the end of the street,
> And I say, 'Cousin Harriet, here is the *Boston Evening Transcript*.'

Browning is often difficult to read. George Meredith is still more difficult; but the modernist with his new rhythms to express new moods—I should shock Robert Graves by applying to a modernist the creed of the 'dead and gone' imagist—and his effort to bring in a hundred persons, summer, autumn, Wagner, Lil's husband, quotations from Shakespeare, Spenser, Goldsmith, Milton, George Meredith, fleeting fancies, nightmare associations, the effect of madness and tiredness, and to make a poem of them, is apt to strain the attention of the plain reader to the breaking-point, and to cause him to revolt against a theory of art that afflicts him with so heavy a burden. Yet, I am afraid that Browning and Walt Whitman between them must be held ultimately responsible, in so far as writers of one generation are definitely influenced by those of a former generation. T. S. Eliot does not hesitate to use the exact words of his predecessors just as they happen to crop up in his mind, without reverence if not without relevance. Could one say that he was influenced by the

Holy Scriptures because he quotes 'There was silence in Heaven' in *Aunt Helen*, or by George Meredith, because in the same poem he quotes one of Meredith's most famous lines? At any rate, it is not that kind of influence that I have set out to trace in this present chapter. I have been thinking of Browning's realistic manner, and how therein he has shown the way to succeeding poets. If they have brought within their scope more than he would have allowed, and gone further than he would have thought legitimate, this enlargement of scope and extension of treatment may have value.

IV

BROWNING THE PSYCHOLOGIST AND HIS INVENTION OF THE DRAMATIC LYRIC

I BEGIN by a reference to the important sentence quoted in the last chapter from a letter written on January 19th, 1870, to Miss Isa Blagden: 'I should judge the conflict in the knight's soul the proper subject to describe.' Browning, you remember, had been reading an Idyll of Tennyson's 'about a knight being untrue to his friend and yielding to the temptation of that friend's mistress after having engaged to assist him in his suit'. Browning says that he and Tennyson 'look at the object of art in poetry so differently!' 'Tennyson thinks he should describe the castle, and the effect of the moon on its towers, and anything *but* the soul.' The letter goes on: 'The monotony, however, you must expect—if the new is to be of a piece with the old ... with Tennyson [as with Morris]—the old *Galahad* is to me incomparably better than a dozen centuries of the *Grail, Coming of Arthur*, and so on. I ought to be somewhat surprised to find myself thinking so, since it seems also the opinion of everybody: even the reviewers hardly keep on the old chime of laudation.'

I think he preferred the old *Galahad* partly because it escapes the 'monotony' of the *Idylls*, but chiefly because in that poem Tennyson does describe the knight's soul, and describes it more or less in Browning's way by letting the knight speak throughout. There is even a conflict in Galahad's soul, though victory is assured, and the energy and spirituality of the knight are the 'notes' of the poem. Energy and spirituality are the 'notes' of many of Browning's poems. Tennyson's *Galahad* may be compared with *The Statue and the Bust*. Whatever be the fate of the irresolute, the men and women of divided aims, Browning says:

> they see not God, I know,
> Nor all that chivalry of his,
> The soldier-saints who, row on row,
>
> Burn upward each to his point of bliss—
> Since, the end of life being manifest,
> He had burned his way thro' the world to this.

Description of the soul was to Browning the object of art in poetry. It was so in 1870—less than a year after the publication of the last volume of *The Ring and the Book*; it was so in 1840, when he finished *Sordello*: 'The historical decoration was purposely of no more importance than a background requires; and my stress lay on the incidents in the development of a soul: little else is worth study. I, at least, always thought so—you, with many known and unknown to me think so—others may one day think so.' [1]

That 'one day' is our day. The modern stress lies on incidents in the development of the soul, not only or chiefly in poetry but in creative literature generally, as well as in the vast field of scientific psychology.

Suppose Browning had taken Tennyson's subject from Malory's *Morte d'Arthur*, how would he have described the conflict in the knight's soul? I wish to posit the question now and to lead up to the answer in the rest of the chapter.

The friend, to whom Browning revealed his most intimate thoughts and hopes, was Alfred Domett. He is known to the reader of Browning as the original of

[1] Introductory letter to J. Milsand of Dijon, written twenty-five years after the writing of *Sordello*.

'Waring' and as referred to in the poem called *The Guardian Angel*. He was born in 1811 and educated at St. John's, Cambridge, but he did not become associated with Browning until 1840, and he left England for New Zealand in 1842. His career in New Zealand was useful and distinguished, and he rose to be Prime Minister in 1862. Browning wrote to him regularly until his marriage with Elizabeth Barrett (Sept. 12th, 1846), when all letters abruptly ceased. Domett returned to England in 1871: 'Waring came back the other day, the same as ever, nearly.'[1] He had preserved the letters sent to him by Browning, and in 1906 they were published by Sir Frederic Kenyon.

Browning's affection for Domett is expressed in *Waring*:

> Meantime, how much I loved him,
> I find out now I've lost him,
> I who cared not if I moved him,
> Who could so carelessly accost him,
> Henceforth never shall get free
> Of his ghostly company.

Browning's picture of him in the same poem may be set side by side with the water-colour drawing made by George Lance, R.A., in 1836. Domett evidently impressed all his associates in some such way as Arthur Hallam impressed his, though Domett's bright-eyed enthusiasm and capacity for hero-worship were qualities not conspicuous in Hallam. It would be interesting to speculate why Browning ceased to write to him in 1846, but there is nothing to go on except the challengable surmises from the course of events.[2]

[1] From a letter to Miss Isa Blagden, March 30th, 1872.
[2] Browning left it to Joseph Arnould to inform Domett that he *was* married.

I have drawn attention to this early friendship, because Domett was a discerning as well as a wholehearted admirer of Browning, and because Browning made reference in his letters to his own poetical work.

Domett's chief effort in poetry is an epic of New Zealand, *Ranolf and Amohia*, published in 1872. Five years later he published another volume entitled *Flotsam and Jetsam*, dedicated 'to (if ever there were one!) "a mighty poet and a subtle-souled psychologist": to Robert Browning'.

The last letter written by Browning to New Zealand contains a valuable confession of poetic faith and an indication of that labour which resulted in the perfection of his chief poetic invention.

'Can you remember what this letter is about which lies open here as fresh as if you had penned it yesterday? It is full of cautions and warnings as touching my wellbeing, mental and physical, all admirable of their kind; and I think that, on the whole, I have profited by them, turned them to practical account . . . for "laid them to heart" I *know* I have. As to the obscurity and imperfect expression, the last number of my "Bells", which you get with this, must stand for the best I could do, *four or five months* ago, to rid myself of these defects—and if you judge I have succeeded to any degree, you will not fancy I am likely to relax in my endeavour now. As for the necessity of such endeavour I agree with you altogether: from the beginning, I have been used to take a high ground, and say, all endeavour elsewhere is thrown away. Endeavour *to think* (the real *thought*), to *imagine*, to *create*, or whatever they call it—as well endeavour to add the cubit to your stature! *Nascitur poeta*—and that conceded to happen, the one object of labour is naturally what you recommend to me, and I to myself—nobody knows better, with what indifferent success. But here is, without affectation, the reason why I have gone on so far although succeeding so indifferently: I felt so instinctively from the beginning that unless I tumbled out the dozen more or less of conceptions, I should bear them about for ever, and year by year get straiter and stiffer in those horrible cross-bones with the long name, and at last parturition would be the curse indeed. Mine was the better way, I do calmly believe, for at this moment I feel as everybody does who has *worked*—"in vain"? no matter, if the work was real. It seems disinspiriting for a man to hack away at trees in a wood, and at the end of his clearing come to rocks or the sea or whatever disappoints him as leading to nothing; but still, turn the man's face, point him to new trees and the true direction, and who will compare his power arising from experience with that of another who has been confirming himself all the time in the belief that chopping wood is incredible labour, and that the first blow he strikes will be sure to jar his arm to the shoulder without shaking a leaf on the lowest bough? I stand at present and wait like such a fellow as the first of these; if the real work should present itself to be done, I shall begin at once and in earnest . . . not having to learn first of all how to keep the axe-head from flying back into my face; and if I stop in the middle, let the bad business of other years show that I was not idle nor altogether incompetent.'

His 'dozen more or less of conceptions' were to emerge through the study of incidents in the development of the soul and were to be expressed dramatically. His direct dramas are by no means failures, but the play was not his proper medium. Yet he wished to let his *personae* talk and to reveal themselves through talk. Flecker says that he was always making desperate attempts to bring the language of conversation into poetry. 'Desperate attempts' may apply to the work of the man with the axe, but only in so far as the work is hard. Browning's attempts were very nearly triumphant. He invented what he called the dramatic lyric, and the only drawback to the dramatic lyric is the difficulty of making the meaning clear. Without any doubt it suited Browning's mind, and he was more successful in it than in the direct dramatic form. And without any doubt it has an attractiveness which has proved irresistible to succeeding writers. But it did not help, as he obviously hoped it would, to save him from the obscure and (thereby) imperfect expression, which Domett cautioned him to avoid, and which this letter proves he wished to avoid.[1]

A play is much more likely to be clear than a dramatic lyric. A play is meant to be acted, and the actors have to make their points at once. There is no turning back to a previous page to refresh one's memory or to clear up an obscurity. Browning's plays *play* as clearly as Shakespeare's, but the play-form does not provide him with the scope for his subtle psychologizing. This psychologizing is the thing he could do, the thing he thought worth doing, and the dramatic lyric is the form through which he could do it. The study of incidents in the development of the soul is apt to be an obscure business. Perhaps it is not the proper business of the poet. But given that a mighty poet undertakes it, he might well think that the language of conversation was

[1] Compare Introductory Note to the first series of Selections, 1872.

the clearest mode of expression: 'If I let this man talk and go on talking and talk himself out, I shall surely make all things clear.' The drawback to the theory is that the soul of one person is a shifting and unstable stage for a drama to be played on, and the imagination and attention of the spectator of the drama are apt to be strained intolerably. Browning could set the various actors moving about, and hear what they said *in full* or construe their replies and remarks and interjections from a lift of the eyebrow or a wave of the hand, but the reader often fails to do so.

Of course we are more accustomed to Browning than we were. In February 1889 the members of the Day's End Club in Exeter met together to read some poems of Browning. They failed to grasp his meaning and they pleaded to him for help. He answered their questions in the margin of the sheet on which they were written.[1]

My Last Duchess (Selections, pp. 2, 3)

Was she in fact shallow and easily and equally well pleased with any favour: or did the Duke so describe her as a supercilious cover to real and well-justified jealousy?

As an excuse—mainly to himself—for taking revenge on one who had unwittingly wounded his absurdly pretentious vanity, by failing to recognize his superiority in even the most trifling matters.

' "Fra Pandolf" by design':

By what design?

To have some occasion for telling the story, and illustrating part of it.

[1] The poet's answers are italicized.

In a Gondola (Selections, p. 58)

Was *she* true, or in the conspiracy?
 Out of it.

Earth's Immortalities (Selections, p. 72)

'Love':

Is the refrain—'(Love me for ever!)' cynical, or sad, or trustful?

A mournful comment on the short duration of the conventional 'For Ever!'

Parting at Morning (Selections, p. 102)

'And the need of a world of men for me':

Is this an expression by her of her sense of loss of him, or the despairing cry of a ruined woman?

Neither: it is his *confession of how fleeting is the belief (implied in the first part) that such raptures are self-sufficient and enduring—as for the time they appear.*[1]

---

[1] This is copied from the original which lies before me. See also article on 'Robert Browning's Answers to Questions concerning Some of his Poems' (*Cornhill*, March 1914) reprinted in *New Poems by Robert and Mrs. Browning*. For ease of reference I append the following passages:

My Last Duchess

Ferrara

That's my last Duchess painted on the wall,
Looking as if she were alive. I call
That piece a wonder, now: Frà Pandolf's hands
Worked busily a day, and there she stands.
Wilt please you sit and look at her? I said
'Frà Pandolf' by design, for never read
Strangers like you that pictured countenance,
The depth and passion of its earnest glance,
But to myself they turned (since none put by
The curtain I have drawn for you, but I)
And seemed as they would ask me, if they durst,
How such a glance came there; so not the first

HIS INVENTION OF THE DRAMATIC LYRIC 119

The difficulties of the members of the Day's End Club came through their unfamiliarity with the form of the poems. In order to appreciate the character of the last duchess they had to realize the character of the man who was speaking of her. It is hardly possible for us to conceive that they should entertain the notion of the duke's 'real and well-justified jealousy'.

In the second part of the poem *Meeting at Night—Parting at Morning* their difficulty arose through a failure to grasp that the man who speaks in the first part speaks

> Are you to turn and ask thus. Sir, 'twas not
> Her husband's presence only called that spot
> Of joy into the Duchess' cheek: . . .
> . . . She thanked men—good! but thanked
> Somehow—I know not how—as if she ranked
> My gift of a nine-hundred-years-old name
> With anybody's gift.

Meeting at Night
I

> The grey sea and the long black land;
> And the yellow half-moon, large and low;
> And the startled little waves that leap
> In fiery ringlets from their sleep,
> As I gain the cove with pushing prow,
> And quench its speed i' the slushy sand.

II

> Then a mile of warm sea-scented beach;
> Three fields to cross till a farm appears;
> A tap at the pane, the quick sharp scratch
> And blue spurt of a lighted match,
> And a voice less loud, thro' its joys and fears,
> Than the two hearts beating each to each.

Parting at Morning

> Round the cape of a sudden came the sea,
> And the sun looked over the mountain's rim;
> And straight was a path of gold for him,
> And the need of a world of men for me.

throughout. In a dramatic lyric there is never any change of speaker. 'Him' in the third line of *Parting at Morning* refers to the sun.

As illustrating the greater familiarity of readers of our day with Browning's characteristic mode of expression, one may notice that Mr. V. C. Clinton-Baddeley, in a twenty minutes' reading from 2LO in January 1930 of selections from Browning's poems, chose *My Last Duchess* and *Meeting at Night* and *Parting at Morning*. He would not have chosen them if he had thought that they would present any difficulty to the casual listener. Browning's reputation for obscurity is evidently diminishing.

I wish to emphasize the point that part of the difficulty of Browning is inherent in the form he invented. Having discarded the play form he chose to write the Dramatic Lyric, or, as it is now the custom to call it, the Dramatic Monologue, and this form he gradually perfected until he found it ready to his hand (with no danger of the 'axe-head flying back into his face') for his mightiest work, *The Ring and the Book*.

We have noticed the disadvantages of the dramatic lyric; let us see its advantages. In other words: What did Browning mean it to be and what did it enable him to do?

I suppose a mode of expression ought not to need explaining any more than the title of a book. But Browning chose to explain this one: In 1863: 'Such Poems as the majority in this volume might also come properly enough, I suppose, under the head of "Dramatic Pieces"; being, though often Lyric in expression, always Dramatic in principle, and so many utterances of so many imaginary persons, not mine.'

Lyric poetry is generally considered to be 'subjective

rather than objective'. It expresses thoughts and feelings of the poet himself. Browning does not express his own thoughts and feelings in the dramatic lyric. It is the utterance of an imaginary person and not of the poet himself. But it is the utterance of the imaginary person's thoughts and feelings. The first dramatic lyric, in point of time, is *Porphyria's Lover*, published in 1836, when Browning was twenty-four. It was not, however, called a dramatic lyric, though it was afterwards included under 'Madhouse Cells' in the collection of Dramatic Lyrics. The first poem in 'Dramatic Lyrics' is *Cavalier Tunes*. Browning may have placed this poem first, because the poem is a song and, therefore, popularly recognizable as a lyric. The second is *My Last Duchess*, a clear example of the kind of poem that afterwards became Browning's chief mode of expression. This would not be popularly recognizable as lyric. Yet it is subjective in the sense of expressing the thoughts and feelings of the imaginary speaker. This is the only sense in which the term 'lyric' can be applied to all the poems Browning gathered together as dramatic lyrics and to the different poems (*Half Rome, The Other Half Rome, Tertium Quid, Count Guido Franceschini, Giuseppe Caponsacchi*, &c.) of *The Ring and the Book*. If 'subjective' is opposed to 'objective', and lyrical poetry said to be subjective in *not* representing a story of people, actions, and events, then most of these poems of Browning cannot be described as lyrical. Browning says they are 'dramatic in principle'. I suppose that he means essentially dramatic: the essence of them is a drama. The drama, however, is unfolded through the talk of a single speaker, and in his talk the speaker does not set out to tell a story but to give his own reflections and aspirations, his own outcries and murmurings. The talk is a study of incidents in the development of the speaker's soul. Its chief design is to reveal the speaker himself. Yet an important design is to unfold the drama and to reveal the other *dramatis personae*. The stage on which the drama is set is the personality of the speaker. We watch the figures of the drama moving about on this stage. That is to say, they are seen through the medium of the speaker's personality.

The verse form of the dramatic monologue does not matter. It may be a stanza form like *Cavalier Tunes* or in heroic couplets like *My Last Duchess* or in blank verse like the poems of *The Ring and the Book*.

Let us examine the second of the *Cavalier Tunes* called 'Give a Rouse'. The speaker is the head of a house loyal to King Charles I. This old cavalier has benefited through his loyalty in goods and house and money and wine. But since the war he has begun to suffer. His son George has been shot by Cromwell's soldiers, and he foresees other calamities. Yet he pledges his king in spite of all, and heartens the others to maintain the cause.

The drama is unfolded in successive pictures: the prosperous, spendthrift, reckless, loyal gentleman *enjoying* his loyalty; the father and son together in their enthusiasm for the King; the son in battle cheering and laughing at the very moment the bullet struck him.

But the cavalier does not set out to unfold this drama. He is giving his own reflections, aspirations, outcries. And the resultant poem is vivid and thrilling, mainly because it reveals the cavalier himself—true to his accepted duty, defiant of circumstances, stifling his own grief, rousing the others to his own unfailing loyalty.

I

King Charles, and who'll do him right now?
King Charles, and who's ripe for fight now?
Give a rouse: here's, in Hell's despite now,
King Charles!

II

Who gave me the goods that went since?
Who raised me the house that sank once?
Who helped me to gold I spent since?
Who found me in wine you drank once?
  Chorus—King Charles, and who'll do him right now? . . .

III

To whom used my boy George quaff else,
By the old fool's side that begot him?
For whom did he cheer and laugh else,
While Noll's damned troopers shot him?
  Chorus—King Charles, and who'll do him right now? . . .

We can see the development of the dramatic monologue and the way in which Browning perfected it by comparing the earliest example of this form, *Porphyria's Lover*, with *Pompilia* of *The Ring and the Book*.

Porphyria's Lover was reprinted as the second *Madhouse Cell*, the first being *Johannes Agricola in Meditation*. 'Madhouse Cell' indicates the abnormality of the person speaking. The abnormality is really typical. For the most part, the dramatic lyric takes the speaker at a moment of crisis: when he or she is wrought up, emotionalized by some happening; and Porphyria's lover has been wrought up past the borderline of sanity.

The story is this: The lover was sitting alone in his room at night. He could hear the wind tearing through the elm tops and vexing the lake. He listened, even then, with 'heart fit to break'. And at the moment of heartbreak, Porphyria glided in. She had come from a 'gay feast', moved by the sudden thought of him, as she knew she would find him, lonely and pale for the love of her. She put his arm round her waist, bared her smooth white shoulder, made his cheek lie there, and spread her yellow hair over his face. Surprise made his heart swell. He was very proud. He knew that Porphyria worshipped him. At that instant she was wholly good and wholly his. He would catch that instant. He found a thing to do. He wound one long yellow string of hair three times round her throat and strangled her. She felt no pain. Then he warily opened her eyes.

>   Laughed the blue eyes without a stain.
> And I untightened next the tress
>   About her neck; her cheek once more
> Blushed bright beneath my burning kiss:
>   I propped her head up as before,
>   Only, this time my shoulder bore
> Her head which droops upon it still:
>   The smiling rosy little head,
> So glad it has its utmost will,
>   That all it scorned at once is fled,
>   And I, its love, am gained instead!
> Porphyria's love: she guessed not how
>   Her darling one wish would be heard.
> And thus we sit together now,
>   And all night long we have not stirred,
>   And yet God has not said a word!

This first example of the monologue is nearer to a straightforward narrative than the later examples. The moment of speaking is not told us until the end of the poem, and we are led on as in the ordinary narrative to the climax. The poem is the effort of a young man making an experiment. It is essentially the same as the dramatic lyrics that follow in that it gives the thoughts and feelings of the speaker, but the poet has not yet familiarized himself with his medium, and, at first reading, one hardly realizes that he is breaking away from the direct narrative form.

A note of youth also is the choice of an abnormal situation, though the *strained* soul is always more interesting to Browning than the calm and normal soul.

The dramatic lyric form in this case enabled him to put before us in a crude and extreme example one of his favourite ideas: Seize and fix the highest moment and thereby glimpse the *summum bonum*, Heaven being our best moment made eternal.[1] The madman evidently thinks that God ought to show some sign of His approval.

The Ring and the Book contains ten dramatic monologues. In three (*Half Rome*, *The Other Half Rome*, *Tertium Quid*) the speakers are commentators on the drama; in two, the speakers are barristers engaged in the trial; in one (*The Pope*) the speaker is the judge to whom is assigned the task of passing sentence, in four (*Count Guido Franceschini, Giuseppe Caponsacchi, Pompilia*, and *Guido*) the speakers are dramatis personae. The background of *Pompilia* is the poet's wife Elizabeth, and yet the character of Pompilia is there just as he found it in the collection of documents now called *The Old Yellow Book*. *Giuseppe Caponsacchi* has for background the kind of person Browning himself hoped to be, and yet Caponsacchi is also true to the character in *The Old Yellow Book*. The character of Guido is alone inconsistent with *The Old Yellow Book*. If one studies the

[1] See *The Last Ride Together*.

hang-dog, sneak-thief face in 'Ritratto dell' infelice Guido Franceschini' one cannot reconcile it with either the Count Guido Franceschini of the first Guido poem or the Guido of the second. But for a penetrating analysis of villainy Guido is supreme. I hazard the theory that for background Guido was the kind of person Browning feared to become. He could not have feared to become the person of the portrait, but the person of the poem has intelligence and energy.

Setting aside these speculations, notice that in *Pompilia* the moment of speaking is indicated at once. What the dramatic monologue enables Browning to do, in this case, is to give Pompilia's own view of her childhood and girlhood, her own view of that dubious pair, Pietro and Violante Comparini, her own view of Giuseppe Caponsacchi, as well as a view, obtainable from no one else, of the events that led up to the assassinations and the assassinations themselves. Supremely, it enabled Browning to give us Pompilia herself from first to last, a complete and detailed picture of his ideal woman.

The impressions of her childhood and girlhood are given as they could not have been given by the use of any other form. Even in a prose transcript it is possible to see the power of the dramatic monologue.[1]

When Pompilia stood scarcely as high as a nunnery bed she used to wonder at a sculptured lion to the right of the church door. The lion seemed to rush out of the wall with half his body and he was in the act of devouring the prostrate figure of a man. What did the marble lion mean? Then there was a Virgin in a lonely niche

---

[1] I have ventured to give this prose transcript of a part of *Pompilia* at some length, because *Pompilia* offers the best illustration I know of what his form of the dramatic monologue enabled the poet to do.

at their street corner. The Virgin was made of thin white glazed clay and the babe that sat upon her knee was broken off. This Virgin rather than the gay ones always got Pompilia's rose.

She had three little girl friends, Tisbe, Giulia, and Tecla. Tisbe was of her own age, a neighbour's child, whom Violante brought to play with her on rainy afternoons. A tapestry hung on the wall of the room where she played, and she and Tisbe agreed to find each other out among the figures. Tisbe was the huntress with a half-moon on her hair-knot and a spear in her hand. She was flying, but without any wings; only as she flew a great scarf was blown to a bluish rainbow at her back. Pompilia herself was a figure turned into a sort of tree, green leaves flourishing out of her five finger-ends and all the rest of her brown and rough. And both Tisbe and Pompilia were half persuaded that the game was real and that they were these things they pretended to be.

Even as a child, when she took her happiness for granted, Pompilia realized Pietro's fondness for her, and, somehow, very dimly, that he needed a child for his own sake—'to make his life of use', as she afterwards phrased it.

She was ill once, and a doctor came with a great ugly hat without a plume, a black jerkin and black buckles and a black sword, and a white sharp beard over his ruff in the front—oh, so lean, so sour-faced and austere! He felt her pulse and made her put out her tongue, then opened a phial and dripped a drop or two of a little black something and she was cured. This was Master Malpichi, a physician without equal in Rome, so they said. What did it matter to her that he was so ugly, with his fierce beard and grim face? It was his physic beautified the man.

Once in the Square of the Spaniards, opposite the Spanish House, she saw a foreigner make a goat perform. The goat was a 'shuddering white woman of a beast' and her master had trained her to climb up and stand straight upon a pile of sticks put close. When she was settled there he took away, one by one, all the sticks except the four upon which her little hoofs really rested, and there she kept firm, while all underneath was air.

At another time when she was crossing the same Square a rough gaunt ragged man, with fiery eyes, rushed at her. There was a crowd of boys and idlers at his heels. He took her hand in his two hands and held it and said: 'Here's the little girl who will let me speak. I am the Pope, Pope Sextus. He who is proclaimed Pope to-day, called Innocent the Twelfth, is Lucifer disguised in human flesh. It was the angels, met in conclave, who crowned me.' She knew that he was deluded, even before the bystanders interposed, crying: 'Take his hands off her, he is a maniac.'

There was an old rhyme she must have heard from some one, when she lived at home—perhaps, from Violante. It was about a virgin who was pursued by Paynims. She hid herself, for the faith of God, in a cave. And a thunderstone wrapped in a flame revealed her couch. The Paynims laughed—'Thanks to the lightning, she is ours at last.' And she cried, 'Wrath of God, assert His love. Servant of God, thou fire, befriend His child.' And the fire she grasped at fixed its flash and became a calm, cold, dreadful sword. The Paynims fell prostrate before her brandished blade, and the souls within

HIS INVENTION OF THE DRAMATIC LYRIC

them died away, and over their bodies, sworded, safe, she walked forth to the solitudes and Christ.

These recollections emerge quite naturally. Pompilia is lying waiting for death. She remembers her childhood, and tells the nuns. But if the reader is familiar with the story of *The Ring and the Book* he will perceive that there is not one of these experiences but has its counterpart in Pompilia's subsequent history. For example, it was the thought of Master Malpichi's efficacious medicine, in spite of his repulsive ugliness, that reconciled her to marriage with the repulsive Guido. By what method, other than the dramatic monologue, could Browning have accomplished this lovely poet's feat?

Some of the dramatic monologues are in the form of soliloquy, but the majority are conversational—that is to say, there are listeners, and the presence of the listeners affects the talk. Often, the remarks of the listeners are indirectly introduced or indicated by the speaker's answers.

In *My Last Duchess* the listener is an envoy from another state who has come to treat with the duke about a second marriage. The duke's talk is carefully calculated to impress this envoy. In *Andrea del Sarto* the listener is the painter's wife, who is impatient to join a 'cousin' waiting in the street below. This cousin's whistle is heard by Andrea. In the first part of *Bishop Blougram's Apology* the listener is a journalist named Gigadibs, and his side of the debate is clearly indicated by the Bishop, and the 'apology' is an answer to him. In *Fra Lippo Lippi*[1] the listeners are the members of the watch who

[1] Notice also Browning's 'crowd psychology', of which there are notable examples in this poem as well as in *The Ring and the Book*.

have arrested Lippo while he was engaged in a nocturnal adventure. Lippo picks out one:

> I'd like his face—
> His, elbowing on his comrade in the door
> With the pike and lantern,—for the slave that holds
> John Baptist's head a-dangle, by the hair
> With one hand ('Look you now', as who should say)
> And his weapon in the other, yet unwiped!
> It's not your chance to have a bit of chalk,
> A wood-coal or the like? or you should see!

The poem is largely conversational in the strictest sense:

> Old Aunt Lapaccia trussed me with one hand,
> (Its fellow was a stinger as I knew)
> And so along the wall, over the bridge,
> By the straight cut to the convent. Six words there,
> While I stood munching my first bread that month;
> 'So boy, you're minded,' quoth the good fat father
> Wiping his own mouth, 'twas refection-time,—
> 'To quit this very miserable world?
> Will you renounce'... 'the mouthful of bread?' thought I;
> By no means! Brief, they made a monk of me...
>
> . . . .
>
> 'Nay,' quoth the Prior, 'turn him out, d'ye say?
> In no wise. Lose a crow and catch a lark.
> What if at last we get our man of parts,
> We Carmelites, like those Calmaldolese
> And Preaching Friars, to do our church up fine
> And put the front on it that ought to be!'[1]

---

[1] The story goes that at the Brownings' house there were present Tennyson, Dante Gabriel Rossetti, and the Brownings. Tennyson read *Maud* and Browning followed with *Fra Lippo Lippi*. One wonders what Tennyson really thought of it. Rossetti made a sketch of Tennyson reading *Maud*, with a quotation from *Maud* subjoined: 'I hate the dreadful hollow behind the little wood.' The sketch is in the Tate

HIS INVENTION OF THE DRAMATIC LYRIC

Count Guido Franceschini speaks before his judges in *The Ring and the Book*. So does Caponsacchi. Guido is talking to his confessors, and, at the end, the black-robed band enters to lead him out to execution. Pompilia is in the House of the Convertites, having been brought there from the villa where she has been mortally wounded by Guido and his associates. She is talking to the Sisters. The Pope is sitting alone in his closet. His talk is mainly a soliloquy, but others are within hail. Beside him on a little table is a handbell, and before ringing it to summon an attendant he pauses to review the case. At the end he rings the handbell and delivers his message for the Governor.

The dramatis personae in *The Ring and the Book* speak at a moment of crisis—one might almost say, at the top of an emotional wave. They all go through the events of the drama in detail. It is usually said that Browning tells the same story over and over again. This is not quite true, because in each of the dramatic monologues the events are looked at from a different angle, and in each case emphasis is laid on one part or other—never the same part. For example, Pompilia gives the impressions of her childhood, which, of course, are not to be found elsewhere; and Caponsacchi records the separate events, in close detail, of the Flight. Pompilia speaks of the Flight, but her emphasis is on another aspect of it. She is pregnant, and her view of a mother and a child she meets at an inn remains as one of the chief things in her account of the Flight.

The emotion of Guido in the last of the dramatic

Gallery. See *The Life of Robert Browning* by W. Hall Griffin and H. C. Minchin, p. 207, and *Elizabeth Barret Browning: Letters to her Sister*, ed. by Leonard Huxley, 1929, p. 230.

monologues may, perhaps, be accounted the most extreme, because he is face to face with almost inevitable death, but Caponsacchi's emotion is the most poignant. He has been brought back from his relegation in Civita Vecchia and called upon to bear witness before the court, just when he has learned that Pompilia is dying.

I emphasize this fact of an emotional crisis because it explains the vivid and detailed exposition of events. Browning is not only a subtle-souled psychologist, but the method of the perfected dramatic monologue is scientifically sound. I may be pardoned for dwelling on this aspect of Browning, because it has often been objected that the telling of the story by Guido, Caponsacchi, and Pompilia is unnatural. Only by a poetic convention, it is said, is Browning allowed to do it.

I appeal to Freud and to my own experience. Freud,[1] following Breuer, confirmed the observation that hysterical symptoms and the form they assumed depended on events in the patient's past life. He found by experiment that if the patient could recall the originating events the symptoms vanished. I heard of this conclusion of Freud's and tested it in my own case. In the summer of 1923 I found myself suffering from certain symptoms. I talked at random to a sympathetic listener, and three or four apparently unrelated and unintelligible 'clues' emerged. After the lapse of some hours these 'clues' became associated, and I recalled a series of events of the summer of 1916 that evidently gave rise to these symptoms, and the symptoms vanished. What amazed me was the vividness of my recollections. I remembered the whole series in the minutest detail,

[1] *The Psychopathology of Everyday Life* and *Introductory Lectures on Psycho-Analysis* by Sigmund Freud.

and visualized everything. And when I told the full story to the same sympathetic listener my excitement was almost uncontrollable. I was at the top of an emotional wave. This experience was sufficient to convince me that Browning's method was psychologically sound.

We are now in a position to propose a tentative answer to the question posited above: Suppose Browning had taken Tennyson's subject from Malory's *Morte d'Arthur*,[1] how would he have described the conflict in the knight's soul?

He would have written a dramatic monologue, taking Lancelot at some moment of crisis and causing him to talk over the whole series of events. Or he might have given Lancelot two speeches, as he gives Guido: one, justifying himself because of the nature of his task and Guinevere's love for him as well as his love for her; and another, showing that all had come to ruin through sexual disloyalty. The conflict in the knight's soul would have come out in both, but in the first, perhaps, only indirectly, because conflicts in the soul are apt not to be acknowledged when the contest is between something that is approved by the common conscience and something that is condemned by it.

I must leave to the next chapter the attempt to trace the influence of the conversational method upon succeeding writers. I shall venture to include prose writers as well as poets.

[1] The reference in Browning's letter of Jan. 19th, 1870, is of course to *Pelleas and Ettarre*, but I have chosen to consider how Browning might have treated the main theme of *The Idylls of the King*.

V

THE CONVERSATIONAL METHOD IN THE TWENTIETH CENTURY

AFTER all, the stress of newness in Browning's description of his monologues as dramatic lyrics is on the word 'lyric'. Tennyson and Rossetti had both made successful use of the dramatic monologue, but Browning in giving the thoughts and feelings of the speaker turned the soliloquy into a colloquy. The monologue became, in some sense, a conversation, and he could bring in, quite naturally, the language of conversation, and yet leave himself free to rise, just as naturally, to sublime utterance. The thoughts and feelings of the speaker were given the widest range. Opportunity was afforded (also quite naturally) for the study of incidents in the development of his soul, for his view of events, for his presentation of evidence, for his refutation of charges, for his excuses for conduct, for his account of human contacts and their reaction upon him, involving his judgement of the other persons concerned. The monologue was a psychological vehicle.

I

This method was applicable to prose-fiction. Henry James, in his centenary lecture on *The Novel in 'The Ring and the Book'* proposed to take Caponsacchi as the centre of interest. He would arrange a chance confrontation with Guido at the beginning of the story, and an interview between Caponsacchi and the Pope, in which they compared notes about Pompilia, at the end of the story. But if Caponsacchi were the centre of interest, everything could be told not only from his point of view but by him. At the moments of crisis we should see the facts through him. That would be of the essence of Browning's method. And that method had already been used in prose fiction and, according to some critics, given us a new type of novel.

One may say that GEORGE MEREDITH's *The Ordeal of Richard Feverel, A History of a Father and a Son*, published in 1859, was the beginning of a new era in novel-writing, and that the method of it was Browning's method applied to prose-fiction.

Lest it should be thought that I am being led away by my own desire to find resemblances and analogies and thereby crushing or distorting the truth ('to crush this a little, it would bow to me') I will quote from J. B. Priestley:[1] '(George Meredith brought into) existence a new method that did nothing less than begin a fresh chapter in the history of the novel. It is a method familiar to all readers of contemporary fiction, and yet, in spite of new developments, he himself still remains its supreme master and his fiction remains the supreme example of its successful use.

'This method describes the action, at all heightened moments, not from the normal detached point of view of a disinterested spectator, but, as it were, from inside of the mind of one of the actors, not as it appears to a merely observant onlooker, but, as it appears in the consciousness of a character taking part in it. He gives us not the fact but the fact coloured by emotion and distorted by thought. Both the poet in him, wishing to express states of mind, or, as Bacon said, "submitting

[1] *George Meredith*, by J. B. Priestley (English Men of Letters, New Series, 1926).

the shows of things to the desire of the mind", and the critic and philosopher, intent upon psychology, grappling with motive, the conflict in the very soul, stand to gain from this change in the point of view. Indeed, it is the only way in which they could adequately express themselves in fiction. And it is really something more than the subjective method now employed by nearly all serious writers of fiction, who make use of the consciousness of their leading characters and give us an inward drama of thought as well as an outward one of speech and action. Meredith does this, but he does not stop here; it is not that he merely tells us what his personages think and feel, but he actually presents the scene to us, if the situation should demand it, completely coloured and shaped by the emotion and thought of the character involved, so that the situation comes to us as it came to the character, we live in the scene and also live in the character.'

This last sentence would stand as a description of almost any of Browning's 'scenes'. Take the scene at the inn in Castelnuovo when Guido has overtaken Caponsacchi and Pompilia. When Caponsacchi is speaking we have the scene 'completely coloured and shaped by the emotion and thought' of Caponsacchi, so that the situation comes to us as it came to him, we live in the scene and also live in the character. We also live in the scene when Guido is speaking, and if the situation does not come to us as it came to him, that is because we live in his character and can make allowances for his distortion of the situation. The psychology is even more subtle than Meredith's.

The phrase, 'conversational method', perhaps conveys to the plain reader an image of a kind of placid fireside talk. Two or three persons are sitting together, and, with intervals of silence, they drop out casual remarks about nothing in particular. But suppose these two or three persons are friends who have many recollections in common, but who have not met for a long time. One of them, meanwhile, has been for a voyage, which has proved to be a critical experience. The companions of his voyage are known to the friends with whom he is conversing. He talks about the voyage. The others hardly say a word. But he answers their unspoken thoughts. The talk becomes a monologue. The speaker may use the homeliest words and images, or at heightened moments may rise to a vivid and exalted eloquence. The situation comes to the listeners as it came to the speaker; they live in the scene and also live in him. And when it is all written down, we have a story like JOSEPH CONRAD's *Youth*.

Youth corresponds to *Porphyria's Lover*, in that it is nearer to the direct narrative form than the later dramatic pieces of Browning. When we come to Conrad's first really successful novel, *Chance*, we may perhaps be led to the conclusion [1] that he consciously adopted Browning's method for his purpose.

Like so many novels of Conrad this story is the story of a voyage. The preliminaries are set out, and we learn what happened after the voyage, but the heart of the story is a voyage of the ship *Ferndale*.

Of the *Ferndale* Powell, called Young Powell in the beginning, was second mate, and Franklin was the chief mate. The captain's name was Roderick Anthony, son of Caerleon Anthony, the poet. He has gone through the ceremony of marriage with Flora de Barral, a

[1] Such conclusions are always challengeable.

daughter of the great de Barral, a financier who has been in prison.

Flora de Barral had been befriended, after her father's downfall, by Mrs. Fyne, Captain Anthony's sister. Flora believes passionately in the great de Barral's innocence, and not only is she given her 'freedom' by Captain Anthony, but allowed to make the *Ferndale* a place of refuge for her father, when he comes out of prison.

The great de Barral, who ships under the name of Smith, is jealous of his daughter's affection, and in his self-centred diseased way watches Captain Anthony, whom he thinks of as his jailer, and eventually plans to poison him. Powell intervenes; Flora is 'restored' to her husband; and de Barral himself drinks the poison.

After the lapse of years Captain Anthony goes down with his ship, and we are left with the prospect of his widow's marriage to Powell, no longer young.

This is the barest bones of the story. The remarkable thing about the book is the method of reaching the objective facts. We never reach them directly. It is hard to say shortly how we do reach them. And among the objective facts I include most of the persons.

There is an 'I' in the story. The man who speaks in the first person singular—and I will call him 'I', if I need to refer to him (for indeed he is not prominent)—is a friend of Marlow's. Marlow is the narrator of *Youth*, reappearing after many years.

Marlow and 'I' meet Powell, who tells them about his first appointment as second mate to the *Ferndale*. This was a great while ago—the time of the main part of the tale. Marlow has met the Fynes. He also remembers the notorious case of the great de Barral, and he has seen something of Flora de Barral.

THE TWENTIETH CENTURY

Henceforward Marlow is the chief speaker. But he does not report always, or even generally, at first hand. He reports Powell, who, in his turn, sometimes reports Franklin. Marlow has the spirit of a commentator. What he reports comes coloured by his own personality, and garnished by his own reflections.

The justification of Conrad's method, as of Browning's *The Ring and the Book*, is its success. That is to say, we do arrive at a very clear and full understanding of all the people of the story. We know them through the speakers, and we know them sometimes at third hand as the speakers wish us to know them. But we know them. And we know them much more thoroughly and subtly because of the constant throwing back and retracing and recolouring.

We also get to know Marlow.

RUDYARD KIPLING, who has made the short story respectable in English, tends more and more to employ the conversational method. His stories are so familiar that it is hardly necessary to give illustrations. I will confine myself to two: one called *The Wrong Thing* from *Rewards and Fairies*, and the other called *The Janeites* from *Debits and Credits*.

In *The Wrong Thing* the chief speaker is the spirit of Sir Harry Dawe (Hal o' the Draft) talking to Mr. Springett the carpenter and the boy Dan. Every one comes in through Hal: the master craftsman, Torrigiano, who is fashioning the iron gates of the King's Chapel in Westminster, Hal's fellow-workman Bob Brygandyne, Hal's bitter enemy Benedetto, and the King, Henry VII himself. The listener, Mr. Springett, is sympathetic and interjects his comments and modern instances. These are reported in full in the ordinary manner. Browning would have hinted at them and brought in Springett also through Hal, or possibly, spanning the centuries as Kipling does here, have made Springett the chief speaker and brought in Hal and all the others through him, if the poet could have allowed himself the dream device.

In *The Janeites* the chief speaker is a mess servant, Humberstall, a man whose mind has been affected by injuries in the War. The members of his 'Circus'—a battery of Heavies—come in through him: Macklin and 'Ammick and Mosse and the Gander. Their feeling for Jane Austen's novels, as well as his own acquired interest in her, comes to us through him. We see all the *dramatis personae* through his eyes, from his mentor, Macklin, and the officers of his battery, to the Sisters on the hospital train in the retreat of March 1918.

'Then I walked a bit, an' there was a hospital-train fillin' up, an' one of the Sisters—a grey-headed one—ran at me wavin' 'er red 'ands an' sayin' there wasn't room for a louse in it. I was past carin'. But she went on talkin' and talkin' about the war, and her pa in Ladbroke Grove, an' 'ow strange for 'er at 'er time of life to be doin' this work with a lot o' men, an' next war, 'ow the nurses 'ud 'ave to wear khaki breeches on account o' the mud, like the Land Girls; an' that reminded 'er, she'd boil me an egg if she could lay 'ands on one, for she'd run a chicken-farm once. You never 'eard anythin' like it—outside o' Jane. It set me off laughin' again. Then a woman with a nose an' teeth on her marched up. 'What's all this?' she says. 'What do you want?' 'Nothing,' I says, 'only make Miss Bates there stop talkin' or I shall die.' 'Miss Bates?' she says, 'What in 'Eaven's name makes you call 'er that?' 'Because she is,' I says. 'D'you know what you're sayin'?' she says, and slings her bony arms round me to get me off the ground. "Course I do,' I says, 'an' if you knew Jane you'd know too.' 'That's enough,' says she. 'You're comin' on this train if I have to kill a Brigadier for you,' and she an' an ord'ly fair hove me into the train, on to a stretcher close to the cookers. That beef-tea went down well! Then she shook 'ands with me and said I'd hit off Sister Molyneux in one, an' then she pinched me an extra blanket. It was 'er own 'ospital pretty much. I expect she was the Lady Catherine de Burgh of the area. Well, an' so, to cut a long story short, nothing further transpired.'

II

Even the phrase 'language of conversation', as applied to poetry, is a tea-caddy definition. For a colloquy need not be colloquial. I suppose the following would be called the language of conversation:

> For instance, men love money—that you know
> And what men do to gain it: well, suppose
> A poor lad, say a help's son in your house,
> Listening at keyholes, hears the company
> Talk grand of dollars, V-notes, and so forth,
> How hard they are to get, how good to hold,
> How much they buy,—if, suddenly, in pops he—
> '*I*'ve got a V-note!'—what do you say to him?
> What's your first word which follows your last kick?
> 'Where did you steal it, rascal?' [1]

or:

>   But, for God?
> Ay, that's a question! Well, sir, since you press—
> (How you do tease the whole thing out of me!
> I don't mean you, you know, when I say 'them':
> Hate you, indeed! But that Miss Stokes, that Judge!
> Enough, enough—with sugar: thank you, sir!)

[1] *Mr. Sludge the Medium.*

or this, with a subtle but absolutely natural 'dig' at the language of conversation as *not* being poetry:

> With Sludge it's too absurd? *Fine, draw the line*
> *Somewhere, but, sir, your somewhere is not mine!*
>
> Bless us, I'm turning poet!

The Sludges recognize poetry when there's a rhyme in it.

Still, the following ecstatical utterance is also the language of conversation:

> Well, and there is more! Yes, my end of breath
> Shall bear away my soul in being true!
> He is still here, not outside with the world,
> Here, here, I have him in his rightful place!
> 'Tis now, when I am most upon the move,
> I feel for what I verily find—again
> The face, again the eyes, again, through all,
> The heart and its immeasurable love
> Of my one friend, my only, all my own,
> Who put his breast between the spears and me.[1]

The strong and vivid image of the spears is just such an image as Pompilia would use in a moment of ecstasy.

Letters are a kind of conversation. It was a very bold and much-criticized mode of Browning's to use a letter for his exposition of the sign of the raising of Lazarus. The letter was dramatic, the letter of an imaginary person, not of Browning himself, but it was a real letter, casual, personal, intimate; and the poet was accused of irreverence, even of flippancy. One who reads *An Epistle containing the strange medical experience of Karshish the Arab Physician* will find Karshish and his sage, Abib, to whom he writes, and the Syrian runagate, to whom

[1] *The Ring and the Book: Pompilia*, ll. 1771-80.

he entrusts the letter, clearly delineated. He will also find the usual breaks for gossip—in this case professional:

>   Scalp-disease
> Confounds me, crossing so with leprosy—
> Thou hadst admired one sort I gained at Zoar—
> But zeal outruns discretion . . . .

The case of Lazarus is approached as a professional would approach it. All this novelty of treatment makes the actual case so much the more impressive. The case becomes actual, because we are invited to look at it as it struck a contemporary, and it is mentioned and discussed in one of twenty-two letters written by the Arab correspondent. Contrast this treatment with Tennyson's, and the difference made by the conversational method is at once apparent. Tennyson does indeed bring in one question that is not found in St. John's writing, but the whole of the beautiful brief poem not only adds nothing to our speculative knowledge or our philosophy of human life but lacks the vividness and completeness of the original record:

> When Lazarus left his charnel-cave,
>   And home to Mary's house return'd,
>   Was this demanded—if he yearn'd
> To hear her weeping by his grave?
>
> 'Where wert thou, brother, those four days?'
>   There lives no record of reply,
>   Which telling what it is to die
> Had surely added praise to praise.
>
> From every house the neighbours met,
>   The streets were filled with joyous sound,
>   A solemn gladness even crown'd
> The purple brows of Olivet.

> Behold a man raised up by Christ!
> The rest remaineth unreveal'd;
> He told it not; or something seal'd
> The lips of the Evangelist.[1]

We shall come again to *Karshish* for another purpose, but notice that the real irreverence is Tennyson's, who suggests that if his question of 'where wert thou?' had been put and answered, the Gospel would have been improved thereby—'Had surely added praise to praise'.

'But zeal outruns discretion.' I must leave these over-discussed Victorians in order to show how the conversational method has influenced their successors. Again, for the sake of continuity, I must begin with those who were writing before the close of the nineteenth century.

W. E. HENLEY has affinities with Browning. He wrote a series of poems under the general title of *In Hospital*, in which he gossips about everybody connected with the hospital. The advantage of this gossip is not merely to secure actuality—in this case the poet is himself a patient in the hospital—but also to give free rein to psychological curiosity. Browning exploited and perfected the conversational method because it provided a vehicle of expression for his psychological interests, and psychological interests are best expressed in talk. Henley says in the 'Advertisement'[2] to his *Collected Poems* that he tried to 'quintessentialise his impressions of the Old Edinburgh Infirmary in unrhyming rhythms, as (I believe) one scarce can do in rhyme'. *In Hospital* contains rhyming rhythms as well. All the rhythms are his talk about things and people—the kind of

[1] *In Memoriam*, XXXI.   [2] *Poems*, Advertisement, 1897.

observations he would drop out at home after he was discharged.

> You are carried in a basket,
>   Like a carcase from the shambles,
>   To the theatre, a cockpit
>   Where they stretch you on a table.
>
> Then they bid you close your eyelids,
>   And they mask you with a napkin,
>   And the anaesthetic reaches
>   Hot and subtle through your being.

Here is the end of a sonnet about a visitor:

> In snow or shine, from bed to bed she runs,
> All twinkling smiles and texts and pious tales,
> Her mittened hands, that ever give or pray,
> Bearing a sheaf of tracts, a bag of buns:
> A wee old maid that sweeps the Bridegroom's way,
> Strong in a cheerful trust that never fails.

He tells of a sailor in *Romance*. It begins in the middle of the sailor's talk:

> 'Talk of pluck!' pursued the Sailor,
>   Set at euchre on his elbow,
>   'I was on the shore at Charleston,
>   Just ashore from off the runner.
>
> 'It was grey and dirty weather,
>   And I heard a drum go rolling,
>   Rub-a-dubbing in the distance,
>   Awful dour-like and defiant.
>
> 'In and out among the cotton,
>   Mud, and chains, and stores, and anchors,
>   Tramped a squad of battered scarecrows—
>   Poor old Dixie's bottom dollar! . . .'

Under the head of *Apparition* he brings in his famous description of R. L. Stevenson:

> Valiant in velvet, light in ragged luck,
> Most vain, most generous, sternly critical,
> Buffoon and poet, lover and sensualist:
> A deal of Ariel, just a streak of Puck,
> Much Antony, of Hamlet most of all,
> And something of the Shorter-Catechist.

'A deal of Ariel' is a pure colloquialism.

JOHN DAVIDSON'S *Fleet Street Eclogues* are conversations. The speakers form a debating society, but their debate is not a series of set speeches, and the remarks they make, in spite of the fact that they speak rhythmically, have much of the spontaneity of unprepared talk. Yet the eclogue method has not become popular. Perhaps its diffuseness and the lack of the binding element of a story allow the reader's attention to stray, just as in an ordinary conversation one may avoid monotony and yet become bored because the talk 'leads nowhere', that is to say, it has no climax.

The eclogue called *St. George's Day*[1] brings in six speakers: Basil, Menzies, Percy, Brian, Herbert, Sandy. The subject is the glory of England, or rather of Englishmen, and in the end all the speakers speak together:

> By bogland, highland, down and fen,
> All Englishmen, all Englishmen!
> Who with their latest breath shall sing
> Of England and the English Spring.

The climax is not genuine. It is like a company of people who have been at variance throughout the year, joining together at Christmas to sing 'Auld Lang Syne'. We are reminded of W. S. Gilbert's gibes in *Pinafore*,

[1] *Fleet Street Eclogues: Second Series.*

without the freedom to laugh at ourselves. Has this anything to do with the method? Is it not rather due to the mood of the poet? The method allows the introduction of various speakers, and those speakers maintain their attitudes without the controlling or reconciling influence of one mind and without the action of a drama of human affairs to play the part of what is sometimes called Fate. The conversation contains many fine passages, but it is indeterminate. The sceptic Menzies seizes on the saying of one of the others, 'We are the world's forlorn hope', and repeats it with ironical emphasis, and this irony is the final impression of the piece. We feel that the beautiful praise of the flowers and the countryside in springtime spoken by the others is perhaps ironical too—that the conversation is not genuine. If the method were that of the dramatic lyric, the opinions of the others would come in coloured by the personality of the speaker. In the method of the dramatic lyric their opinions are known through him and they are discounted or extenuated because he is the controlling influence, and we know how he regards the others, and can make our allowances in accordance with our knowledge. If, for example, Menzies were the speaker throughout and quoted the others or indicated their views and enthusiasms, we should not have the impression of unreality, because we know how Menzies looks at life. Or if the speaker were the poet himself, the effect would be similar. But if we suspect that the poet is really speaking his own mind through one of the characters and merely playing with us in letting the others speak, the names become names of puppets and not of genuine persons.

John Davidson handles the eclogue method with great

skill. He makes it the vehicle of many differing points of view. It affords him an opportunity for the expression of his passionate love of humanity. Yet it is subtly disappointing. And the disappointment is, at least partly, due to the method. A poetical debate in which the speakers have no particular relation to one another lacks vitality. Nor is it easy to find a subject that can provide unity for mere unrelated voices. If the eclogue lacks vitality and unity we must come to the conclusion that Davidson's development or adaptation of the conversational method has failed.

RUDYARD KIPLING adheres to the single speaker. In his earlier *Barrack Room Ballads* he dared to make use of dialect—the dialect of Tommy Atkins. He ran the risk of doggerel. Browning had run the risk of doggerel even in a religious poem such as *Christmas Eve*. Take some of Kipling's first lines:

> I've a head like a concertina, I've a tongue like a button-stick.
>
> I went into a public-'ouse to get a pint 'o beer.
>
> My name is O'Kelly, I've heard the Revelly.
>
> Wot makes the soldier's 'eart to penk, wot makes 'im to perspire?

The dialect poems of William Barnes were written by a man to whom the Dorset talk was his native tongue; the Cockney poems of Rudyard Kipling were written by a literary craftsman. He was just as ready to write in the Yorkshire dialect for Learoyd or the Irish brogue for Mulvaney as in the Cockney dialect for Ortheris. But the so-called Cockney dialect prevails in his poems. It is hardly the Cockney dialect, it is just uneducated. Uneducated people may have read the poems and liked

THE TWENTIETH CENTURY

them. I have a pirated copy of *Barrack Room Ballads* that was sold in the street for a penny. The Ballads are the kind of poetry that corresponds to the music of 'The Man that broke the Bank at Monte Carlo' or 'It's a long, long way to Tipperary'. They may have contributed to give the people a taste for poetry. For they are true poetry. Yet there is sometimes a false note:

> I am sick o' wastin' leather on these gritty pavin' stones,
> An' the blasted Henglish drizzle wakes the fever in my bones;
> Though I walks with fifty 'ousemaids outer Chelsea to the Strand,
> An' they talks a lot o' lovin', but wot do they understand?

The travelled, leisured Englishman may pretend to be bored by his own country and assume the pose of preferring every country to his own, but the ordinary uneducated Englishman not only does not talk that way—he does not understand how any Englishman can. I remember being asked by a gunner to visit his home when I was on leave from France. The gunner spoke with affection of his people and regarded the place where he lived with respect. His people struck me as ignoble and grasping, and the place where he lived was a roofed-in hole under the shadow of a railway arch. But the gunner was looking forward to going home as his chief joy.

I remember hearing a sergeant of the Artists' Rifles recite to a parcel of Tommies Rudyard Kipling's *Chant Pagan* from *The Five Nations*.

> I will arise an' get 'ence—
> I will trek South and make sure
> If it's only my fancy or not
> That the sunshine of England is pale,
> And the breezes of England are stale,
> An' there's somethin' gone small with the lot . . .

The soldiers heard him in silent bewilderment. They applauded perfunctorily and were glad when it was over. They simply did not believe that the sunshine of England was pale and her breezes stale, still less that something had gone small with the lot.

Rudyard Kipling sometimes uses the language of the Tommy to express his own sentiments—not Tommy's. One can more easily learn Tommy's mode of speech than Tommy's real thoughts.

Kipling is nearer to the truth in what may be called vulgarly his 'Dutch Uncle' mood. He talks naturally like a Dutch uncle and he expresses the Dutch uncle's sentiments:

> If you can talk with crowds and keep your virtue,
>   Or walk with Kings—nor lose the common touch,
> If neither foes nor loving friends can hurt you,
>   If all men count with you, but none too much;
> If you can fill the unforgiving minute
>   With sixty seconds' worth of distance run,
> Yours is the Earth and everything that's in it,
>   And—which is more—you'll be a Man, my son! [1]

Of course, not many of us talk with crowds and fewer of us walk with kings, but we like to imagine ourselves as doing both these things. The doctrine of self-sufficiency and consequent indifferentism is another chant pagan—Stoic this time—and the Gospel of work is Kipling's favourite Gospel ('He is a good man; I shall work him hard'), but in another Gospel the inheritance of the earth is said to belong to the meek. Unfortunately for the peace of mankind, that other Gospel is not

---

[1] *If* ——, the poem that follows *Brother Square-Toes* in *Rewards and Fairies*.

popular. Kipling's doctrine is more suitable for those who desire a place in the sun—or in the limelight.

Kipling has followed the exact method of the dramatic lyric in his *M'Andrew's Hymn*, though the imaginary audience is God. M'Andrew's hymn is the 'Song o' Steam', which, strangely enough, he thinks a man like Robbie Burns could sing, but the hymn is in the form of a conversation between M'Andrew and God. M'Andrew alternately argues and beseeches, justifying himself and calling upon God to 'obsairve' of what service he is to his kind, and grovelling for forgiveness because of his 'steps aside at Gay Street in Hong-Kong', and, still more, because of his temptation to sin against the Holy Ghost:

> 'Your mither's God's a graspin' deil, the shadow o' yoursel',
> 'Got out o' books by meenisters clean daft on Heaven an' Hell.
> 'They mak' him in the Broomilaw, o' Glasgie cold an' dirt,
> 'A jealous, pridefu' fetich, lad, that's only strong to hurt.
> 'Ye'll not go back to Him again and kiss His red-hot rod,
> 'But come wi' Us' (Now, who were *They?*)' an' know the Leevin' God,
> 'That does not kipper souls for sport or break a life in jest,
> 'But swells the ripenin' cocoanuts an' ripes the woman's breast.'

The Engine is the chief of the dramatis personae that come in through M'Andrew, but there are others: his 'mither's God', and the God of whom the whispering devils speak, Sir Kenneth of the 'Board' and, especially, the first-class passengers, for whom M'Andrew has contempt.

> That minds me of our Viscount loon—Sir Kenneth's kin—the chap
> Wi' Russia leather tennis-shoon an' spar-decked yachtin'-cap. . . .
> 'Mister McAndrew, don't you think steam spoils romance at sea?'
> Damned ijjit! I'd been doon that morn to see what ailed the throws,
> Manholin', on my back—the cranks three inches off my nose.

But the chief revelation is of M'Andrew himself. He contrives to indicate his whole career and to bring out every side of himself in his colloquy with God. For example,

> Commeesion on my stores? Some do; but I cannot afford
> To lie like stewards wi' patty-pans. I'm older than the Board.
> A bonus on the coal I save? Ou ay, the Scots are close,
> But when I grudge the strength Ye gave I'll grudge their food to *those*.

Those, the Engines, are his passion. He has even burned the plans of his 'Deeferential Valve-Gear' because he found he could not invent and look to his engines as well. He hears in the engines the great lesson of life:

> 'Law, Orrder, Duty an' Restraint, Obedience, Discipline!'
> Mill, forge an' try-pit taught them that when roarin' they arose,
> An' whiles I wonder if a soul was gied them wi' the blows.

The other dramatic lyric in the same collection, *The Mary Gloster*, is not so successful. It smacks too much of the 'ballads' of George R. Sims. These Sims ballads were extremely popular when I was a boy and may have prepared the way for the popularity, the much 'giddier' popularity, of Kipling.

The adherence of JOHN MASEFIELD and W. H. DAVIES to the conversational method has been sufficiently indicated in a previous chapter. Masefield is not without his gross lapses from verisimilitude.

A finer poet than either is A. E. HOUSMAN, in spite of a certain monotony of tune and the depression of his outlook. In *A Shropshire Lad* more than two-thirds of the poems are talks, giving the actual words of the speaker; and of these at least twelve are conversations brought in through a single speaker. The collection of poems is called *A Shropshire Lad* because the speakers are young peasants of that county.

The conversations are:

(1) A dialogue between a peasant and his lass. (V.)
(2) A young man—a farm-labourer—who has killed his brother, says farewell to his friend. (VIII.)
(3) A peasant recalls the talk between his dead sweetheart and himself and what happened afterwards. (XXI—*Bredon Hill*.)
(4) A talk between the spirit of a dead man and his living erstwhile comrade, who cheers the dead man's sweetheart. (XXVII.)
(5) A man who is about to travel abroad asks how he shall help another. (XXXII.)
(6) A soldier has found a 'new mistress', the Queen, whose soldier he is going to be, and he recalls the words of his old sweetheart and answers her. (XXXIV.)

(7) A man talks with himself. (XLIII—*The Immortal Part*.)
(8) A man apostrophizes a youth who has committed suicide. (XLIV.)
(9) A countryman in London talks with a Grecian statue. (LI.)
(10) A man who has killed himself for love talks with his lover. (LVI.)
(11) A man talks with his soldier friend about behaviour in battle. (LVI—*The Day of Battle*.)
(12) In praise of ale; a conversation and a tale about Mithridates.

Of *Last Poems*, forty-one in number, thirty are 'talks' and seven or eight conversations.

The propriety of Housman's language of conversation has been challenged. For Housman does not translate the thoughts of his speakers, as some poets do, but he purports to give the words his speakers themselves would naturally use.

The well-known *Bredon Hill* begins:

> In Summer time on Bredon
> The bells they sound so clear;
> Round both the shires they ring them
> In steeples far and near,
> A happy noise to hear.
>
> Here of a Sunday morning
> My love and I would lie,
> And see the coloured counties,
> And hear the larks so high,
> About us in the sky.

It has been objected that 'coloured counties' is the poet's phrase and not the peasant's, and that the peasant would not have said '*about* us in the sky'. Many things are said of peasants that are not true. Sydney Smith, Canon of St. Paul's and Rector of Combe Florey in Somerset, said: 'For sentiment a ploughman has nothing more nearly approaching to it than the ideas of broiled bacon and mashed potatoes.' I used to live in Combe Florey and I went with Cecil Sharp to hear several folk-singers there. All these singers were peasants. The last we visited was a farm-labourer, and when we came to his cottage his three sons were beginning their supper, a mash of vegetables with strips of bacon on top. We awaited the master, who, his wife told us, sometimes sang an old song. He presently appeared. 'Yes,' he said, 'I can mind *The Lark in the Morn*'. No, his supper could wait. He did not want to keep the gentlemen while he ate his supper. So he sang *The Lark in the Morn*. Cecil Sharp asked him when such a song came into his mind. 'Oh, sometimes when I'm out to plough.' His father sang it before him, and he had had it from his father, both of whom lived and died in the village. That would carry us back to the days of Sydney Smith. But Sydney Smith knew nothing of it, or he could not have uttered that egregious falsehood about the ploughman and his sentiment.

Lascelles Abercrombie (in *Poetry and Contemporary Speech*) mentions two descriptions of a climbing rose. The cultivated man called it 'an awfully jolly little thing', and the peasant called it an 'innocent little blow'.

I think we may conclude that Housman is more likely to be right than his critics. Nevertheless, the poet who dares to employ the accent and idiom of speech to adopt into poetry what Abercrombie calls the 'expressive irregularities and careless experiments of conversation', must beware of pitfalls. THOMAS HARDY uses the conversational method.

> 'What did you do? Cannot you let me know?'
> 'Don't ask! . . . 'Twas midnight, and I'd lost at cards.'
> 'Ah. Was it crime—or seemed it to be so?'
>   'No—not till afterwards.'
> 'But *what*, then, did you do?'
> 'Well—that was the beginning—months ago;
> You see, I had lost and could not pay but—so.
> And there flashed from him strange and strong regards
> That you only see when scruples smash to shards . . .'[1]

The last two quoted lines are not really close to the accent and idiom of speech.

Contrast this:

> 'A said to me, who knew her well,
>   'O why was I so weak!'
> 'A said to me, who knew her well,
>   And have done all her life,
> With a downcast face she said to me,
> 'O why did I keep company
> Wi' them that practised gallantry,
>   When vowed a faithful wife!'
>
> 'O God, I'm driven mad!' she said,
>   'To hear he's coming back;
> I'm fairly driven mad!' she said:
>   'He's been two years agone,
> And now he'll find me in this state,
> And not forgive me. Had but fate
> Kept back his coming three months late,
>   Nothing of it he'd known!' . . .[2]

Even the inversion of the last line is true to rustic speech,

[1] *Reluctant Confession* from *Winter Words*.
[2] *The War-Wife of Catknoll* from *Winter Words*.

THE TWENTIETH CENTURY

and 'to practise gallantry' is still a common expression among unsophisticated southern folk.

WALTER DE LA MARE employs the conversational method with a difference. In his best-known poem, *The Listeners*, the Traveller says: 'Is there anybody there?' and then again, 'Is there anybody there?' and, after a long pause,

> Tell them I came and no one answered,
> That I kept my word.

And yet this twice-repeated ordinary question and his statement that he had kept his word in coming, become 'unearthly scattered talk' in view of the 'phantom listeners' that dwell in the lone house.

He manages to introduce this 'unearthly' note even when he is colloquial:

> 'I'm thinking and thinking,' said old Sam Shore,
> 'Twere somebody *knocking* I heard at the door.'

> From the clock popped the cuckoo and cuckooed out eight,
> As there in his chair he wondering sate . . .
> 'There's no one I knows on would come so late,
> A-clicking the latch of an empty house
> With nobbut inside 'un but me and a mouse . . .
> Maybe a-waking in sleep I be,
> And 'twere out of a dream came that tapping to me.' [1]

Newbolt says that this 'poet's life is a search in all places that are deep and dark; no one since Shakespeare has asked so many secrets of the universe'. Here is his

[1] *Twelve Poets*, 1918.

colloquial way of asking a question that has never been answered:

>   It's a very odd thing—
>   As odd as can be—
>   That whatever Miss T. eats
>   Turns into Miss T. . . .

In his songs about childhood—and his first volume was *Songs of Childhood*—he can use the ordinary language and describe quite ordinary happenings and yet suggest, just as Blake does, something beyond our immediate ken, something unexpected, perhaps, in the shallow sense, but not unexpected if we consult our deeper sympathies.

>   They took us to the graves,
>   Susan and Tom and me,
>   Where the long grasses grow
>   And the funeral tree:
>   We stood and watched; and the wind
>   Came softly out of the sky
>   And blew in Susan's hair,
>   As I stood close by.
>
>   Back through the fields we came,
>   Tom and Susan and me,
>   And we sat in the nursery together,
>   And had our tea.
>   And, looking out of the window,
>   I heard the thrushes sing;
>   But Tom fell asleep in his chair,
>   He was so tired, poor thing.[1]

Even when he is writing about beasts with an effect of humour, there is nearly always the suggestion of something beyond.

[1] *Songs of Childhood.*

Seem to be smiling at me, he would,
  From his bush in the corner, of may—
Bony and ownerless, widowed and worn,
  Knobble-kneed, lonely and grey;
And over the grass would seem to pass
  'Neath the deep dark blue of the sky,
Something much better than words between me
  And Nicholas Nye.

But dusk would come in the apple boughs,
  The green of the glow-worm shine,
The birds in nest would crouch to rest,
  And home I'd trudge to mine;
And there, in the moonlight, dark with dew,
  Asking not wherefore nor why,
Would brood like a ghost, and as still as a post,
  Old Nicholas Nye.[1]

Or, take the last two stanzas of *The Pigs and the Charcoal Burners*:

He watched 'neath a green and giant bough
  And the pigs in the ground
Made a wonderful grisling and gruzzling
  And greedy sound.

And when, full-fed, they were gone, and Night
  Walked her starry ways,
He stared with his cheeks in his hands
  At his sullen blaze.

RUPERT BROOKE was well qualified for the conversational method. He loved 'to talk and talk and talk'.[2] His gift of humour comes out in his letters. But he seldom 'let himself go' in poetry. He was too much occupied in trying to be a poet. 'I tried to be a poet. And because I'm a clever writer, and because I was

[1] *Peacock Pie*.   [2] See letter from Tahiti.

forty times as sensitive as anyone else, I succeeded a little.' His sensitiveness is clearest in *The Great Lover*. But sometimes it is mere irritability as in *The Voice*:

> You came and quacked beside me in the wood.
> You said 'The view from here is very good!'
> You said, 'It's nice to be alone a bit!'
> And, 'How the days are drawing out,' you said.
> You said, 'The sunset's pretty, isn't it?'
> . . . .
> By God! I wish—I wish that you were dead!

His *The Old Vicarage, Grantchester*, has become popular —hackneyed. It is in the conversational manner. It has an air of spontaneity ('this hurried stuff', he called it); one feels that he is not 'trying' to write poetry. That is its attractiveness: he allows his gift of humour a free rein and he is no longer sensitive to the opinions of that imagined coterie of critics who decide what it is to be a poet.

> And in that garden, black and white,
> Creep whispers through the grass all night;
> And spectral dance, before the dawn,
> A hundred Vicars down the lawn;
> Curates, long dust, will come and go
> On lissom, clerical, printless toe;
> And oft between the boughs is seen
> The sly shade of a Rural Dean . . .
> Till, at a shiver in the skies,
> Vanishing with Satanic cries,
> The prim ecclesiastic rout
> Leaves but a startled sleeper-out,
> Grey heavens, the first bird's drowsy calls,
> The falling house that never falls.
>
> God! I will pack and take a train,
> And get me to England once again! . . .

He comments on Browning's references to God in a letter to Miss Asquith: 'Did you ever notice how the Browning family's poems all refer suddenly to God in the last line? It's laughable if you read through them in that way. "What if that friend happened to be—God?" "What comes next? Is it—God?" "And with God be the rest." "And if God choose, I shall but love thee better after death", etc., etc. I forget them all now. It shows what the Victorians were.'[1] Rupert Brooke preferred to use 'God' as a convenient expletive. There are three such uses in this poem (*The Old Vicarage, Grantchester*). The Brownings did not *mean* their references to God to be laughable. Rupert Brooke's references remind me of the bibulous person in the front row of the stalls who almost at the end of a performance of *The Profligate*[2] exclaimed, 'My God, I have seen this play before!' But a great change took place in Rupert Brooke's outlook in 1912. 'What if that friend happened to be—God?' came to have a new significance for him. I must leave any further remarks on this change to a later chapter.

Rupert Brooke also let himself go in *Sonnet Reversed* and the scraps of humorous verse and parody which he included in letters to his friends. He is much more attractive in this 'talky', hurried stuff than he is in his realistic efforts, such as *Wagner* and 'The damned ship lurched and slithered . . .' and 'When I see you, who were so wise and cool. . . .' I believe these efforts were a kind of bravado. Their ugliness was designed to show that he could be Elizabethan and was sick of Victorianism.

[1] Memoir prefixed to *The Collected Poems of Rupert Brooke*, p. xcvi.
[2] See Sir J. Forbes Robertson's Reminiscences.

HUMBERT WOLFE's best poem, *Requiem*, is mainly of the conversational order. At one point he seems to have been reading Browning and put the book down in order to take up the pen. This is how the first part of *The Builder* ends:

> Childe Rolande is at the gate. The paynim gloom
> grapples his throat, but still he sounds again
> man's last rejoinder that, outfacing doom,
> awakes the startled hosts of Charlemagne
>   crying in the night
> 'The heathen dark has wrong, Christians have right.'

And the second part begins:

> Theories of Art! Believe me, they're no theories!
> To know yourself, to clutch what now and here is
> and set it down for yourself—that's all there is
> in all that chatter about mysteries!
> Take my Gioconda (Mind! the paint is wet,
> and stand well back! She isn't finished yet!)
> What made me paint her just like that, d'you think?
> Shade, line and colour! Fools to waste their ink!
> All that is in it—that's the stuff of the trade,
> as a man of bone and flesh is moulded and made.
> Yes, but does God stop there? Does he design
> this as an exercise in colour and line
> and rest content with that? And dust His thumb
> as though He'd finished working out a sum! . . .

The first passage is a reference to Browning's poem *Childe Roland to the Dark Tower Came*. The title of Browning's poem is a line in Shakespeare's *King Lear*. It is one of several instances of a little hint suggesting a great poem. But Humbert Wolfe's reference is not to *King Lear*. The passage before the one already quoted runs:

The desire remains for beauty they did not know,
they failed and builded better than they knew,
    who failing wind
the secret slug-horn at the ramparts of the mind.

Browning's poem ends:

There they stood, ranged along the hill-sides, met
    To view the last of me, a living frame
    For one more picture! in a sheet of flame
I saw them and I knew them all. And yet
Dauntless the slug-horn to my lips I set,
And blew. *Childe Roland to the Dark Tower came.*

The second part beginning 'Theories of Art! . . .' is very Browning. Compare passages previously given from *My Last Duchess* and *Fra Lippo Lippi*.

His *The Saints—She* has something of the simple sublimity of *Pompilia*, though the poet is speaking and not the saint herself. He begins, 'Do you remember?' as if to prompt her to such recollections as Pompilia has of her childhood:

Do you remember the Dom Rémy you knew,
    the plain and the small mountain-range of ricks,
    the poplars at their goose-step, two by two,
    the brown hen-church that folded her stone-chicks,
        your father's farm
so dear, so small it almost fitted in your arm?

Do you remember (even through the flame)
    after the long day's labour in the field
    how with the Angelus you heard your name
    mixed with the bells, and hid your face and kneeled
        when sweet and high
a peasant heard 'ecce ancilla Domini'?

The Respectable Woman speaks for herself on her death-bed. Sometimes we feel that the poet is interpreting her thoughts for us:

> It should have been easy to die moderately,
>   having lived without excess. To escape the extreme
>   experience of Death's command to see,
>   beyond these modified tones, the single beam
>   whose flagrant knife
>   slashes into aching fragments the pattern of life.

At the end she seems to speak words such as she might verily have spoken:

> But death comes suddenly with a great wind,
>   stripping the spirit naked to the light,
>   and I must suffer not less than those who sinned
>   the exposure that I gave my life to fight,
>   and yet I know
>   I did not err, though God Himself should tell me so.

The same transition is true of many others, *The Common Woman, The Soldier, The Harlot*—sometimes the poet translates their thoughts into his own phrases and sometimes they seem to speak their own words. The effect is a curious inconsistency and confusion. Wolfe cannot decide between traditionalism and free thinking, though to accuse him of a mere imitative brilliance and not to recognize the sincerity and frequent and high beauty of his poetry is jaundiced criticism.

The 'letter' form for a poem is, of course, old—at least as old as Horace. It was characteristic of Browning that he should adopt it for the discussion of a sacred subject, the sign of the raising of Lazarus.

CHARLES HAMILTON SORLEY wrote a delightful letter:[1]

> This from the battered trenches—rough,
> Jingling and tedious enough.

[1] *Marlborough and Other Poems.*

He recalls his Odyssey and what they did 'down Sparta way' and the splendid Mess after the day's labours and the war-song of the old bard. The old fight was beginning again. They were sons of one school across the sea. But for warmth and welcome and wassail he has to imagine the return to his old place—

> And soon, O soon, I do not doubt it,
> With the body or without it,
> We shall all come tumbling down
> To our old wrinkled red-capped town.

'Behold a man raised up by Christ!' The reunion will be as real as the foregathering in the house of Lazarus when that friend of Jesus was loosed and let go.

ROBERT GRAVES uses the letter form. The first letter is to Siegfried Sassoon 'from Bivouacs at Mametz Wood, July 13th, 1916', recalling a meeting 'down Fricourt way', when they two plotted journeys for 'golden-houred "Après-la-guerre"'. So he goes on, 'Well, when it's over. . . .' I wish I were at liberty to quote it all, except the 'Fragment included at the end', which is an abominable picture.

The second letter is an amusing 'satiric complaint in the old style' to an editor that he has not paid the poet for his contribution. The third is called *The College Debate*: 'That this House approves the Trend of Modern Poetry' (from a letter addressed to Edith Sitwell). The Dean of Saul Hall, of course, condemns everything that has been written during the last thirty years—'Yours is an age of pigmies, dwarfs and apes'. The Head Librarian thinks we have, still surviving, two grand singers, 'Watson still writes, Bridges is yet alive'. A junior don defends Hardy and Housman, and he is aware of

Brooke, Squire and Flecker, De la Mare and Masefield, but he has no patience with the younger men,

> This post-war group. Sassoon is crude and queer,
> And Eliot's mad or wholly insincere,
> And Free Verse isn't Poetry, that's clear,
> Blunden shows promise, but he's quite small beer,
> There's D. H. Lawrence doesn't write a bit well,
> While as for that fantastic . . .

She finds champions who dispose of Tennyson and his peers, press the attack on Watson and Bridges, Hardy and Housman, snipe at Brooke and Masefield, 'sadly backnumbered',

> With patronage for doting De la Mare,
> Since never Genius dawns. Lo there! Lo there!

Graves seems not to remember the injunction of Someone: 'Go not after them.' But perhaps the lady did.

The fourth is a letter from Wales (*Richard Rolls to his friend, Captain Abel Wright*). Here Graves is becoming more difficult to read. The conversational method allows for stray associations, wisps of thought, wisps of talk:

> We stopped blackberrying and someone said
> (Was it I or you?) 'It is good for us to be here.'
> The other said, 'Let us build Tabernacles'
> (In honour of a new Transfiguration;
> It was that sort of moment); but instead
> I climbed up on the massive pulpit stone,
> An old friend, but unreal with the rest,
> And prophesied—not indeed of the future,
> But declaimed poetry, and you climbed up too
> And prophesied. The next thing I remember
> Was a dragon scaly with fine-weather clouds
> Poised high above the sun and the sun dwindling
> And then the second glory. . . .

This sunset is compared with a 'gala-show' when they had watched the French making a mass-attack at Notre Dame de Lorette in a thunderstorm.

The last is a short *Letter to a Friend* and brings us to the modernist manner. It begins:

> Gammon to Spinach,
> Kentucky to Greenwich,
> 'Neither have I met you,
> Nor can I forget you
> While the world's round.'
> Spinach in reply. . . .

The modernist claims the freedom to use any kind of language and any kind of metre or verse. The form should correspond to the different moods. Browning may be ultimately responsible. If one thinks of the last stanza of *Master Hugues of Saxe Gotha* or the wild rhyming and strange 'associations' of *Pacchiarotto*, one cannot but connect Browning with the 'madness' of T. S. Eliot or the difficult references of Gerard Hopkins. Modernist verse is as if one let oneself go in conversation, saying out loud the odds and ends that drift into one's mind, or even drift from one's mouth without seeming to pass through the conscious mind. Here is an example, which I am free to quote in full, for what it is worth. It is supposed to be a representation of an episode called 'Carnival in Paris' by a Scandinavian composer, Svendsen.

> *Con brio* prepares us for gusto in pleasuring,
> Dancers and prancers stepping it anyhow,
> Themes of delirium,
> Whirling and twirling,
> Sobersides Jackself become Tom-a-Bedlam,
> Or whatever be French for the loosening, quickening.—

(Oh, it's so sickening
Not having sounds for 'em!)
Music has chances. Well, have a go at it!
Try to put horns and bassoons—they're too slow at it.
Give way to strings,
They're the things for a six-eight.
Comes the wood-wind: he's a looker-on.
He got the spirit at first, then grew critical,
Wondered that Jack, steady Jack, should be mischievous
Tom, thought of Home and the lack
Here of quietness, joys of the fireside
(Mother and all that!) could not abide
Frivolous women and satyrs and bacchanals
(You know!): 'Come from the North I do,
So I'm ashamed of you,
Throwing your legs about,
Give you a tune like a hymn
Made of semibreves.'
But no! I am writing a thing called A Carnival,
Supposed to be all of a rush and a junketing.
Leave knitting and good talk and 'When shall we meet
    again?'
Get to your feet again,
Abandon the proper,
And don't put a stopper
On mirth like a copper.
'Move on there!' We'll show you we're moving.
Hullo, where's your helmet? It's gone? Keep your head
    on straight.
Ha, Ha!

VI
BROWNING'S OPTIMISM

IN an introduction to a volume of selections from Browning published in 1903, Mrs. Alice Meynell wrote: 'The most inspired and inspiring of the qualities of his genius is his singular and splendid courage.' Later on[1] she said: 'It is no wonder that the proffer of Browning's optimism, half-heartedly made again on the day of his centenary, did again fail. His "All's right with the world" is as vain as the pessimist's "All's wrong with it". It is out of the range of customary life. Intelligible joy and grief are in the midways, and in the midways there is cause for as much sadness as our human hearts can hold.' Concerning the 'range of customary life' another quotation from the same writer may be permitted: 'Browning became the most interesting writer of his day to many who sought his pages, not for the sake of the chant, the spirit, or the rapture, but for the sake of an enquiry into actual incidental, accidental human nature in action.'

Browning's singular and splendid courage arises from his optimism. That courage is infectious. The courage of the stoic is not infectious. But the courage of the shallow optimist is likely to break. There were persons who before the War had deliberately shut their eyes to the unpleasant, had, indeed, made a veritable cult of the pleasant, and when the War came they were broken. Their view of life was proved to be false. They could not sustain the disillusion. But Browning's optimism was not shallow. It is true that he was not tested, as Mrs. Meynell was, by the shattering cataclysm

[1] *Second Person Singular and Other Essays*, 1922.

of the Great War. Yet his optimism was consonant with a close inquiry into actual incidental accidental human nature in action. That is to say, he kept within the range of customary life. I do not know on what evidence Mrs. Meynell based her judgement that the 'proffer of Browning's optimism' made in 1912 'did again fail'. Why 'again'? Had it failed before? If it had failed before and if it failed then, Mrs. Meynell has not given the true reason for its failure.

The shallow optimist may shut his eyes to the sadness there is in the 'midways' of life. Browning has faced not only that sadness but 'he has laid bare what there is in man of sordid, selfish, impure, corrupt, brutish, and he proclaims, in spite of every disappointment and every wound, that he still finds a spiritual power without him, which restores assurance as to the destiny of creation'.[1] Again: 'Browning has dared to look on the darkest and meanest forms of action and passion from which we commonly and rightly turn our eyes, and has brought back for us from this universal survey a conviction of hope.'

One wonders if even Shakespeare made so remorseless an inquiry into human nature. Here are two passages of a much later date than Westcott's writing. The first makes mention of the courage which Mrs. Meynell admired in 1903: Francis Paget[2] thanks Miss Laurence for a photograph of Browning, 'helping me to know something of the fire and intensity that came out in the great poems, and that made his simple geniality and kindness so beautiful. It seems a singularly noble

[1] Westcott, *On Some Points in Browning's View of Life*, Nov. 1882. ('I cannot have been sufficiently grateful for Dr. Westcott's paper, one of the most valued honors of my life.' Browning to Rev. J. W. Williams, 17 April 1883.)

[2] *Life of Francis Paget*, 1912, p. 111.

character to recall—with its magnificent courage and vigour and brilliancy in work, its unfading devotion to one love, its constant care for the gladness of other peoples' lives. I am very grateful for the privilege of having known him.'

The second passage concerns Browning's inquiry into human nature: 'We may form diverse estimates of Browning's work: we may be sometimes baffled by *Paracelsus*, and inclined to despair of *Sordello*; but does not much of the difficulty come of this—that he is trying to lead us through the tangled forest of an inner life, haunted by strange forms of temptation, lit by wandering lights, amidst broken paths and clues; that he is bold enough to hint at significant fragments of experience and character and purpose, of which his piercing insight makes him sure, though even he may see them but by glimpses?'[1]

I

Mrs. Meynell's quotation, 'All's right with the world', is, of course, from *Pippa Passes*. We may begin conveniently with *Pippa Passes* in an attempt to see what Browning's optimism really is. This is the song that Ottima and Sebald heard:

>The year's at the spring
>And day's at the morn;
>Morning's at seven;
>The hill-side's dew-pearled;
>The lark's on the wing;
>The snail's on the thorn:
>God's in his heaven—
>All's right with the world!

The singer is a young girl from the silk-mills of Asolo.

[1] *Ut supra*, p. 206.

She is out on her one day's holiday of the whole year—a spring day. She has leapt out of bed determined to make the best of it, not to squander a wavelet of it, a mite of her twelve hours' treasure. The song is surely not unnatural on the lips of such a child at such a time. Older, less innocent, and more sophisticated persons have experienced similar sensations on similar occasions and have been ready to declare,

>God's in his heaven—
>All's right with the world!

There is nothing particularly optimistic in it, nothing outside the customary range of life, unless we exclude from life holidays and joy in the spring and larking on Hampstead Heath.

The true optimism of *Pippa Passes* is in the whole conception. *Pippa Passes* is a dramatized parable of the Sower, except that no seed falls upon the wayside or on the stony ground or among the thorns, but that it all gets in and gets down and springs up—not one good seed is lost. Pippa appears at critical moments in the spiritual life-history of Ottima and Sebald, of Jules and Phene, of Luigi and his mother, of the Bishop and Maffeo; and her appearance and her singing produce an instantaneous effect. There is no failure. Her voice determines the actions and fashions the destinies of all these men and women.

Her first passing is by the room where Ottima and Sebald are together, remorseless after their abominable crime, and he is just going to crown her as magnificent in sin. The words that arrest him are not 'All's right with the world!' but 'God's in his heaven':

>God's in his heaven! Do you hear that? Who spoke?
>You—you spoke!

> Oh—that little ragged girl!
> She must have rested on the step . . .

I am ready to admit that it is an enthusiast's view of life. In the parable, some seeds do fall in unfruitful places, and the Speaker of the parable lays a warning stress on the places in the human heart that baulk the immediate purpose of the Sower, but He gives no hint that these places abound or that the larger area of the ground is not good. Browning was fully alive to the delays and postponements caused by the obstinacy of evil men—the thorns must be rooted up, the hard-trodden path tilled, the stones taken out of the field—but he chose in this poem to jump the immediate and to imagine the work accomplished at a word, as in the sublime statement of the primal decree: 'God said, Let there be light, and there was light.'

So far from 'All's right with the world' being the expression of Browning's philosophy of hope, his optimism has, strictly speaking, little to do with the 'world'. He recognizes rarely the larger life of humanity. He is concerned with the life and death of the single soul.

Life as it is constituted, the events of life as they happen, are best for 'carrying on'. The regretful retrospect that causes a man to say, 'Oh, if only I had my time over again!' has no counterpart in Browning's poetry. The cry

> Ah Christ, that it were possible
> For one short hour to see
> The souls we loved, that they might tell us
> What and where they be

is never echoed by him. 'La vie est bonne, nous dit-il, et la mort, sans doute, meilleure.'[1]

[1] *Robert Browning: Étude sur sa pensée et sa vie,* par Mary Duclaux.

Let us, for the estimate of life's ordinary experiences, take the case of Lazarus, who has had an experience out of the ordinary.[1] The elders of the tribe brought in Lazarus, obedient as a sheep, to bear the inquisition of Karshish. Karshish acknowledges the man's gentleness and kindness and utter abhorrence of cruelty, his prone submission to the will of God; but makes it plain that his vision has indisposed him for a balanced view of affairs. Lazarus has lost his sense of proportion, he is out of place, and is merely waiting for death,

> For that same death which must restore his being
> To equilibrium, body loosening soul
> Divorced even now by premature full growth.

The corollary is that a man is in place and fit for life's duties, having a proper sense of proportion and a duly balanced mind, who has *not* been disturbed by something out of the ordinary course of a man's ordinary life. Lazarus

>   is witless of the size, the sum,
> The value in proportion of all things,
> Or whether it be little or be much.
> Discourse to him of prodigious armaments
> Assembled to besiege his city now,
> And of the passing of a mule with gourds—
> 'Tis one! Then take it on the other side,
> Speak of some trifling fact,—he will gaze rapt
> With stupor at its very littleness,
> (Far as I see) as if in that indeed
> He caught prodigious import, whole results:
> And so will turn to us the bystanders
> In ever the same stupor (note this point)
> That we too see not with his opened eyes.

     .   .   .   .

[1] An espistle.

> He holds on firmly to some thread of life—
> (It is the life to lead perforcedly)
> Which runs across some vast distracting orb
> Of glory on either side that meagre thread,
> Which, conscious of, he must not enter yet—
> The spiritual life around the earthly life:
> The law of that is known to him as this,
> His heart and brain move there, his feet stay here.
> So is the man perplext with impulses
> Sudden to start off crosswise, not straight on,
> Proclaiming what is right and wrong across,
> And not along, this black thread through the blaze,—
> 'It should be' baulked by 'here it cannot be'.

If we test a man by his serviceableness, we find those most serviceable who accept their experiences and abide on the ground of their own proper nature. Hervé Riel was a coasting pilot. Because he was a good coasting pilot and was content to be that, he saved Damfreville's fleet.

> ... from Malo Roads to Croisic Point, what is it but a run?

That line gives the secret of his service. He was accustomed to make that run; he had learned to do it well; he was content to do it.

Pheidippides was a patriot too. The very name of Athens sent a blaze through his blood. And Athens he served in precisely the best manner in which he could serve. And no one else could serve Athens that way so well as he did. He was a noble, strong man who could run like a god. Racing was his mode of service.

The 'clown' (*Echetlos*), who ploughed for Greece on Marathon day, was adept at ploughing. The others had the skill of spear-play. He knew nothing of that. But plough he could and did, and was content to plough.

These men served. No one can say that the service of one was greater or smaller than the service of another. They abode on the ground of their own proper nature: the one a coasting pilot, the next a professional runner, the third a ploughman. No service would have been possible to any had he wished to be other than he was meant to be.

This is the thought of *The Boy and the Angel*. One finds the corollary truth in *Pippa Passes*: 'All service ranks the same with God.' (I am glad Mrs. Meynell did not object to that.) But the chief conviction of *The Boy and the Angel* is that the best service is rendered when a man abides on the ground of his own proper nature. Not even the angel Gabriel can take the place of Theocrite, the craftsman. Theocrite, doing his appointed work, adds his indispensable note to the song of creation.

In *Rabbi Ben Ezra* Browning uses the image of a cup being shaped on a potter's wheel. By means of this image he summarizes the intelligible joys and griefs of a man's life.

> What though the earlier grooves
> Which ran the laughing loves
> Around thy base, no longer pause and press?
> What though, about thy rim,
> Skull-things in order grim
> Grow out, in graver mood, obey the sterner stress?

Disease, pain, love, the cry of despair, the hopeless longing—these are the 'skull-things'. And these experiences, like the 'laughing loves', are

> Machinery just meant
> To give thy soul its bent,
> Try thee and turn thee forth, sufficiently impressed.

The so-called difficulties of life are an essential and

necessary part of it. Man's struggle to know is a necessary part of it. He knows partly but conceives beside;—

> Creeps ever on from fancies to the fact,
> And in this striving, this converting air
> Into a solid he may grasp and use,
> Finds progress, man's distinctive mark alone,
> Not God's, and not the beasts'; God is, they are,
> Man partly is and wholly hopes to be.
> Such progress could no more attend his soul
> Were all it struggles after found at first
> And guesses changed to knowledge absolute,
> Than motion wait his body, were all else
> Than it the solid earth on every side,
> Where now through space he moves from rest to rest.
> Man, therefore, thus conditioned, must expect
> He could not, what he knows now, know at first.[1]

The visionary of *Easter Day* says at the end that whether the vision be false or true, whether it was a dream and distemperature, due to my watching and the strange Northern light, still it has left me

> happy that I can
> Be crossed and thwarted as a man,
> Not left in God's contempt apart,
> With ghastly smooth life, dead at heart,
> Tame in earth's paddock as her prize.

Browning's optimism is not 'wise passiveness'. A man may indeed sigh for rest at the end of his life, may even regard the body as a prison-house and look forward to deliverance from it, as he seems to do in *Pisgah Sights*, but Browning's normal gospel is:

> As the bird wings and sings,
> Let us cry 'All good things
> Are ours, nor soul helps flesh more, now, than flesh helps soul'.

[1] *A Death in the Desert.*

And while we are in the flesh our duty is to strive with all our energies for our life's set prize. In *The Statue and the Bust*—a poem for which Thomas Hardy had a special admiration—he illustrates this doctrine by the story of two lovers, whose end in view was a crime. They drifted and let the years slip by and never attained their object.

> The counter our lovers staked was lost
> As surely as if it were lawful coin:
> And the sin I impute to each frustrate ghost
>
> Is—the unlit lamp and the ungirt loin,
> Though the end in sight was a vice, I say.
> You of the virtue (we issue join)
> How strive you? *De te, fabula!*

This story has the same motive as the parable of the Unjust Steward. The steward's end was a crime. But he pursued his end with undeviating persistence. He bent all his energies that way. And so his master commended him. The comment on the story is, 'The children of this world are more prudent in their own generation than the sons of the light'. You of the virtue, you who are striving for the eternal tabernacles, how strive you? *De te, fabula!* Are you as single-minded and energetic in the pursuit of your object as the steward was in the pursuit of his? Because the eternal tabernacles are not for those who are slack and undetermined. You must be ready to burn your way through the world if you want to see God.

In *The Patriot* Browning deals with a failure. The Patriot recognizes that the disesteem of the world leading to an ignoble death is 'safer' than a worldly triumph. He has had experience of both. He is now on the way to execution. A year ago he entered the city in a very ecstasy of popular acclaim. And what has happened during the year? He has been serving them, but they have changed—that is all. But he concludes it was better to serve that year, to do his best in the sight of God, even though it led to this bitter end, than to have died in the moment of triumph.

> I go in the rain, and, more than needs,
>   A rope cuts both my wrists behind;
> And I think, by the feel, my forehead bleeds,
>   For they fling, whoever has a mind,
> Stones at me for my year's misdeeds.
>
> Thus I entered, and thus I go!
>   In triumphs, people have dropped down dead.
> 'Paid by the world, what dost thou owe
>   Me?'—God might question; now instead,
> 'Tis God shall reply: I am safer so.

Browning calls this 'an old story'. One wonders whether he was thinking of a very old story—of an execution that was not done in a corner. The Patriot of that day entered with palm-branches mixed in His path, and in less than a week He went out with a rope cutting both His wrists behind, and something pressing on His forehead that hurt worse than stones.

The poet's own life is mainly contemplative. Browning did not often write of himself, but in describing Guercino's picture of the Guardian Angel for his friend Alfred Domett (though he did not send Domett a copy) he says:

> I took one thought his picture struck from me,
> And spread it out, translating it to song.

There are references to Mrs. Browning: 'My Angel with me too', and 'My love is here'.

The Guardian Angel is teaching a little child to pray. The poet muses on the angel's ministry. If the angel, when he has done with the child, would find in him 'another child for tending'; if only he could feel the 'bird of God' guarding him out of all the world and bending low and laying his hands together and lifting them up to pray, and holding him, as a lamb, in the spread of his garment,

> If this was ever granted, I would rest
> My head beneath thine, while thy healing hands
> Close-covered both my eyes beside thy breast,
> Pressing the brain, which too much thought expands,
> Back to its proper size again, and smoothing
> Distortion down till every nerve had soothing,
> And all lay quiet, happy and suppressed.
>
> How soon all worldly wrong would be repaired!
> I think how I should view the earth and skies
> And see, when once again my brow was bared
> After thy healing, with such different eyes.
> O world, as God has made it! All is beauty:
> And knowing this, is love, and love is duty.
> What further may be sought for or declared?

I have referred to *Saul* in another connexion, with its glorification of man's life—'the mere living'—and of the common joys and sympathies of men. In *The Last Ride Together* the lover goes farther and conceives heaven as life's best moment made eternal.

> And yet—she has not spoke so long!
> What if heaven be that, fair and strong
> At life's best, with our eyes upturned
> Whither life's flower is first discerned,
>   We, fixed so, ever should so abide?

> What if we still ride on, we two
> With life for ever old yet new,
> Changed not in kind but in degree,
> The instant made eternity,—
> And heaven just prove that I and she
> Ride, ride together, for ever ride?

II

'La vie est bonne, nous dit-il, et la mort, sans doute, meilleure.'

There can be no reasonable doubt that Browning believed in a life after death, and believed also that the life after death is better than this one. When he speaks in his own person, as he does in *Prospice*, he states his belief in his own life after death, i.e. in what we call a personal immortality. He looks forward to reunion with his wife, who has died. He speaks of this reunion many times in letters (to which we shall have opportunity to recur in a later chapter). Elizabeth is living, after her death, and so instantly and sympathetically alive is she that he appeals to her for help in the writing of his greatest poem.[1] In the personal Epilogue to his last volume, *Asolando*, he says that fools think we are 'imprisoned' by death. On the contrary, we are set free —we sleep to wake.

It is the life after death that gives the *meaning* to this life. The lover's satisfaction in many of the love-poems depends upon the after-life, e.g. *Cristina* and *Evelyn Hope*. The old scholar of *A Grammarian's Funeral* is said by his disciples to await a life in which he can put to the proof all he has learned in his earthly life. 'There shall never

---

[1] *The Ring and the Book*: 'O Lyric Love . . .'

be one lost good', spoken by Abt Vogler, the musician, implies immortality. So does

> Look thou not down but up
> To uses of a cup,

spoken by the old rabbi, Ben Ezra. The immortality implied is not a colourless Sheol but a glorious sphere of usefulness. Pompilia declares, 'No work begun shall ever pause for death'—not even pause, much less cease.

In some of the religious poems, Christ is personally alive, that is to say, the Jesus of Nazareth who walked in Galilee has risen from the dead. The dead St. John[1] lies 'breast to breast' with Him. The visionary of *Christmas Eve* sees Him, and recognizes Him and is guided by Him. His resurrection is the theme of *Easter Day*. The poem called *Cleon* voices the unsatisfactoriness of subjective immortality. And it is in view of a personal immortality that the Pope[2] judges Guido and Ixion[3] interprets suffering.

As these are two extreme instances we may pay a more detailed attention to them. Guido is the chief criminal with whom the Pope is required to deal. We have heard of Guido's detestableness from many witnesses—Caponsacchi likens him to the Judas Iscariot who betrayed Jesus—and the Pope reaffirms his loathsome criminality. And he condemns him to death *because* such a suddenness of fate provides him with the last chance:

> For the main criminal I have no hope
> Except in such a suddenness of fate.
> I stood at Naples once, a night so dark
> I could have scarce conjectured there was earth
> Anywhere, sky or sea or world at all:

---

[1] *A Death in the Desert.*   [2] *The Ring and the Book.*   [3] *Ixion.*

BROWNING'S OPTIMISM

But the night's black was burst through by a blaze—
Thunder struck blow on blow, earth groaned and bore,
Through her whole length of mountain visible:
There lay the city thick and plain with spires,
And, like a ghost disshrouded, white the sea.
So may the truth be flashed out by one blow,
And Guido see one instant and be saved.

And yet it is not the last chance. There is no last chance. No soul can be lost irretrievably.

Else I avert my face, nor follow him
Into that sad obscure sequestered state
Where God unmakes but to remake the soul
He else made first in vain; which must not be.

For the infirmities and permanent disabilities of life Browning finds compensation, as in *Deaf and Dumb*.[1] In *Ixion* he sets out to interpret suffering.

The Greek legend of Ixion provides one of the best-known instances of typical punishment. Ixion was a king of the Lapithae, natural father of Pirithous and supernatural father of the Centaurs. He boasted of the favours of Hera, being deceived by Zeus, and suffered the penalty of the burning wheel, on which he was condemned to revolve for ever in the lower world.

The idea that underlies this legend seems to be that the body which has been prostituted to the service of unlawful pleasure becomes the instrument of pain. Mrs. Orr[2] thought that Browning's poem was written in refutation of the doctrine of eternal punishment. In

---

[1] See page 72.
[2] '(Browning) told me about Mrs. Sutherland Orr (Leighton's sister) and what an astonishing interpretation of him was her handbook.' (Mary Gladstone, op. cit. p. 454.)

the end Ixion sees beyond his torment to an issue of good:

> What is the influence, high o'er Hell, that turns to a rapture
> Pain—and despair's murk mists blends in a rainbow of hope?
> What is beyond the obstruction, stage by stage tho' it baffle?
> Back must I fall, confess 'Ever the weakness I fled'?
> No, for beyond, far, far is a Purity all-unobstructed!

J. T. Nettleship derided the notion that there was any necessity for Browning to refute this doctrine. One may notice in this connexion that in the last part of the poem Ixion discards Zeus, who has inflicted the punishment on him, as supreme power.

> Out of the wreck I rise—past Zeus to the Potency o'er him.

Zeus he recognizes as a cruel tyrant, less scrupulous, less divine than man, and he hails the Potency o'er him. This Potency dwells in the light; and it is to the light that he aspires to rise. Zeus, because of power callously, irresponsibly, revengefully used, will sink, despite his godship.

Ixion aspires to the light, because the light becomes visible through his pain. His pain came by way of punishment, a punishment indeed resented, but none the less acknowledged as following on what was judged to be his crime. Physical pain, the pain of the senses, is here representative of all suffering. A body on a burning wheel! Jesus uses the same sort of symbol in the parable of Dives. The rich man made petition that Lazarus should dip the tip of his finger in water and come and cool his tongue because he was tormented in a flame. This torment has some claim to be called logical. For the pleasures of Dives had come through the senses. He was so busily occupied in pampering the senses that he neglected the obvious need of the helpless beggar. And now in Hades the seat of torture is the sense that he had indulged. On earth he had fared sumptuously every day; after his death he longs in vain for a drop of water.

Ixion rises to a height of faith not because he disregards his pain—it is too insistent and fierce to be disregarded—but because he comes to disregard its origin and to look through it as through a mirror. There is fashioned out of it a rainbow of hope. High over hell is the Potency dwelling in light. And as he spins round on the horrid wheel, his tortured body, ever renewed for more torture, flies off in a vapour of sweat and tears and blood. This iris, born of his agony, arches his torment—an iris, ghost-like, cold, white, startling the darkness. And beyond this is the Light. He knows that the Light is there, because, refracted through the iris of pain, the murk mists of despair, it turns the iris, it blends the mists into a splendour of hope.

> High in the dome, suspended, of Hell, sad triumph, behold us!
> Here the revenge of a God, there the amends of a Man.
> Whirling forever in torment, flesh once mortal, immortal
> Made—for a purpose of hate—able to die and revive,
> Pays to the uttermost pang, then, newly for payment replenished,
> Doles out—old yet young—agonies ever afresh;
> Whence the result above me: torment is bridged by a rainbow,—
> Tears, sweat, blood,—each spasm, ghastly once, glorified now.

The 'revenge of a God' is this whirling, tormented body, mortal flesh made immortal so that it could pay the penalty to the uttermost pang and dole out agonies ever afresh. The 'amends of a Man' is the rainbow, the result of this torment—the rainbow of tears, sweat, and blood, the rainbow of which each constituent was a ghastly spasm of pain. Every spasm is glorified now.

This rainbow is the central idea of the poem. It is announced in the beginning as the amends of a man; it is developed in the end as the mainspring of constant and unbaffled striving through all failure. Man's strength may be checked in the body, as Ixion's was, or in the soul, the medium whence his own entity strives for the Infinite Being, for the free and all-embracing. Just as he is on the threshold of the higher life, full of courage to press on, to burst through pangs to the Infinite Pure—to take the Kingdom of God by violence —then he finds nothing but the old evils he has thought to escape: pride, revenge, hate, cruelty. Such is the character of human failure. Man pays the price of endeavour as Ixion did, 'thunderstruck, downthrust, Tartaros—doomed to the wheel'. Still, in spite of every obstruction, nay even because of the things that he suffers, man looks out from the apparent triumph of evil and sees the rainbow of hope. It is fashioned of tears, sweat, and blood. So far as we know, it could not be there, arching man's torment, unless man suffered the torment. This is the issue of suffering and the meaning of it.

It may be objected that most of these poems are dramatic and that the opinions of the persons speaking are not the opinions of the poet. Shakespeare, in treating of the same subject of immortality (including—if we regard the Ghost as a contribution to the reasoned philosophy of the subject—penal suffering) puts two different aspects of it in the mouths of two speakers in *Hamlet*. The prince in the 'To be or not to be' speech says:

> For in that sleep of death what dreams may come
> When we have shuffled off this mortal coil,
> Must give us pause . . .

The dreams are obviously dreadful. Horatio bids the dying Hamlet farewell in these words:

> Good-night, sweet prince,
> And flights of angels sing thee to thy rest!

Which is Shakespeare's view? Hamlet, moreover, speaks of the 'undiscovered country, from whose bourne no traveller returns', when, as we have been led to think, he has already recognized and exchanged speech with one traveller who has returned. Is he, for the moment, regarding the Ghost as we regard ghosts in a Christmas story?

But whatever the difficulties with regard to Shakespeare's personal beliefs, we can be reasonably sure of Browning's, because his poems are, for the most part, not dramas but dramatic lyrics, and because he has not only written so many dramatic poems with the same tendency but has also written personal poems.

A personal poem with a tendency slightly different from any we have considered that treats of death and life after death is *La Saisiaz*. Here Browning completely abandons his air of certainty. He reminds me of a sergeant-major who said to me, 'About this resurrection, I may believe in it and then I mayn't. I believe in it for three months at a time, say, and then I only hope it will be.' In *La Saisiaz* Browning deals with this probability or hope. His conclusion is the peak of his optimism. Scientific faith, or absolute certainty, is impossible. Neither is it fitted for man's spiritual good. But this probability or hope *is* fitted for man's spiritual good—is exactly suited to the due conduct of our life upon the earth.

III

What is the relation of Browning's optimism to Christianity? Many Christians claim him as a Christian poet *par excellence*. He himself seems to have denied that he was a Christian.[1] Optimism does not make a man a Christian. Dean Inge, who is a professing Christian, scouts optimism, even mocks at it with the old quip that an optimist is one who buys from a Jew and sells to a Scotchman and expects to make a profit. Optimism may be the result of happy circumstances and a healthy body and a robust temperament. Neither does belief in immortality make a man a Christian. Plato believed in the immortality of the soul and wrote the *Phaedo* to prove it—which Browning says, in *La Saisiaz*, he finds it impossible to do. Is a Christian one who believes in Jesus Christ as the Son of God? Or is he one who merely reveres the character of Jesus? Or must we confine Christians to professing and practising members of a Christian church? Well, in the first place, I would point out that when Browning takes a Gospel subject, i.e. a subject that is suggested by one of the four Gospels of the New Testament, he does not keep within the limits of the Gospel view. I will illustrate this by a single

[1] *The Life of Robert Browning*, by W. H. Griffin and H. C. Minchin, p. 296.

example from Browning's account of the death of the apostle Saint John.

A Death in the Desert has been described as the best commentary on St. John's Gospel. The poem is a defence of Christianity, in face of questionings and denials, by a whole-hearted believer and prophet. Dealing with the idea of spiritual progress:

> I say that man was made to grow, not stop;
> That help, he needed once, and needs no more,
> Having grown but an inch by, is withdrawn:
> For he hath new needs, and new helps to these . . .
>
> . . . .
>
> I say, that as the babe, you feed awhile,
> Becomes a boy and fit to feed himself,
> So, minds at first must be spoon-fed with truth:
> When they can eat, babe's-nurture is withdrawn.

Miracle was necessary at first, for the establishment of faith. When faith grew, miracles were withdrawn; 'they would compel, not help'.

This is not the view of miracles expressed in St. John's Gospel. St. John uses the word 'sign'. Signs are not credentials of divine mission in the sense that we believe in Jesus Christ and accept the truths He taught because He performed signs. St. John seeks to show that the so-called miracles were teaching-signs—that the signs themselves taught in an objective, external and therefore eternal form the truths that Christ came to teach.

The signs in St. John's Gospel—omitting the supplementary chapter—are seven, and grew naturally out of the needs of the moment. The first was given to provide wine at a wedding-feast, the second to restore a dying boy to his father; the third to help a sick man who had been ill for thirty-eight years and had vainly tried to make use of the supposed healing properties of a holy well; the fourth to supplement the food of a large crowd of pilgrims; the fifth to calm the terror of his own disciples; the sixth, to assist a blind man to gain his sight; the seventh to raise from the dead a friend of His called Lazarus.

The last four are all interpreted, that is to say, the truth that each is meant to teach is plainly stated: 'I am the Bread of life'; 'I am, fear not'; 'I am the Light of the World'; 'I am the Resurrection and the Life'. The form of the interpretation (I am . . .) suggests the oneness of Jesus with the Father.

Repeated appeals were made to Jesus to show convincing 'signs'—to perform such acts as should convince men of His mission in the world. That the signs recorded by St. John were not convincing he makes clear in the case of the feeding of the pilgrims. After the feeding, 'they said therefore unto him, What then doest thou for a sign, that we may see and believe thee? what workest thou?'

One may perhaps sum up St. John's view as: Miracles (or signs) were given for the establishment of truth (not faith) and that when once the truth has been established there is no further need of signs. Even this is a slight distortion. It conveys the idea that the signs had a kind of expository object in their performance, when, as a matter of fact, they were acts done to meet human needs. A Japanese missionary told me that in the East they will match you miracle for miracle—that the Gospel miracles make no appeal, and that it is the teaching of Christ that is alone convincing. But the signs of St. John's Gospel are not in the same category as the budding rod of Aaron; Jesus was not an amateur thaumaturgist challenging the professionals. He was one who was touched with a feeling of our infirmities and acted accordingly. St. John, reflecting upon these acts, saw that they served another purpose:—they revealed the great truths of God.

The view Browning puts into the mouth of the dying disciple is not the view expressed in that disciple's Gospel. But it is a view that any Christian may hold.

When we turn to the cardinal article of belief in the resurrection from the dead and compare the various poems in which the article is discussed with the discussion in the New Testament, we find that Browning's view is not at all the same as the Christian attitude.

Browning's constant preoccupation is: What is the relation of belief, or, if belief is impossible, of hope, to the conduct of our life here? The New Testament writers are also concerned with conduct. The fact of Christ's resurrection, which is the pledge of ours, is the basis of human freedom as well as the promise of glory. 'Now *is* Christ risen from the dead . . . If Christ be not raised, ye are yet in your sins.' The *probability* of a future life, and the results that follow from a courageous and hopeful attitude towards death, are not once mentioned. Saint Paul does indeed argue from the existence of a 'natural' body to the existence of a 'spiritual' body, but it is not so much an argument as a statement of fact: 'As we have borne the image of the earthy, so shall we bear the image of the heavenly.' I have already drawn attention to the beliefs that Browning seems to hold in some of his personal poems and in many of his letters. He looks forward to reunion with his wife, and he seems to rely upon his wife's help for the writing of his greatest poem. What I am now contending is that his philosophy of hope in *La Saisiaz* (a personal poem) and in the dramatic poems *Easter Day*, *Karshish*, and *Bishop Blougram's Apology*, and, indirectly, in *Cleon*, is not the philosophy of religion we gather out of the New Testament. That philosophy involves the *certainty* of our life 'in Christ' now, and of the fullness of life hereafter, because He died and rose again *for us*.

I do not affirm that the New Testament philosophy of religion is superior to Browning's philosophy or that Browning's view is incompatible with Christianity. But the Christian interpretation of the life and death of Christ is not the same as the teaching of Browning, even if we confine ourselves to *A Death in the Desert*. The dying disciple interprets the life and death of Christ thus:

> To me, that story—ay, that Life and Death
> Of which I wrote 'it was'—to me, it is;
> —Is, here and now: I apprehend nought else.
> Is not God now i' the world His power first made?
> Is not His love at issue still with sin,
> Visibly when a wrong is done on earth?
> Love, wrong, and pain, what see I else around?
> Yea, and the Resurrection and Uprise
> To the right hand of the throne—what is it beside,
> When such truth, breaking bounds, o'erfloods my soul,
> And, as I saw the sin and death, even so
> See I the need yet transiency of both,
> The good and glory consummated thence?
> I saw the power; I see the Love, once weak,
> Resume the Power: and in this word 'I see,'
> Lo, there is recognised the Spirit of both
> That moving o'er the spirit of man, unblinds
> His eye and bids him look.

That is to say, the life and death and resurrection and ascension of Christ have become a kind of symbol of a contest and a conquest that is always going on. The New Testament interpretation of the life and death and resurrection and ascension is that the Son of God was incarnate and that His life was a self-emptying and His death a sacrifice, and that His resurrection and ascension completed His triumph over sin and death. In this way the Christ became the Saviour of the world. By His life He showed men what they were meant to be, and through His sacrifice and triumph He gave them the power to be what they were meant to be, and their restored inheritance is no less than eternal life in the presence of God. No New Testament writer sees the 'need' of sin and death. One of the writers says that by man came death and that by man—meaning Jesus Christ—came also the resurrection of the dead. But that is not an acknowledgement of the 'need' of death. And, here too, the emphasis is on the sacrifice of Jesus Christ as leading to the resurrection. The interpretation in the poem is not incompatible with Christianity. The life and death of Christ has often appealed to men as a symbol of an everlasting contest and triumph, but so has the life and death of many another hero. And every heroic soul has in him the capacity to serve others. There is a mood in which one looks on sin and death as 'needful' because of the good and glory that grow out of them. But that mood may occur to a Jew like Rabbi Ben Ezra as well as to a disciple of Christ.

The word 'Christian' is used so vaguely that it has been necessary to point out the difference between Browning's 'probability' and the New Testament 'certainty', as also the difference between Browning's interpretation (though it be through the mouth of St. John) of the life and death of Jesus Christ and the New

Testament interpretation of it, in order to understand how Browning came to deny that he was a Christian.

I apologize for this tedious case, especially for the long exposition of the St. John Gospel view of miracles. Yet miracles are a stumbling-block, and it is as well to know how one early-Christian writer regarded them. I must also apologize for accepting the report of Robert Buchanan in this matter of Browning's Christianity. W. Hall Griffin contends that this report is apocryphal or that Browning made the denial in a fit of temper! I have accepted the report and, by giving what many people may reprobate as too narrow an account of the Christian religion, I have sought to justify Browning's denial. And, after all, a poet who chooses to put his chief convictions about life and death into the mouth of a Jew is declaring plainly enough that he does not confine himself to the Christian attitude.

IV

A word or two may be permitted here about the general effect of Browning's optimism. As I have hinted, he has been usually—and perhaps rightly—regarded as a great exponent of the Christian religion. A Christian, it is thought, should be an optimist, and, therefore, it is argued, so supreme and undeviating an optimist as Browning must be a Christian. Many readers—and preachers—have looked to him for a reinforcement of their faith. At any rate, he is always encouraging. And he is not merely encouraging because he speaks of what is beautiful and joyous, and neglects to face the ugly and venomous facts of life. He dares to face such facts, and from his close scrutiny of them he brings to us, in Westcott's phrase, an 'assurance of hope'. That is why so many readers have willingly undertaken the toil of learning his 'way' and of deciphering his meaning. They have been told that he is 'difficult'. Critics have exhausted themselves in proving that he is 'unmusical'. But the persevering reader has found something so infectiously brave about him that he has gone on reading and communicated his 'madness' to others. Mary Gladstone is a good example of this infection in the '70's, and there are many examples now. Such readers often discover that his difficulty has been exaggerated, and more often they find with delighted surprise that he can rise to a perfection and beauty of expression that give the effect not only of inevitableness but of spontaneity as well. His optimism is, however, the lure and the sustaining force.

I began this chapter by citing remarks from Mrs. Alice Meynell's *The Second Person Singular and Other Essays*. She spoke of the failure of the proffer of Browning's optimism. I will close by a quotation from a French critic, Mary Duclaux, who wrote in 1922—the same year as Mrs. Meynell's book of essays. I have already extracted one sentence. This is the full passage:

'Mais ce qui surtout l'a rendu cher aux contemporains de sa vieillesse, ce qui rend son vers, encore aujourd'hui, vivace et efficace quand la poésie des autres grands "Victoriens" nous paraît surannée, c'est que Browning a été le chantre obstiné de l'espérance.[1] La poésie

---

[1] Here is an appeal (1930) from Lady Lawrence to the same effect: 'I have undertaken with the help of the Ladies' Committee to raise £50,000 for the rebuilding and extension of the Robert Browning Settlement, the living memorial to one of England's greatest poets. Browning Hall, for the past 40 years the centre of various social and religious activities which provide amenities otherwise far beyond the reach of residents in the crowded streets and mean tenements of Walworth, is on the

anglaise du XIXe siècle a été fort belle, mais éloignée de la Vie et de ses humbles besoins: chimérique avec Shelley, folle de beauté avec Keats; Coleridge, mal éveillé, nous enchante avec les débris d'un songe; Tennyson, rêveur harmonieux, Rossetti, le subtil analyste du cœur secret, Matthew Arnold, avec ses doutes et sa culture exquise, sont tous des êtres solitaires. Byron, Wordsworth, Browning, seuls, sentent avec un plein cœur d'homme, parlent une langue sans fard. Et Browning a par surcroît cette grâce: il nous rassure. La vie est bonne, nous dit-il, et la mort, sans doute, meilleure! Cet optimisme nous impressionne d'autant plus qu'il ne nous cache aucune des laideurs, des misères de l'existence. Sa foi robuste triomphe, et si parfois elle nous semble un peu trop entêtée, un peu voulue, peut-être, si, au fin fond de nous-mêmes, nous préférons la résignation enchantée d'un Prospéro, néanmoins elle donne à son chant un timbre exultant, un tressaillement vital, un essor vers l'Infini, qui le font, tout imparfait, tout obscur qu'il soit parfois, ce que la poésie de nos jours est bien rarement: un aliment de l'âme.'

verge of collapse and has been condemned by the London County Council. Unless help is forthcoming quickly, all its activities must come to an end, and the practical side of Browning's philosophy of hope will be destroyed.'. . . (*The Times*). By the way, the address for donations is 105 St. Clement's House, Clement's Lane, E.C. 4.

VII

OPTIMISM AND REACTION AGAINST OPTIMISM IN THE TWENTIETH CENTURY

IT is not difficult to collect out of the writings of later-day poets passages which express a belief in life comparable to Browning's, but on a large survey one may perhaps admit that Browning's level has not been maintained even by the poets who take a sanguine view of events. Then there has been in the poetry of Thomas Hardy and A. E. Housman a definite reaction against optimism.

Perhaps the publication in 1859 of Charles Darwin's *Origin of Species* is critical for modern thought in this respect. The theory of evolution was not strictly new. I do not mean merely that Darwin was anticipated by Wallace, but that the idea of evolved forms of life had been suggested long ago—one may find it in Lucretius. Evolution, as Darwin propounded it, implies mutation of species, and mutation of species depends upon natural selection, and natural selection is the result of a struggle for existence. Immutability of species seems to be acknowledged in the biblical account of origins, and at first sight it is difficult to reconcile Darwin's book and orthodox traditional beliefs.

Darwin himself, who went to Cambridge that he might prepare for Ordination in the Church of England, found that he was distracted from that aim not only by his paramount interest in natural history, but by the observations, continued during twenty years, which were afterwards embodied in *The Origin of Species*. His studies resulted in an atrophy of aesthetic perception.

Whereas formerly he had taken pleasure in the poetry of Wordsworth and Coleridge, and, especially, in the plays of Shakespeare, he was unable in his later days to read poetry at all. He found Shakespeare dull to the point of nauseation. He also abandoned his belief in the Christian revelation. He seems to have repudiated the description 'atheist', but he considered himself an agnostic, though an unaggressive one.

The effect of his researches upon Darwin, one of the most sincere and lovable men who ever applied their powers to the study of science, may be paralleled by the effect upon his readers and upon those who heard of his doctrines. 'Darwinism' has become reasonably well known even to people who have not read his books. The thought of life as a struggle for existence has proved much more depressing than the thought of evolution, and his explanation, the result of a most amazing mass of observations and experiments, has had a greater effect than the theory of evolution. When 'the struggle for existence' is not qualified by a belief in immortality, life is presented to the consciousness of man as ruthless and hopeless. There is another region of faculty in man, and it is in this region that we find a revolt against the reasoned results of Darwinism. Men's belief in immortality is largely intuitive—Browning once declared that his was—and it is in the subconscious area of mind or spirit that men cherish idealistic convictions, that sooner or later determine their outlook on life.

Even so, their convictions may be in conflict with the prevailing tone of contemporary thought, and thereby suffer some blunting or diminution of enthusiasm. Browning was born in 1812 and was forty-seven when *The Origin of Species* was published. There is a reference here and there to evolution, but his habit of mind was untroubled by it.[1] T. E. BROWN, of Clifton, was born in 1830. This notable poet[2] has the same sanguine and optimistic temperament as Browning, and he followed Browning (as also did Hardy) in a reaction from the conventional poetical vocabulary. Brown was inoculated (so to say) against the depressing effects of Darwinism by his temperament; he was also protected by his vocation—he was a priest of the Church of England and a schoolmaster at Clifton College. GEORGE MEREDITH was born in 1828. His attitude towards Darwinism is difficult to define because it is elusive. His poem *Earth and Man* deals with evolution and with the struggle for existence. Meredith defends earth's cherishing of her best endowed. In other poems —*A Faith on Trial* and *The Wind on the Lyre*—he speaks of the ultimate attainment to God through earth; but he admits that spiritual truth cannot be apprehended by the logical faculty. We shall come again to these poems in a later chapter. What I wish to emphasize here is that Meredith is a poet of evolution, but he is eager to declare that a poet is a poet and neither optimist nor pessimist. He has a kind of hard brightness of detachment when you think he is coming to grips with the consequences of Darwinism.

Not so THOMAS HARDY. He was born in 1840. 'If it be possible', he wrote in 1876, 'to compass into a sentence all that a man learns between 20 and 40, it is that all things merge in one another—good into evil, generosity into justice, religion into politics, the year into the ages,

[1] Osbert Burdett thinks he became in his later life a rallying-point against Darwinism (*The Brownings*).
[2] His best poem is *Betsy Lee* (1872).

the world into the universe. With this in view the evolution of the species seems but a minute and obvious process in the same movement.'

Again: ' "All is vanity", saith the Preacher. But if all were vanity, who would mind? Alas, it is too often worse than vanity; agony, darkness, death also.

'A man would never laugh were he not to forget his situation, or were he not one who has never learnt it. After risibility from comedy, how often does the thoughtful mind reproach itself for forgetting the truth? Laughter always means blindness—either from defect, choice, or accident.'[1]

This is enough for the moment. The obstinate and complete reaction against optimism must be examined later on in greater detail. I quote these typical words now because they indicate the influence Hardy brought to bear upon the younger men. It was not until 1898 that Hardy published a book of poems, but he had been writing novels since 1871 and his fame as a novelist was secure in 1896. Hardy may have done much to discredit Browning's optimistic 'stuff'. It was not because Browning was out of the range of customary life, but because Hardy regarded life as a different kind of process with a different kind of end. And, as I began by saying, even among those who were not disposed to go all the way with Hardy, optimism suffered a check.

JOHN DAVIDSON, 'the first realist', was poor and neglected. It is not surprising that his poetry concerns the sadness and inequality and futility of life. However, he preserves some remnants of Browning's faith.[2]

Three of his ballads may be instanced: *A Ballad of Heaven*, *A Ballad of Hell*, and *A Ballad of an Artist's Wife*.

[1] *The Early Life of Thomas Hardy*, pp. 146–8.   [2] See above, pp. 53, 54.

But his optimism arises from his passionate belief in the ordinary man. He cannot credit his own conclusions. The tears of the artist's wife are not really 'useless'.

> 'Who was she?' God himself replied:
> 'In misery her lot was cast;
> She lived a woman's life, and died
> Working My work until the last.'
> It was his wife. He said, 'I pray
> Thee, Lord, despatch me now to Hell.'
> But God said, 'No; here shall you stay,
> And in her peace for ever dwell.'

When Davidson writes in his own person his fears are indistinguishable from Housman's: we spin ropes of sand; we lie down with the dead for ever. In the Dedication to *The Testament of John Davidson* (1908) he writes: 'I trust that your chagrin and mortification are, indeed, intolerable, chagrin and mortification being in all ages a root and fount of greatness in life, in polity, in art, in war.'[1]

Sir Walter Raleigh speaks of Browning as a 'vulgar (yes, vulgar) bustling Western if ever there was one'. He has, apparently, a much greater admiration for RUDYARD KIPLING, for he condemns R. Le Gallienne's book on Kipling: 'When "a towering falcon in her pride of place is by a mousing owl hawked at and killed" the thing portends calamity to the world of letters.' Sir Walter Raleigh plays the mousing owl so far as Browning is concerned, but his description of 'bustling Western' might apply to Kipling. Kipling preaches a Gospel of Work and the merit of the Western is to 'bustle'. His optimism is an optimism of applied energy. Browning

[1] For the essential optimism of JOHN MASEFIELD and especially his belief in conversion, I must refer the reader to Chapter II.

abhorred the 'unlit lamp and the ungirt loin'. The phrase is scriptural. The exhortation in the New Testament is to men who wait for their lord. They must be ready on the instant when the call comes. Browning means by the phrase that men should strive to the uttermost for their life's set prize. Kipling confines his attention mainly to the builders of Empire, whom Browning knew not. The merit of these builders is 'to strive, to seek, to find, and not to yield'. If men keep up their courage and work hard, all will be well. Kipling has the advantage of visualizing an empire, while Browning only visualizes an individual striving for a prize. The New Testament visualizes men who are dedicated to the service of a spiritual master. But the optimism of applied energy is common to all three. Work, the primal curse, is turned to a blessing.

Another and more beautiful side of Kipling's optimism is his belief in children. Browning was allured by youths, boys and girls, and believed in the perfection of their life. Pippa and David, Pompilia and Theocrite, are perfect in their generation. Kipling believes in smaller and younger persons, and when he writes about them or allows them to speak, one gets an impression that life is too good to end.

RUPERT BROOKE also mocked at Browning. I have quoted his mockery. He seems to have disliked the 'soul-ful bits' in Browning as much as Sir Walter Raleigh did. But in 1912 comes a change. He was working up to the change, as witness a letter to F. H. Keeling, in 1910: 'What is pessimism? . . . Are you telling us that the world is, after all, bad, and what's more horrible, without enough seeds of good in it? I, writing poetry and reading books and living at

Grantchester all day, feel rather doubtful and ignorant about "the world"—about England, and men, and what they're like... But I feel a placid and healthy physician about it all (only I don't know what drugs to recommend). This is because I've such an overflowing (if intermittent) flood of anti-pessimism in me. I'm using the word now in what I expect is its most important sense, of a feeling rather than a reasoned belief. The horror is not in *believing* the Universe is bad—or even believing the world won't improve—on a reasoned and cool examination of all facts, tendencies, so much as in a sort of general *feeling* that there isn't much potentiality for good in the world, and that anyhow it's a fairly dreary business,—an absence of much appreciation and hope, and a somehow paralysed will for good... I have a remedy....

'The remedy is Mysticism, or Life, I'm not sure which. Do not leap or turn pale at the word Mysticism, I do not mean any religious thing, or any form of belief. I still burn and torture Christians daily. It is merely the *feeling*—or a kindred one—which underlay the mysticism of the wicked mystics, only I refuse to be cheated by the *feeling* into any kind of *belief*. They were convinced by it that the world was very good, or that the Universe was one, or that God existed. I don't any the more believe the world to be good. Only I do get rid of the despair that it isn't—and I certainly seem to see additional possibilities of its getting better.

'It consists in just looking at people and things as themselves... What happens is that I suddenly feel the extraordinary value and importance of everybody I meet, and almost everything I see...'

The change, to put it bluntly in Mr. Marsh's words,

was that he discovered goodness to be the most important thing in life—'that immortal beauty and goodness', as he wrote much later, 'that radiance to love, which is to feel that one has safely hold of the eternal things'. Henceforward the only thing he cared for—or rather, felt he ought to care for—in a man was the possession of goodness; its absence, the one thing he hated, sometimes with fierceness.

It is significant that this change proved disconcerting to his friends.

The change had its effect on his poetry. *Mary and Gabriel* of the later time is a very beautiful poem. It has real feeling and is not merely pictorial like Dante Gabriel Rossetti's, still less disgusting like Thomas Hardy's poem about Christ's mother and His birth. The picture of the angel and the woman is there, clear and splendid; there is also a record of Mary's emotions:

> 'Twixt tears and laughter, panic hurrying her,
> She raised her eyes to that fair messenger.
> He knelt unmoved, immortal; with his eyes
> Gazing beyond her, calm to the calm skies;
> Radiant, untroubled in his wisdom, kind.
> His sheaf of lilies stirred not in the wind.
> How would she, pitiful with mortality,
> Try the wide peace of that felicity
> With ripples of her perplexed shaken heart,
> And hints of human ecstasy, human smart,
> And whispers of the lonely weight she bore,
> And how her womb within was hers no more
> And at length hers?
>   Being tired, she bowed her head
> And said 'So be it!' . . .

To the same period belongs this from *The Great Lover*:

Love is a flame:—we have beaconed the world's night.
A city:—and we have built it, these and I.
An emperor:—we have taught the world to die.
So, for their sakes I loved, ere I go hence,
And the high cause of Love's magnificence,
And to keep loyalties young, I'll write those names
Golden for ever, eagles, crying flames,
And set them as a banner, that men may know,
To dare the generations, burn, and blow
Out on the wind of Time, shining and streaming . . .

And, best known of all, *The Soldier*:

And think, this heart, all evil shed away,
  A pulse in the eternal mind, no less
    Gives somewhere back the thoughts by England given;
Her sights and sounds; dreams happy as her day;
  And laughter, learnt of friends; and gentleness,
    In hearts at peace, under an English heaven.

WALTER DE LA MARE's poems, though the theme of so many of them is the rare-sweet air of an imagined country, convey a joyousness which is more positive than Brooke's anti-pessimism. In *The Imagination's Pride* he is not afraid to be cheated into some sort of belief:

Comfort thee, comfort thee. Thy Father knows
  How wild man's ardent spirit, fainting, yearns
For mortal glimpse of death's immortal rose,
  The garden where the invisible blossom burns.
Humble thy trembling knees; confess thy pride;
  Be weary. O, whithersoever thy vaunting rove,
His deepest wisdom harbours in thy side,
  In thine own bosom hides His utmost love.

He also has a poem about the birth of Christ, *Before Dawn*:

> All flowers and butterflies lie hid,
> The blackbird and the thrush
> Pipe but a little as they flit
> Restless from bush to bush;
> Even to the robin Gabriel hath
> Cried softly, 'Hush!' . . .
>
> No snowdrop yet its small head nods,
> In winds of winter drear;
> No lark at casement in the sky
> Sings matins shrill and clear;
> Yet in this frozen mirk the Dawn
> Breathes, Spring is here!

He has an unexpected turn of thought in *Hospital*. His thought is often unexpected on a superficial reading. It is only by catching the spirit of the poem that the seemingly surprising thought falls into its place. Witness the last line in this passage:

> Ghosts may be ours; but gaze thou not too closely
> If haply in chill of the dark thou rouse to see
> One silent of foot, hooded, and hollow of visage,
> Pause, with secret eyes, to peer out at thee.
>
> He is the Ancient Tapster of this Hostel,
> To him at length even we all keys must resign;
> And if he beckon, Stranger, thou too must follow—
> Love and all peace be thine.

And here is a very echo of Browning's favourite doctrine of the survival of the good or the eternal usefulness of the good:

> Never ebbed sweetness—even out of a weed—
> In vain.

But Browning's philosophy of hope is most notably re-stated by the two 'classicists', LAURENCE BINYON and Robert Bridges, who would not in any way of poetic succession call themselves his disciples. I will quote a passage or two from Binyon's magnificent ode, *The Sirens*, printed at the Stanton Press in 1924 and published by Macmillan in 1925. The Prelude is 'a night of my youth':

> I am known to the Unknown; chosen, charmed, endangered:
> I flow to a music ocean-wild and starry,
> And feel within me, for this mortality's answer,
> Sea without shore . . .

In 'the trumpet summoning lost ships':

> But we have tasted wild fruit, listened to strange music;
> And all shores of the earth are but as doors of an inn;
> We knocked at the doors, and slept; to arise at dawn and go.
> We spilt blood for gold, trafficked in costly cargoes,
> But knew in the end it was not these we sailed to win;
> Only a wider sea; room for the winds to blow,
> And a world to wander in . . .

When he is hymning the Finders, he acclaims

> Touch of the mind that seeks behind
> The world for the befriending Mind.

Later on we hearken to the eternal lovers rejoicing,

> Out of the hollows of unpenetrated Night
> From afar calls to them, though they have known it not,
> A voice that is theirs, yet is not theirs, a new voice
> Never yet heard, yet older than all things;
> Laughter of a child's voice, sweeter than any sound
> On the earth or in the air, voice of eternal joy
> Victorious over the bowed wisdom of mortals,
> A well beyond the world, that springs and sings.

In the section called 'The Undiscovered World' we are bidden contemplate the journey of the Magi:

> What image shaped they of the World's Desire,
> What presence throned in majesty and might,
> As they went musing, deep in hope and dread,
> And under vast cope of the wheeling skies
> Found but a naked child, a child new-born?
> Wisdom resigned the crown of her enthroning;
> All her impassioned question was forsworn;
> In wonder she saw all things with new eyes.

And in the 'Mystery of Dawn':

> O undiscovered world that all about us lies
> When spirit to Spirit surrenders, and like young Love sees
> Heaven with human eyes!
> World of radiant morning! Joy's untravelled region!
> Why lies it solitary? and O why tarry we?
> Why daily wander out from Paradise?

The 'world-besieging storm' at the end and the trumpets of calamity prepare us for a revelation:

> Vision that dawns beyond knowledge shall deliver him
> From all that flattered, threatened, foiled, betrayed.
> Lo, having nothing, he is free of all the universe,
> And where light is, he enters unafraid.

So in *The Idols*, his second great ode, the whole problem is resolved into something quite definite and simple, something that corresponds to what Browning calls in *Abt Vogler* 'the C Major of this life'. *The Secret*, which the poet told me he considered the 'best of his short things', being founded upon a real experience, has the same theme as *The Idols*, and in *The Death of Adam* the conclusion is that

> Their burning deep unquenchable desire
> Shall be their glory, and shall forge at last
> From fiery pangs their everlasting peace.

OPTIMISM IN THE TWENTIETH CENTURY

Sirmione (in *England and Other Poems*) sounds an even deeper note:

> And silent rings a cry from star to sun,
> Through all the worlds, light, life and love are one!

And also that a power has

> Moulded us for each other's need, and linked
> Our brief breath with the eternal will . . .

Akin to Browning's chief conviction is the following from the same poem:

> In whom no deed was willed, *no lonely thought*
> *Attempered and to sword-blade keenness brought,*[1]
> But it has helped us, even us, for whom
> They shine in glory from the ages' gloom.

In finding illustrations of optimism in the poetry of ROBERT BRIDGES[2] I propose to confine myself to his fullest and ripest work, *The Testament of Beauty*, and in putting down or indicating passages I must leave the reader to be lured on to the whole work, wherein may be found the riches of one of the richest minds of our time. A serene joy in life and nature has always been a mark of Bridges's poetry. He had to live through the War of 1914–18. His *Testament of Beauty* is of great significance as having been written (or, at any rate, finally revised) when he had had ample time to reflect on that series of events. We cannot be wrong in regarding *The Testament of Beauty* as a record of the poet's own convictions. He declares its personal character himself,

---

[1] The italicized words might be a description of Binyon's own work.
[2] Dr. Robert Bridges, O.M., died between the writing of Chapter II and this one.

and he also claims that every poem echoes the life of the poet.

> The manner of this magic is purest in musick,
> but by the learner is seen more clearly in poetry,
> wherein each verbal symbol exposeth its idea;
> so that 'tis manifest by what promptings of thought
> the imaginativ landscape is built and composed,
> and how horizon'd: And the secret of a poem
> lieth in this intimat echo of the poet's life. (IV. 987)

Bridges's view of *childhood* suggests the intrinsic glory of human life—a glory that cannot go down in death.

> Thus Rafaël once venturing to show God in Man
> gave a child's eyes of wonder to his baby Christ;
> and his Mantuan brother coud he hav seen that picture
> would more truly hav foreshadow'd the incarnation of God.
> 'Tis divinest childhood's incomparable bloom,
> the loss whereof leaveth the man's face shabby and dull.
> (I. 331)

And, again, of the mother:

> Wherewhile a new spiritual personality
> in its miraculous significance, the child
> is less the mother's own than a treasur entrusted,
> which she can never love too fondly or serve too well;
> Nay, rather is she possess'd by her own possession,
> and in her VITA NUOVA *such things are reveal'd
> that all she hath thought or done seemeth to her of small worth.*
> The unfathomable mystery of her awaken'd joy
> sendeth her daily to heaven on her knees in prayer:
> and watching o'er the charm of a soul's wondering dawn
> enamoureth so her spirit that all her happiness
> is in her care for him, all hope in his promise;
> and his nobility is the dream-goal of her life. (II. 137)

Again:

>Yet for the gift of his virgin intelligence
>a child is ever our nearest pictur of happiness:
>'tis a delight to look on him in tireless play
>attentivly occupied with a world of wonders,
>so rich in toys and playthings that naked Nature
>wer enough without the marvelous inventary of man;
>wherewith he toyeth no less, and learning soon the lore
>of cypher and alphabet anon getteth to con
>the fair uncial comment that science hath penn'd
>glossing the mazy hieroglyph of Nature's book;
>and as he ever drinketh of the living waters
>his spirit is drawn into the stream and, as a drop
>commingled therewith, taketh of birthright therein
>as vast an heritage as his young body hath
>in the immemorial riches of mortality. (II. 462)

Of *War*:

>Children, for all their innocency and gentleness,
>in their unreason'd Selfhood think no scorn of war,
>but practise mimicry of it in their merry games . . .
>(II. 568)

. . . .

>My little chorister, who never miss'd a note,—
>I mark'd him how when prayers wer ended he would take
>his Bible, and in his corner ensconced would sit and read
>with unassumed devotion. What was it fetch'd him?
>Matthew Mark Luke and John was it? The parables,
>the poetry and passion of Christ? Nay 'twas the bloody books
>of Jewish war, the story of their Judges and Kings;
>lured by those braggart annals, while he conn'd the page
>the parson's mild discourse pass'd o'er his head unheard.
>(II. 576)

Reason's account of War:

> And of War she would say: it ranketh with those things
> that are like unto virtue, but not virtue itself:
> rather, in the conscience of spiritual beauty, a vice
> that needeth expert horsemanship to curb, yet being
> nativ in the sinew of selfhood, the life of things,
> the pride of animals, and virtue of savagery,
> so long as men be savage such it remaineth;
> and mid the smoke and gas of its new armoury
> still, with its tatter'd colours and gilt swords of state,
> retaineth its old glory untarnish'd—heroism,
> self-sacrifice, disciplin, and those hardy virtues
> of courage honour'd in Brasidas, without which
> man's personality were meaner than the brutes. (II. 869)

The poet gives a picture of an assembly of guests at the country seat of some great politician, and the contrast between the ideal nakedness of a classic statue the politician has set up in the grounds and the parasols and silks of aimless idlers, and he compares this contrast to the appearance of a true soldier among vain, profiteering seekers after comfort and wealth:

> —'tis very like among common concourse of men,
> who twixt care of comfort and zeal in worldly affairs
> hav proved serving two masters the vanity of both,
> when a true soldier appeareth, one compact at heart
> of sterner virtues and modesty of maintenance,
> mute witness and martyr of spiritual faith, a man
> ready at call to render his life to keep his soul. (II. 895)

He speaks of the plagues of Athens and London, and that men knew not that it was the 'crowded foulness of their own bodies punished them so', but we knew that it was mankind's crowded uncleanness of soul that brought our plague of the war and yet 'could not cure nor stay', and so when the fierce fight wore out there was no sober return to health.

> Amid the flimsy joy of the uproarious city
> my spirit on those fierce jubilant days of armistice
> was heavier within me, and felt a profounder fear
> than ever it knew in all the War's darkest dismay. (II. 998)

He appreciated the old ways of agriculture, the effigy of plough-teams that endeared November's melancholy to him, but he is quick to recognize the *new poetry of toil*.

> Or what man feeleth not a new poetry of toil,
> whenas on frosty evenings neath its clouding smoke
> the engin hath huddled up its clumsy threshing-coach
> against the ricks, wherefrom laborers standing aloft
> toss the sheaves on its tongue; while the grain runneth out,
> and in the whirr of its multitudinous hurry
> it hummeth like the bee, a warm industrious boom
> that comforteth the farm, and spreadeth far afield
> with throbbing power; as when in a cathedral awhile
> the great diapason speaketh, and the painted saints
> feel their glass canopies flutter in the heav'nward prayer.
> (III. 374)

He gives a description of that picture of Titian's which some mystic named L'AMOR SACRO E PROFANO, and he says:

> Thus Titian hath pictured the main sense of my text,
> and this truth: that as Beauty is all with Spirit twined,
> so all obscenity is akin to the ugliness
> which Art would outlaw; whence cometh that tinsel honour
> and mimicry of beauty which is the attire of vice. (III. 1118)

And he speaks of the higher 'Ethick' which by personal alliance with *beauty* has made escape,

> soaring away to where
> The Ring of Being closeth in the Vision of God. (IV. 246)

He reasons with the mystic—the renouncing mystic—and says,

> Ther is no motiv can rebate
> or decompose the intrinsic joy of activ life,
> whereon all function whatsoever in man is based. (IV. 460)

He traces the origin of a belief in the *Communion of Saints*, which

> foldeth the sheep in pastures of eternal life, (IV. 1252)

and seeks images in illustration not only from prayer, and from a service in Lent in a city church, but also from our English sport and tens of thousands sitting huddled to watch the fortune of the football.

He has a beautiful eulogy of *Love*:

> But love's true passion is of immortal happiness,
> whereof the Greeks, maybe—whose later poets told
> of a heav'nly Aphroditè—had some dim prescience
> before man ever arrived at thatt wisdom thru' Christ,
> and now teacheth to his children as their birthright,—a gift
> whose wealth is amplified by spending, and its charm
> rejuvenated by habit, that dulleth all else. (III. 300)

And this heavenly love is not alien from the second call of nature's love:

> And so mighty is this second vision, which cometh
> in puberty of body and adolescence of mind
> that, forgetting his Mother, he calleth it 'first Love';
> for it mocketh at suasion or stubbornness of heart,
> as the oceantide of the omnipotent Pleasur of God,
> flushing all avenues of life . . . (IV. 1340)

It is this welcome hour of bliss that 'standeth for certain pledge of happiness perdurable'.

There is a testament of beauty in the *little works of man*,
which
     strewn on the sands of time, sparkle
like cut jewels in the beatitude of God's countenance.
              (II. 507)
The chief testament, however, is in the Son of Man:
 So it was when Jesus came in his gentleness
with his divine compassion and great Gospel of Peace,
men hail'd him WORD OF GOD, and in the title of Christ
crown'd him with love beyond all earth-names of renown.
 For He, wandering unarm'd save by the Spirit's flame,
in few years with few friends founded a world-empire
wider than Alexander's and more enduring;
since from his death it took its everlasting life.
His kingdom is God's kingdom, and his holy temple
not in Athens or Rome but in the heart of man.
They who understand not cannot forget, and they
who keep not his commandment call him Master and
  Lord.   (I. 771)
He rescues man from the dilemma of pagan thought,
 that ther can be no friendship betwixt God and man
because of their unlimited disparity.   (IV. 1388)
From this dilemma, this 'poison of faith',
 Man-soul made glad escape in the worship of Christ;
for his humanity is God's Personality,
and communion with him is the life of the soul.
 . . . .
        Christ yet walketh the earth,
and talketh still as with those two disciples once
on the road to Emmaus—where they walk and are sad;
whose vision of him then was his victory over death,
thatt resurrection which all his lovers should share,
who in loving him had learn'd the Ethick of happiness;
whereby they too should come where he was ascended
to reign over men's hearts in the Kingdom of God.
              (IV. 1391)

216   OPTIMISM AND REACTION AGAINST

It is a shock to draw away from this high and inspiring faith—comparable in its directness and simplicity to the dying declaration of Pompilia—to the doubts and questionings of Thomas Hardy and the resolute hopelessness of A. E. Housman. It is, of course, merely conjecture that the influence of Darwin is chiefly responsible. If the theory of evolution accounts for the pessimism of the poets, their view is in strange and rather striking contrast to that of Sir Oliver Lodge and Eddington, who, by the way, happens to be an old pupil of mine. I wish I could claim a share in the direction of Eddington's mind towards the 'Ethick of happiness'. He said once that I had taught him the 'love of literature', but he has arrived at his own certainties, and his great intellectual powers and genius of discernment tend to strengthen the hold of smaller men. He says in his Swarthmore Lecture: 'Our story of evolution ended with a stirring in the brain organ of the latest of Nature's experiments, but that stirring of consciousness transmutes the whole story and gives meaning to its symbolism. Symbolically it is the end, but looking behind the symbolism it is the beginning. . . . After exhausting physical methods we returned to the inmost recesses of consciousness, to the voice that proclaims our personality; and from there we entered on a new outlook. We have to build the spiritual world out of symbols taken from our own personality, as we build the scientific world out of the symbols of the mathematician.'[1]

THOMAS HARDY's last book of poems, *Winter Words*, was not issued until after his death. In the Preface to *Winter Words*—it is wholly his own preface—he expressed

[1] *Science and the Unseen World*, by Arthur Stanley Eddington (New York, The Macmillan Co., 1929), pp. 38 and 82.

the intention of issuing the book on his birthday. He did not say what birthday but left the number blank. The Preface is interesting because the aged poet 'goes for' the critics who have accused him of gloom and pessimism. He roundly says that they have not read him, and he proposes to uncover a few places in this very volume which disprove their conclusions. He also disclaims the formulation of any philosophy of life either in this book or in any of his writings.

I have often wondered what were those places the poet would have uncovered to the complaining critic. I can think of a humorous piece about Liddell and Scott, who made the Greek Lexicon; of a poem that shows intense sympathy with a drowning dog; of a poem written on his eighty-sixth birthday called, 'He never expected much'; of another about some bell-ringers, who, having drunk themselves thirsty until closing-time on New Year's Eve, afterwards swigged the sacramental wine and could not produce a sound from the bells, though they pulled and pulled; of a drinking-song. I have sought for cheering pieces, but all the others are less cheering than these.

As for the disclaimer of the formulation of any philosophy in any of his writings, one may class Thomas Hardy, as Mr. A. C. Ward does in his handbook on 'Twentieth Century Literature', as belonging to the Interrogators. To ask questions is not to formulate a philosophy. But the fact that his unvarying answer to the chief question is in the negative does in some sense constitute a philosophy. It has been said that the distinguishing mark of his poetry is a 'satisfying flatness'. I do not find it either satisfying or flat. But those who do, interpret their satisfaction as due to the 'interesting

spectacle of a mind continually probing and exploring'
and the flatness as 'produced by the persistent pressure
of the Spirit of Negation'.

What does that mean? I do not refer to the continually probing mind, to what Hardy himself, quoting Wordsworth, calls the 'obstinate questionings', but to the persistent pressure of the spirit of negation. What does it mean? How would the man-in-the-street or the man-in-the-third-class-railway-carriage put it?

I happen to have had an experience which enables me to give some sort of answer. I was travelling south by train from Sunderland. At Leeds I left the train to collect some victuals, and when I returned I found the carriage full of men, one of them in my seat. He courteously gave it up to me and wandered elsewhere. Most of the men were ex-service men and they began to talk about pensions and the hardships that had been suffered in respect of Government allowances. I made up my mind not to join in the conversation. But presently an old man with a rather dribbly mind said, 'What's this I hear about giving up the Bible?' A man opposite me (call him B) said, 'You mean the Prayer Book.' 'Well, then, the Prayer Book,' amended the old man, and turned to me with a challenge, thus: 'You might be a man of good life, I wouldn't wonder'—he judged from my collar and so I bowed as well as I could —'what do you think of it?' I said, 'Have you read the new Prayer Book?' 'No,' he said, 'I can't say as I have.' 'Have you read the old one?' At that there was a general laugh, and the old man ceased to dribble. Then B, following some obscure connexion, said, 'Why did they bury that poet—I've forgotten his name—in Westminster Abbey when he didn't believe in God?'

'You mean Thomas Hardy,' I said. 'Yes, that's the man.' 'Have you read Thomas Hardy?' 'No, but my wife has. And she says he said, "If there is a God . . .", meaning that he didn't believe there was one.' 'Well, I said, 'a man may change his mind. And one never knows how the change may come. I remember being In Y wood in 1916 . . .' 'Oh, yes,' said another man, 'Y wood. I know Y wood right enough. I was there . . .' 'We've heard all about that,' said B. 'What we want to hear now is what this gentleman has to say about belief in God.'

So I told him my experience in Y wood—which is not perhaps pertinent to the present discussion.

But what is pertinent is B's remark about Thomas Hardy. Because it is probable that what B or B's wife meant by not believing was the same as the persistent pressure of the spirit of negation.

Some poets have affected to disregard the 'message' of poetry. Flecker said that his theory of poetry prompted him to the creation of beauty to the total disregard of the 'message'—the message, apparently, being an irrelevant or even contemptible element. How can one disregard the message of poetry? For example, could one disregard in *Hassan* the Procession of Protracted Death and concentrate as freely on the beauty of it as if it were the Procession of Unending Joy? Or, could one see, *first*, if ever, the beauty of Rafi's whisper to Pervaneh and the talk of sensual cruelty in Act IV, Sc. 2? Nor can one resist the pressure of the 'Spirit of the Years' in *The Dynasts*. One might resist the 'Spirit Sinister', but not the 'Spirit of the Years'.

'It was thought proper to introduce,' says Hardy in the Preface to *The Dynasts*, 'as supernatural spectators of the terrestrial action, certain impersonated abstractions, or Intelligences, called Spirits. They are intended to be taken by the reader for what they may be worth as contrivances of the fancy merely. Their doctrines are but tentative, and are advanced with little eye to a systematized philosophy warranted to lift "the burthen of the mystery" of this unintelligible world. The chief thing hoped for them is that they and their utterances may have dramatic plausibility enough to procure for them, in the words of Coleridge, "that willing suspension of disbelief for the moment which constitutes poetic faith". The wide prevalence of the Monistic theory of the Universe forbade, in this twentieth century, the importation of Divine personages from any antique Mythology as ready-made sources or channels of Causation, even in verse, and excluded the celestial machinery of, say, *Paradise Lost*, as peremptorily as that of the *Iliad* or the *Eddas*. And the abandonment of the masculine pronoun in allusions to the First or Fundamental Energy seemed a necessary and logical consequence of the long abandonment by thinkers of the anthromorphic conception of the same.

'These phantasmal Intelligences are divided into groups, of which one only, that of the Pities, approximates to the "Universal Sympathy of human nature—the spectator idealized" of the Greek Chorus; it is impressionable and inconsistent in its views, which sway hither and thither as wrought on by events. Another group approximates to the passionless Insight of the Ages. The remainder are eclectically chosen auxiliaries whose signification may be readily discerned. In point of literary form, the scheme of contrasted Choruses and other conventions of this external feature was shaped

OPTIMISM IN THE TWENTIETH CENTURY 221

with a single view to the modern expression of a modern outlook, and in frank divergence from classical and other dramatic precedent which ruled the ancient voicings of ancient themes.'

It is an affectation to say that you have no philosophy of life to present, or, that you present none—and this philosophy constitutes the 'message' of the writing—when you invent a scheme 'with a single view to the modern expression of a modern outlook'. So the Fundamental Energy is not styled God or He but It, and the modern notion of It is expressed as follows:

Spirit of the Pities.
       Meet is it, none the less,
To bear in thought that though Its consciousness
May be estranged, engrossed, afar or sealed,
Sublunar shocks may wake Its watch anon.

Spirit of the Years.
Nay. In the Foretime, even to the germ of Being,
Nothing appears of shape to indicate
That cognizance has marshalled things terrene,
Or will (such is my thinking) in my span.
Rather they show that, like a knitter drowsed,
Whose fingers play in skilled unmindfulness,
The Will has woven with an absent heed
Since life first was; and ever will so weave.

This utterance of the Spirit of the Years concerning the Supreme Mover agrees with what Hardy wrote on October 17th, 1896, concerning *The Dynasts*, then beginning to take shape in his mind.[1] 'Poetry. Perhaps I can express more fully in verse ideas and emotions which run counter to the most crystallized opinion—hard as a rock—which the vast body of men

[1] See *The Later Years of Thomas Hardy*, p. 57.

have vested interests in supporting. To cry out in a passionate poem that (for instance) the Supreme Mover or Movers, the Prime Force or Forces, must be either limited in power, unknowing, or cruel—which is obvious enough, and has been for centuries—will cause them merely a shake of the head; but to put it in argumentative prose will make them sneer, or foam, and set all the literary contortionists jumping upon me, a harmless agnostic, as if I were a clamorous atheist.'

When Hardy wrote his Preface to *Winter Words* he must have forgotten a letter written in May 1907 to Mr. Edward Wright. This letter acknowledges the formulation of a philosophy and also contains an interesting reference to Darwin's book. He claims that his philosophy is the same as denoted in his previous volumes, and is an expression of what the 'thinking world' has come to adopt. He gives no references, except to Darwin, to support the claim that the 'thinking world' agrees with him. It is probably true, as Keyserling says, that 'there cannot occur to any one a thought which is not implicit in the general possibilities of the spirit of the age'. But the 'thinking world' is not to be identified with the general possibilities of the spirit of the age or even with the spirit of the age itself. Hardy, for example, treats all theologies as on the same level: Greek, Jewish, and Christian, and says they have all been 'used up'. Nevertheless, a considerable section of the 'thinking world' is attached to the Christian theology, and a marked modern tendency is to regard Jesus Christ as a teacher of unique originality: 'The words of Jesus, even superficially examined, are veritable treasuries of sober, healthy common sense; probed to their depths, they are the highest manifestation of the

OPTIMISM IN THE TWENTIETH CENTURY 223

art of magical expression. This means that they are so conceived that their meaning, when it penetrates deep enough, must transform spirit and soul in accordance with their own peculiar laws; in the case of Jesus, surface and depth were in perfect harmony.'[1]

Here are the relevant passages from the letter[2] to Mr. Edward Wright:

'I quite agree with you in holding that the word "Will" does not perfectly fit the idea to be conveyed—a vague thrusting or urging internal force in no predetermined direction. But it has become accepted in philosophy for want of a better, and is hardly likely to be supplanted by another, unless a highly appropriate one could be found, which I doubt. The word that you suggest—Impulse—seems to me to imply a driving power behind it; also a spasmodic movement unlike that of, say, the tendency of an ape to become a man and other such processes.

'In a dramatic epic—which I may perhaps assume *The Dynasts* to be—some philosophy of life was necessary, and I went on using that which I had denoted in my previous volumes of verse (and to some extent prose) as being a generalized form of what the thinking world had gradually come to adopt, myself included. That the Unconscious Will of the Universe is growing aware of Itself I believe I may claim as my own idea solely—at which I arrived by reflecting that what has already taken place in a fraction of the whole (*i.e.* so much of the world as has already become conscious) is likely to take place in the mass; and there being no Will outside the mass—that is, the Universe—the whole Will becomes

---
[1] Hermann Keyserling, *The World in the Making*, p. 247.
[2] *The Later Years of Thomas Hardy*, p. 124.

conscious thereby: and ultimately, it is to be hoped, sympathetic.

'I believe, too, that the Prime Cause, this Will, has never before been called "It" in any poetical literature, English or foreign.'

I do not wish to deny Hardy's claim to originality in calling God 'It'—though I heard a man call God 'It' in the slang sense long before the publication of *The Dynasts*—but his 'It' only declares the impersonality or heartlessness of the President of the Immortals. The philosophy of *The Dynasts* is really the same as that of *Tess*:

'She—and how many more—might have ironically said with Saint Augustine: "Thou hast counselled a better course than Thou hast permitted."'

And, at the end: ' "Justice" was done, and the President of the Immortals, in Aeschylean phrase, had ended his sport with Tess.'

Still, we may retain the hope that It, the Will, or the President of the Immortals, will one day wake up and not continue to drowse over Its (or her) knitting, or to go on playing the pianoforte with Its fingers while It is thinking or talking of something else and Its head does not rule them; and that when It wakes up, It may become sympathetic and not find sport in the hanging of 'pure women'.

The philosophy of A. E. Housman is implicit. I do not wish to illustrate it at any length, partly because Housman's pessimism is sometimes even a little peevish and always depressing, and partly because, as I have already striven to show, there is much else in his poetry —a perfect, if limited, technique, a deep appreciation of natural appearances, an appealing love of humanity.

Yet these excellencies are seriously countered by the constant sense of the futility of life and the nothingness of death:

> Now, and I muse for why and never find the reason,
>   I pace the earth, and drink the air, and feel the sun.
> Be still, be still, my soul; it is but for a season:
>   Let us endure an hour and see injustice done.[1]

'The blackbird in the coppice' looked out to see the ploughman stride, and sang to him, and he picked up a stone and killed it.[2]

> Then my soul within me
>   Took up the blackbird's strain,
> And still beside the horses
>   Along the dewy lane
>   It sang the song again:
>
> 'Lie down, lie down, young yeoman;
>   The sun moves always west;
> The road one treads to labour
>   Will lead one home to rest,
>   And that will be the best.'

This is the least bitter note about death. And yet, strangely and beautifully, through all his hopelessness persists the poet's love of his fellow-men:

> East and west on fields forgotten
>   Bleach the bones of comrades slain,
> Lovely lads and dead and rotten;
>   None that go return again.
>
> Far the calling bugles hollo,
>   High the screaming fife replies,
> Gay the files of scarlet follow:
>   Woman bore me, I will rise.[3]

[1] *A Shropshire Lad*, XLVIII.   [2] Ibid. VII.   [3] Ibid. XXXV.

Housman says, in his Preface to *Last Poems*: 'I publish these poems, few though they are, because it is not likely that I shall ever be impelled to write much more. I can no longer expect to be revisited by the continuous excitement under which in the early months of 1895 I wrote the greater part of my other book, nor indeed could I well sustain it if it came. . . .'

One feels that, perhaps. Yet the quality is the same, the perfection the same, the spirit the same.

The wording of *Reveille* (already quoted p. 91) approaches by exception more nearly to Hardy's.

But here—in *Last Poems*—is the old tune:

> Oh stay at home, my lad, and plough
> The land and not the sea,
> And leave the soldiers at their drill,
> And all about the idle hill
> Shepherd your sheep with me.[1]

The same view of Nature:

> For nature, heartless, witless nature,
> Will neither care nor know
> What stranger's feet may find the meadow
> And trespass there and go,
> Nor ask amid the dews of morning
> If they are mine or no.[2]

One fears that Housman's idea of the universe has bitten into the younger men, especially the more vocal of them, since the War of 1914–18. But one believes that beneath this one may get to some stratum, in which are forming new ideas of suggestion, impulse, conduct, attainment, relationship, beauty; of the limits of selfishness; of the possibilities of happiness; of the core of life

[1] *Last Poems*, xxxviii.   [2] Ibid. xl.

under the outward vesture; of the reality of death and life, both of the mind and of the body; of what has the quality of permanence and indestructibility; of the meaning of the past and the disregard of the past; of the value of the present and the allurement of the future. These ideas, concreted in experience, event and character, may become the stuff of poetry. Such poetry should prove a fresh nourishment of the soul.

VIII
BROWNING'S REPUTATION AS A LOVER

I PROPOSED in the first chapter of this book to dwell on the love-story of the Brownings, because it is only now that the love-story is making its way into the public mind and producing an effect probably greater than the reading of their poetry. The reputation of Robert Browning as a lover is almost wholly in the twentieth century. Indeed, it might be said to be almost wholly in the second quarter of the twentieth century! The courtship part of the love-story has been known for many years to the comparatively few readers of the two volumes of love-letters, published just before the close of the nineteenth century, and there are not many readers[1] who would not echo George Meredith's words that they were a splendid couple and that it is a love-story far surpassing all the efforts of writers of fiction. But during 1929 and 1930 several books have been issued, re-editing the courtship in popular form. I have already mentioned *The Brownings* by Osbert Burdett and *Andromeda in Wimpole Street* by Miss Dormer Creston. Then there are Miss Isabel Clarke's study and Miss C. Lenanton's novel, *Miss Barrett's Elopement*. And we have had a new play, by Rudolf Besier, *The Barretts of Wimpole Street*, dealing with the love-story of Elizabeth Barrett and Robert Browning and that 'strange creature, Mr. Barrett', as the producer of the play called him. The play was given at the Malvern Festival, 1930.

[1] Sir Walter Raleigh is an exception. 'The harm she did to Bob!' &c. See *Letters of Sir Walter Raleigh, ut supra*. Perhaps Raleigh had not read the love-letters.

Hope End House, the 'strange creature's' old home, is six miles from Malvern.

I do not propose in this chapter to retrace the courtship in any detail. My object is to supplement the courtship story by some comments on the married life of the Brownings drawn from the letters of Elizabeth Barrett Browning to her sister Henrietta, and to complete the survey by quotations from a remarkable series of letters written by Robert Browning after his wife's death, mainly to Miss Isa Blagden, who had been one of Elizabeth's closest friends.

I

But I may first refresh the reader's memory about the essentials of the Andromeda part. Browning was a veritable Perseus. Elizabeth Barrett had had a serious nervous breakdown (as it used to be called) after the death by drowning at Oddicombe near Torquay of her favourite brother. She was confined to her room and thought to be a hopeless invalid. Her father seems to have taken a morbid pleasure in her invalidism, because it kept her always near him and under his immediate direction in his house in Wimpole Street. He was a man of possessive temperament. He wanted his children for his very own. Elizabeth was in this condition of mewed-up invalidism when Browning began to write to her in January 1845. She had a considerable reputation as a poet and critic—a greater reputation than he had. In his first letter Robert Browning told her that he loved her books and he loved her too. They went on exchanging letters, some of which, especially his, make stiff reading, until by the intervention of their splendid friend, Kenyon, he was allowed to visit her. His visits did not put a stop to the letters. Only one of his is missing. He seems to have made some overbold proposal, which frightened Elizabeth, and this letter was destroyed.

By degrees he encouraged her to physical efforts. She took to getting up and walking about and at length to walking out. She was attended by her faithful maid, Wilson, and a tiresome little dog, of which she was inordinately fond, called Flush. Mr. Barrett, though he knew about the 'pomegranate man'—this was his humorous way of referring to the author of *Bells and Pomegranates*—did not suspect whereto these events were tending. At first, Elizabeth tried to conceal from Robert the real condition of her father's mind. But, as the courtship proceeded, she was compelled to face the facts and to make them known to him. Her disclosure is extraordinarily poignant. The truth was thrust upon her through Mr. Barrett's refusal to allow her to go to Pisa, after such a visit had been recommended by her doctor.

By March 1846 Robert and Elizabeth were planning their marriage. Her decision was hastened, if not caused, by her father's talk of removing his whole family to the country. The strange creature began to take notice. 'Dearest'—this was her intimation to Robert—'it was plain to me yesterday evening when he came into this room for a moment at seven o'clock, before going down to his own to dress for dinner, plain that he was not altogether pleased at finding you here in the morning. There was no pretext for objecting gravely, but it was plain he was not pleased.'

This at last roused Robert. He had not shown anger before. He tumbles over himself in a long sentence:

'. . . that a father choosing to give out of his whole

day some five minutes to a daughter, supposed to be prevented from participating in what he probably, in common with the whole world of sensible men, as distinguished from poets and dreamers, consider every pleasure of life, by a complete foregoing of society—that he, after the Pisa business and the enforced continuance, and as he must believe, permanence of this state in which any other being would go mad. . . .' This is a third of the sentence, which ends: '. . . my Ba, it is SHOCKING.'

I quote these words, because they reveal, in that recognition of her state as one in which any other being would go mad, the real extent of his anxiety. In view of this revelation his patience and care and self-control are seen to be all the more admirable.

It is tempting to linger over this correspondence. His references to his own father and mother are in marked contrast to her sketches of the ogre in her home. Here is one: '. . . because since I was a child I never looked for the least or greatest thing within the compass of their means to give, but given it was. . . .'

But I must content myself with a brief summary. They discussed money. His income from poetry was negligible. He believed that he could obtain a pension or an official post. She said he must not give up his leisure. She had an income independently of her father—about £360 a year—this was a late confession—and they could live. What she dreaded was her father's tongue, if she told him she was going to marry. She said she would die before his words. Robert's reply was: 'Let us go quietly away.'

His anxiety brought on headaches: he had never suffered in his life before. His headaches may have contributed more than anything else to her determination to 'take September' as the month for marrying. But she must be attended by Wilson, an expensive servant. And she was spending £40 a quarter on herself. Robert was to borrow £100 from his father for journey-money. His father and mother of course knew about the project, and Robert assured her that 'if you care for any love, purely love, you will have theirs'. She replied: 'May your father indeed be able to love me a little, for *my* father will never love me again.'

Robert bought a marriage licence on September 10th and they were married on September 12th at St. Marylebone Parish Church. She and Wilson stole out together and called at a chemist's and went on to the church where Robert and his cousin, James Silverthorne, met them. Robert went home after the ceremony. Elizabeth drove to her friend, Mr. Boyd's. Mr. Boyd was in the secret and he sustained her with a drink of Cyprus wine. Wilson went home. Elizabeth's sisters, having missed her and Wilson, came to Mr. Boyd's to find her. They did not see the ring on her finger—she had taken it off—and though she trembled with fright at their grave faces she kept up somehow and drove with them to Hampstead.

A week passed. Robert would not visit her again. He could not bring himself to ask for her as Miss Barrett. They exchanged letters. He wrote last on September 19th. On that day they 'eloped'. The elopement was not Miss Barrett's, but Mrs. Browning's. She and Robert were never separated afterwards. He did not write to her again because there was no need. She wrote many times to her father, but he did not answer—did not even open her letters. Nor did he mention her in his will. He told Kenyon, much later, that his daughter 'should have been thinking of another world'.

II

The letters of Elizabeth Barrett Browning to her sister Henrietta[1] cover nearly the whole of Elizabeth's married life. These letters contain descriptions of the Brownings' life and of society in Italy and in Paris 'where they were during Napoleon III's *coup d'état*; Elizabeth's vivid concern with the cause of liberty in general and Italian freedom in particular, her maternal pride in her little son, and, over all, the unalterable attachment to her sisters and even to the unbending old father, whose perverted sense of family unity was so disastrous to his children'.[2]

But my sole object now is to gather out of the letters her tributes to her husband. The first letter was written from Pisa, when the Brownings had been married nearly a month. Mrs. Jameson had helped Robert to take care of his wife, having 'shepherded' them in Paris and travelled with them to Pisa by easy stages. I quote from a letter of November 24th, 1846:

'This morning, when we were at breakfast, sitting half into the fire and close together, and having our coffee and eggs and toasted rolls, he said suddenly, in the midst of our laughing and talking, "Now! I do wish your sisters could see us through some peep hole of the world!" "Yes," said I, "as long as they did not hear us through the peep hole!"—for indeed the foolishness of this conversation would—on which he laughed and began, "abstract ideas", etc. *That* was for you to hear,

[1] *Elizabeth Barrett Browning: Letters to her Sister 1846–1859*, ed. L. Huxley (1929).   [2] Publisher's notice.

you understand, to have the reputation of our wisdom. . . .'

A delightful beginning! Not a bit the 'fubsy old Browning' of Sir Walter Raleigh's perverse imagination.[1]

'It is not a bad thing, be sure, for a woman to be loved by a man of imagination. He loves her through a lustrous atmosphere which not only keeps back the faults, but produces continual novelty, through its own changes. Always, he will have it, that our attachment was "predestinated from the beginning", and that no two persons could have one soul between them so much as we. . . .'

She quotes 'dear Mr. Kenyon's' opinion of Robert as 'an incarnation of the good and the True'—'which is the truest truth of my husband, and draws from me a deeper gratitude still'.

'I am happier than ever I was in my life . . . I never in my earliest dreams dreamed of meeting a nobler heart and soul, or a deeper affection—do remember, if you please, that I have been married nearly three months, though the first week (as I remind Robert) went for nothing! . . . Who would have prophesied that, some six months ago?'

In some discussion of going to Venice, she had to apologize: 'And I turned round, observing graciously— "whenever I blame you, I find myself in fault afterwards". To which he answered with the greatest quietness (of course, I *expected* him to say "my darling, when you find fault with yourself, you are most in fault of all," or something pretty of that kind) but he just answered— "It is a satisfaction, at any rate, that you should admit it". So I admired his infinite "modesty". . . .

[1] See *Letters of Sir Walter Raleigh (1879–1922)*, ed. Lady Raleigh, p. 164.

'As to faults, Henrietta, you and Arabel, may laugh as you please at my blindness. Of course he is quite capable of doing and thinking wrongly, and he will tell me things of himself, of which I saw at once "that was wrong, very wrong". . . . But for defects of character, for deficiencies in the heart and moral being—for such faults as make themselves habitually felt in persons—and in most persons—I will say, and it is honestly speaking, I never perceived one sign of such things in him, and do not perceive them now more than the first day. Faults towards me he never committed, and I believe will never commit; and, by faults towards me, I simply mean an ungentle or impatient word, a cold look, an exception to the usual tone of tenderness. He says (said it just when I was observing the exact contrary), that it has been the greatest *advantage* to us to be shut up in this seclusion without any distractions—that we have *learnt one another* better by it, than we should have done if we had taken the usual course of married people who live so for three weeks or a month, and then proceed to other amusements. I had been calling it "rather a trial"—he said that it could only be so in cases of unreal and fanciful attachments. . . .'

On March 31st, 1847, she speaks of a temporary relapse. 'He was so dreadfully affected by my illness, as to be quite overset, overcome—only never too much so, to spend every moment he was allowed to spend, by my bedside—rubbing me, talking to me, reading to me —and all with such tenderness, such goodness. Wilson says "I never saw a *man* like Mr. Browning in my life"; and I hear that the Doctor made a remark to the same effect. . . .'

In April from Florence: 'Well—but I was talking of

Mrs. Jameson. . . . I am sure she looked on in utter astonishment, while Robert seized on me to place me on the sofa. She told me before she went away that every hour of her intercourse with him, from first to last, had raised him higher in her estimation and her affection. Dear Mrs. Jameson! . . .'

A letter written on November 23rd and 24th, 1847, is nearly all about Robert and Father Prout and Mrs. Boyle and 'Aunt Nina' (Robert's name for Mrs. Jameson). Elizabeth says that Robert is 'perfect' to her, that she is at liberty to talk out aloud all the *bêtises* that come into her head, that she tells her dreams even and has visions of letters in the candle according to Wilson's instructions. This freedom to talk nonsense is a very pleasing sign, and, perhaps, her freedom to tell him her dreams had an important effect upon his poems.

'If I wanted to offend him I should do something in the way of respect and obedience.

'Now I will tell you. The other day he said to me (in relation to Flush or some equally weighty subject I think it was):—

'"I do wish, Ba, you wouldn't do so and so." To which I answered:

'"Well, I won't do it any more," was ever a more unexceptionable answer? Yes, and it was meekly delivered too. But *he* didn't like it at all, nevertheless, and cried out quite quickly:

'"Don't say such words to me, Ba."

'"What ought I to say, then?"

'"Say that you will do as you please as long as you please to do it."

'So you see what a difficult position mine is. You see! My vow of obedience is only appealed to on great occasions such as finishing a mutton-chop, or cutting one more slice of bread and butter—and it's almost a pity that so much good vowing should have gone for almost nothing.'

About the idea of debt (Florence, January 4th, 5th, 6th, 1848): 'There's dearest Mr. Kenyon who renews his offer that we should draw on him whenever we want money. We feel it, of course, as much as if it were required, which, I thank God, it is not!—for I should have hard work to console Robert if we were even shoe-deep in pecuniary difficulty from any cause. He exaggerates the importance of being clear on all sides. We are not at all alike in that respect. Not that he cares for money the least more than I do—but the idea of "debt" is a sort of "Croque-mitaine" to him—and says "fee fa fum" in the dark. . . . There never was any one who looked round a corner with a more imaginative obliquity, when the idea of money-difficulty is suggested in any form, than Robert does. It is we who remind our creditors of their claims on us instead of its being the other way. We send down to our hostess on the very morning, that she may come to have the next two months rent prepared. The same with everything.'

In March: 'If I had no one to talk to I should talk to myself, certainly: but Robert is always glad to hear me. Otherwise I should love *him* less.'

In the same letter she gives an account of Robert's indignation at a foolish communication which caused her a transitory terror—she thought the great thick letter for which Robert paid half-a-crown, was about 'Papa'—it had a black edge an inch deep and Papa's griffin seal. Robert snatched it from her hand, read some way in it and dashed it into the fire, calling the writer an 'inconsiderate fool' as if the man ought to have known that the seal was Papa's and a black-edged letter so sealed would cause Ba to grow as white as a sheet!

And at the end: 'He says to me sometimes—"Now, Ba, wouldn't it have been *wrong* if we two had not married?" And really we seem in some mysterious way to get closer and closer every new four and twenty hours.'

She interrupts a letter about Ledru Rollin, the republican, to speak of something she calls 'aristocratic' in Robert. 'Sometimes, in joke, I call him an aristocrat—I cry out *"à bas les aristocrats"*—because he really cares a good deal about external things—perhaps it is an artist's sense of grace that he has, only that I choose to make fun of it. For instance about houses, and furniture, and horses and carriages, he is far more particular than I ever was or can be. Then I laugh—and then he says it is for my sake. So it may be, and is, ungrateful that I am—only that he certainly looks to the things minutely,—he has a feeling about them, not altogether Spartan.'

Piedmontese and Austrian armies were on their way to Florence just before 'Pen' (Robert Wiedemann Barrett) Browning, their only child, was born. His birthday was March 9th, 1849. 'Political' Italy engrossed her even through that time. The Austrians did not arrive in Florence until May 3rd. She was sick at heart, and so was Robert, at the prospect of the country. But, of course, Pen occupies a large place in her subsequent letters. 'Robert reproaches me with talking to him in Italian—he hates the idea of his not speaking English with his earliest breath. Robert being highly patriotic, you are to understand, and especially when the farthest from England.'

In February 1850 they were discussing moving from Florence. She thinks they might carry their furniture up the Rhone. 'Oh, he would have done that or anything for me—he is so perfectly, so beyond example and expression good and kind to me, that if I were to let him see any strong wish of mine upon any subject, he would fulfil it out of a sort of necessity of the heart: so that on this very account, I like rather to watch his inclinations than to express mine.'

But they were still in Florence in November. 'We have fires now, though the weather is lovely for November, and I take long walks every day. We have fires now, and as soon as the lamp comes, Robert sits in his arm chair, and I curdle myself up on the sofa, or perhaps on a cushion on the hearth and we say to one another:

'"Oh, how delightful this is! I do hope nobody will come to-night"—and so, we read, and talk, and Robert can't keep from letting out the end of Copperfield, and I scold him and won't hear a word more. Then the door opens, and enter Baby holding by Wilson's finger.'

On July 21st, 1851, she wrote from Paris that the Tennysons had called on them. 'He had Robert's poems with him, and had been reading them aloud the previous evening. We were all friends at once; and really he was more than a friend, for he pressed on us the use of his house and two servants at Twickenham as long as we stayed in England, and even wrote a note (insisting that we should take it) to his servants, to the effect that they should give up possession to us forthwith. We took the note—it is an autograph at once of genius and kindness.'

They were in Paris again in November, and Robert is reported to be particularly critical about her bonnets!

She writes from Florence on March 4th, 1853 to announce that Helen Faucit, the actress (with whom, and her husband Sir Theodore Martin, Browning stayed in a later year at Llantysilio),[1] was going to play in *Colombe's Birthday* at the Haymarket Theatre. 'If there is a success it will be a good thing for us in a pecuniary point of view, and if not, there will be no harm done.'

And in the same letter: 'Here am I, in the seventh year of marriage, happier than on the seventh day!'

There is an especially charming letter of May 14th, chiefly about Pen, or Penini, as she calls him.

'To-morrow Robert and I have a scheme in our heads, of going to Pistoia and Prato by the railroad, and of dining at a caffé somewhere "like two lovers", Robert says. In order to which we leave our respectability and Penini behind us. He won't like being left, I can tell you. He thinks he has a right to be with us wherever we go, and as he enjoys everything just as much as we do, I really am inclined to think so.'

Writing on February 12th, 1855, when she is convalescent after a month's illness she makes mention of Robert's anxiety and his wonderful care for her and also (for the first time apparently) speaks of rapping spirits and whispering voices manifested to a Mr. Kirkup—an artist and archaeologist—and says that although Robert insists that the clairvoyant is a 'humbug' she suspends her opinion. In July when they were in London she saw David Dunglass Hume, who stood for

[1] There is a tablet in Llantysilio Parish Church, stating that Robert Browning worshipped there.

'Mr. Sludge the Medium' of Browning's poem. Readers of that poem will not be surprised that Elizabeth writes to Henrietta on the condition, 'that when you write to me you don't say a word on the subject—because it's a *tabooed* subject in this house—Robert and I taking completely different views, and he being a good deal irritated by any discussion of it. . . .'

There follows an account of the exhibition, which caused Robert to cry out against Hume's *humbugging*. 'For my own part I am confirmed in all my opinions. To me it was wonderful and conclusive; and I believe that the medium present was no more *responsible* for the things said and done, than I myself was.'

There is more about spirit manifestations, this time to a Mr. Jarves, in a letter of August 30th. Even Robert admits that Jarves is perfectly *veracious*. 'By the way—the subject is still *in suspense* in this house. Some of these days perhaps Robert will be a medium himself, and then he will believe. Till then I shall never stir the question more. . . .'

Still in London on October 3rd, she announces the publication of *Men and Women*, described by M. Milsand as 'superhuman' poems, and also speaks of a surprise visit of the Laureate. 'He read us the whole of *Maud*, and exquisitely—the voice hangs in my ear still. We dined and smoked together and were so happy and affectionate as possible; and I didn't get to bed on the second day till three o'clock in the morning. So that altogether I nearly died of the joy of it. But I seriously love Tennyson.'

'And yet Arabel says she likes Robert better. One of the reasons being that Robert doesn't smoke pipes—no, nor cigars, let me add.

'Sometimes I have exhorted him to smoke, by the bye. It would do him good occasionally.'

It is worth while noting that despite the serious difference of opinion about mediums and spirit manifestations Robert wrote *One Word More* at the end of *Men and Women*, and this dedicatory poem is the most beautiful of all his tributes to her, while she was alive.

In a letter from Paris on December 6th, 1855, she addresses herself to the defence of Lazarus, as she briefly calls Browning's *Epistle of Kharshish*. 'The way in which Lazarus is described as living his life after his acquaintance with the life beyond death, strikes me as entirely sublime, I confess.'

There is an amusing reference to her belief in spiritualism in a letter (also from Paris) of April 11th, 1856:

'Robert and I were so excessively amused the other day by an American visitor who brought us a letter from Florence—a raw intensely American American, who came into the room without gloves and sate down and did the conversation in the manner of the "highest black circles". Of course we threw him on the spirit-subject, and he informed us how all Florence had been "infatuated" &c. but—and, there, he addressed himself to me in a prepossessing manner—"but I observe that believers in these things are usually of *one-horse-power*—" to the extreme amusement of Robert who sate by listening. He thought he was saying something particularly agreeable to me of course. And as he is rather of one-ass power himself, I didn't take the unintended affront much to heart.'

Robert 'talked himself into quite a hatred of Hume', but Elizabeth still persisted in believing him to be a wonderful medium.

Mr. Kenyon died at the end of 1856, and rendered a real service to literature by making these two poets independent—he left them both substantial legacies. His death afflicted Elizabeth, but a greater blow was the death of Mr. Barrett in the following year. She said in a letter which Robert must have seen, as he enclosed it with a note to Henrietta, that it had been a great help to her that of late years she had 'apprehended more of the ways of life in that world'.

Later on, February, 1858, Robert became exceedingly unwell. 'He was persuaded to try homoeopathy. He submitted, with a smile of scorn, to give it a fair trial. By degrees the scorn disappeared—there seemed to be "really something in it"—undeniably he "felt better". Now he has a regular healthy appetite. If he begins by being an homoeopathist he will end by being a spiritualist, I prophesy to him. So positive he used to be on this subject.'

Elizabeth had a bad illness in 1859, brought on by the failure of her hopes for Italy, and Robert nursed her with devoted care. Henrietta died in 1860, and this was the worst blow of all.

Of the last hours of Elizabeth herself, Robert wrote to Charles Macready from Florence on July 18th, 1861: 'Do not imagine that I am prostrated by this calamity. I have much or everything to do as directly in my wife's interest as if she were enjoining it on me when we talked over our plans the last evening of all . . . . I dare believe from much I cannot write that God did really take her to Himself without even the momentary awe of a warning—while, by some inexplicable way, I was permitted to lose nothing through her ignorance that she was about to leave me.'

On July 20th he wrote to Miss Haworth: 'Through the night she slept heavily, and brokenly, that was the bad sign. But then she would sit up, take her medicine, say unrepeatable things to me, and sleep again. At four o'clock there were symptoms that alarmed me; I called the maid and sent for the doctor. She smiled as I proposed to bathe her feet—"well, you are making an exaggerated case of it". Then came what my heart will keep till I see her and longer—the most perfect expression of her love for me within my whole knowledge of her—always smilingly, happily and with a face like a girl's—and in a few minutes, she died in my arms, her head on my cheek.'

III

I have already quoted from the volume of letters written by Robert Browning to Miss Isa Blagden. This volume was arranged for publication by Mr. A. Joseph Armstrong and printed at the Baylor University Press, Waco, Texas, in 1923. Isa Blagden was born in 1816, and Robert's letters extend from 1855 to 1873, the year of Isa Blagden's death. He wrote concerning them: 'Remember I read your letters twice and then burn them: mine, I trust, earnestly conjure, you will never show: but you will not.'

Isa Blagden published a volume of poems and five novels, and there are references to her literary work in Robert's letters: '... if you would try and work earnestly with what faculties you have the reward would come as promptly to you as to any one; but you do not, and you fancy *that some people get their reward without such labour*, which I do not know an instance of.' But the letters before Elizabeth's death are usually about

Elizabeth. Isa Blagden spent the last afternoon of Elizabeth's life with her. After Elizabeth's death Robert made an arrangement with Isa Blagden—though probably not before the summer of 1862—that she should write to him on the 12th of each month, and that he should answer on the 19th. Both dates would recall E. B. B., as on the 12th (of September, 1846) Robert and she were married, and on the 19th (September, 1846) they left England together.

I propose to quote from these letters and also from three others written to Miss Blagden, not included in the Baylor volume, but issued from the collection of Mr. T. J. Wise, in order to make it clear that there was only one woman in Robert Browning's life even after her death. He was the constant lover.

Robert wrote at intervals of a few days after the final announcement of Henrietta's death (December 3rd, 1860), speaking of Ba's grief and her way of hiding herself, and her anxiety to be good and reasonable. Early in 1861 he thinks that Ba will soon get better. In June, after a relapse, he pronounces her 'infinitely better', but tells Miss Blagden not to come as she must not speak.

His first letter after Ba's death is written from near Dinard on August 22nd, 1861: 'I will not however try to write about myself: you know how I could talk, but there seems a cold wind to blow, and all my soul shuts up when the business is to write. I am better of course than just when we arrived in Paris, or than when we left. I go round in the same order of ideas, and arrive always at the same conclusion, but I don't feel the miserable contrast between then and now, as when first coming on the old Paris nights, peculiarities, nothings that only grow to be somethings from their first association. . . .'

And from the same place, on August 31st: 'I am better in many respects: I should not count it "better" to be with one regret the less, nor shall I ever be.'

His father and sister, Sarianna, were staying with him. On September 9th he speaks of Pen's happiness and cheerfulness. 'He amuses himself with my father, whose kindness and simplicity make him a wonderful child's friend certainly: they sketch together, go home and paint etc. and Pen's loud merry laugh is never out of my ears. . . .' On September 17th: 'Pen has bathed and ridden daily, he swims quite well for so little a fellow, and seems perfectly healthy and strong. I seem hardly to remember the velvet tunic and short trousers, the curls and the hat and the feather of three months ago. Three months!' (E. B. B. died on June 29th.)

On September 19th, 1862, he writes from Ste Marie, Pornic: 'With respect to Florence, I cannot tell how I feel about it, so do I change in my feelings in the course of a quarter of an hour sometimes: particular incidents in the Florence way of life recur as if I could not bear a repetition of them,—to find myself walking among the hills, or turnings by the villas, certain doorways, old walls, points of sight, on a solitary bright summer Sunday afternoon—there, I think that would fairly choke me at once: on the other hand, beginning from another point of association I have such yearnings to be there! Just now, at the approach of Autumn, I feel exactly like a swallow in a cage, as if I *must* go there, have no business anywhere else, with the year drawing in. How thankful I am that all these foolish fancies never displace for a moment the solid fact that I can't go but have plain duty to do in London,—if there could be a doubt about that, I should drift about like a feather: at times (to give you a notion of what I might do if free to be foolish) I seem as if I should like, by a fascination, to try the worst at once, go straight to the old rooms at Casa Guidi, and there live and die! But I shall shake all this off and say to myself (sometimes aloud), "Don't be afraid, my good fellow, you'll die too, all in good time:" so I go on.'

On November 19th of the same year, from 19 Warwick Crescent, he writes about the tablet to E. B. B., to be set up in Florence. 'Even now, I can't tell you the thrill of pain and pleasure I feel about it: the presence of this is now habitual to me, I can have no doubt that it is my greatest comfort to be always remembering her; the old books and furniture, her chair which is by mine, all that is a comfort to me, but in this case, it was as if, besides my feeling on my own account the deepest gratification at this act, determined and carried into effect, I also sympathized with *her* pride and pleasure. And how must I feel to *you*, my own dearest of friends, whose work it has been? I know you "Thank God," as you say, from your very heart, and so do I: all I can say is, I shall love the dust of Florence, the letters which make up its name, every man, woman and child it holds. There—I've done. . . .'

The next month: '. . . but I can't help going on and talking about Florence, and the friends or acquaintances *there*, the other matters absolutely go out of my head and I should have to dig into it uncomfortably deep to get at what was said and done only last week.'

He refers to the writing arrangement on April 19th, 1863: 'You don't quite believe me, I see, that writing to you is next best thing to hearing from you, or you would not wonder that I remember it was *the day on the day*.'

He also speaks rather enigmatically in the same letter of his 'alleviations'. 'As for Pen, I love him dearly, but if I hated him, it would be pretty much the same thing. There are most unspeakable alleviations in my case, so plain a course to pursue, the effects of it so immediately consoling, and the power to carry it out, almost as complete as I could desire: so it is little wonder and no subject of praise that I don't turn out of the one strip of light into the darkness on either side.'

Early in the next year he writes again about the Florence tablet, and praises Leighton's whole conduct in connexion with the matter as entirely noble and generous. 'I have just learned from Brini of the payment of a second instalment which denotes that the work is two-thirds finished: I have determined at last that the central medallion shall be appropriated, not to a portrait, but to an ideal head of "Poetry": a portrait proves to be impossible, one, that is, which we would accept: there is nothing to be done but to submit to a necessity, for any playing with the truth *there* would be hateful to me.'

The next entirely relevant letter is on December 19th, 1864. I have quoted from it already, but for the reader's convenience I will repeat some passages here: 'Yes, dearest Isa, it is three Christmasses ago, *fully* now: I sometimes see a light at the end of this dark tunnel of life, which was one blackness at the beginning. It won't last for ever. In many ways I can see with my human eyes why this has been right and good for me, as I never doubted it was for Her, and if we do but re-join any day, the break will be better than forgotten, remembered for its uses. The difference between me and the stupid people who have "communications" is probably nothing more than that I don't confound the results of the natural working of what is in my mind, with vulgar external experiences. . . . Well, for myself, I am certainly not unhappy, any more than I ever was: I am, if the phrase were now to be coined first, *"resigned"*, but I look on everything in this world with altered eyes, and can no more take interest in anything I see there but the proof of certain great principles, strewn in the booths at a fair: I could no more take root in life again, than learn some new dancing step. On the other hand, I feel such comfort and delight in doing the best I can with my own object in life, poetry, which, I think, I never *could* have seen the good of before, that it shows I have taken the root I *did* take, *well*. I hope to do much more yet: and that the flower of it will be put into Her hand somehow. I really have great opportunities and advantages, on the whole, almost unparalleled ones, I think, no other disturbances and cares than those I am most grateful for being allowed to have. . . .'

In a letter from Ste Marie he speaks (on Sept. 19th, 1865) of its being 'a delicious day, much as it was when I left England all those years ago, eighteen in number. Well, dearest Isa, one travels and travels and gets nearer to heaven, I hope.'

He breaks the sequence of 12th and 19th letters to tell her on June 20th, 1866, about his father's death. He pays a lovely tribute to his father's character and then says: '*He was worthy* of being Ba's father—out of the whole world, only he, so far as my experience goes. She loved him—and *he* said, very recently, while gazing at her portrait, that only that picture had put it into his head that there might be such a thing as the worship of saints and images. . . .'

A letter of September 19th, 1867, concerns a scandalous story of a man and his second wife, and mentions a rumour about himself: 'No goose tells you that I *am* married—only that I shall be—and six years hence the same goose can cackle "So it *was* to be—only it was broken off". I never saw Miss Ingelow but once, at least four years ago, at a musical morning party, when I said half a dozen words to her: only heard of her, as I told you, by her writing a note to accompany her new book, a day or two before I left London.'

Then follows a most violent reprobation of the idea of a second marriage for himself: 'It is funny people think I am likely to do nothing naughty in the world, neither rob nor kill, seduce nor ravish, only honestly *marry*—which I should consider the two last—and perhaps the two first—naughtinesses united, together with the grace of perjury. Enough of it all.'

In the same letter he speaks of Miss Blagden's 'right sense' of the Bagni . . . and also of the Lima, where he used to bathe.

'I was there three times, α, β, γ, δ, ϵ, ζ, ι. There! Those letters indicate seven distinct issues to which I came with Ba, in our profoundly different estimates of things and persons. I go over them one by one and must deliberately inevitably say, on each of these points I was, am proved to be, right, and she wrong. And I am glad I maintained the truth on each of these points, did not say "what matters whether they be true or no, let us only care to love each other". If I could ever have such things out of my thoughts it would not be to-day—the day, twenty years ago, that we left England together. If I ever seem too authoritative or disputative to you, dearest Isa, you must remember this, and that only to those I love very much do I feel at all inclined to lay down what I think to be the law, and speak the truth. But no good comes of anything else, in the long run, while as for seeing the truth, it seems to me such angelic natures don't, and such devilish ones do, it is no sign of the highest nature. On the contrary, I do believe the very highness blinds, and the lowness helps to see.'

On February 19th, 1868, he writes: 'How I should like, what is not unrealizable as most dreams, to go for a little and see Florence, quite unknown by anybody, only seeing the few friends. . . .'

And, exactly a year later, he makes reference to another rumour of a second marriage: 'There is a curious lie flying about *here*, concerning poor me; I am going to marry Miss A., daughter of Ly. B., mother also of Ly. C. &c. &c. I heard of it three times last week. I never even heard there was such a person as any one of the three, never heard their names even. You will soon have it retailed you as indubitable fact. . . .'

On July 19th, 1870, he refers to Ba's hopes for Italy: 'All I trust is that Italy will get Rome easily and naturally. Oh, oh Ba—put not your trust in princes. . . .' (Just as if she were alive!)

On August 19th, 1870, writing from Saint-Aubin-sur-Mer he speaks of the Villa Alberti at Siena, 'one of the places I love best to remember. . . . I have a pen and ink drawing of it, dated and signed the last day Ba was ever there. "My fig tree!" She used to sit under it, reading and writing. Nine years—or ten years, rather, since then!'

Robert Browning lived on until December 12th, 1889. But among his last poems were echoes of the old days with Ba and the same poignant hope for the renewal of them.

> Others may need new life in Heaven—
> Man, Nature, Art—made new, assume!
> Man with new mind old sense to leaven,
> Nature—new light to clear old gloom,
> Art that breaks bounds, gets soaring-room.
>
> I shall pray: 'Fugitive as precious—
> Minutes which passed,—return, remain!
> Let earth's old life once more enmesh us,
> You with old pleasure, me—old pain,
> So we but meet nor part again!'[1]

---

[1] This may be an echo of the anxieties from which he was never entirely free throughout the whole of his courtship and married life. Even a fleeting indisposition of hers threw him into a fever of apprehension.

IX
BROWNING'S REPUTATION AS A MYSTIC

THE word 'mystic' is the Greek μύστης, applied to an initiate in the religious mysteries who was to keep silence (μυεῖν) about what he knew. A mystic is defined in the English Dictionary as 'one who believes in spiritual apprehension of truths beyond the understanding'.

The idea of 'keeping silence' still attaches to the mystical state, in so far as the appeal of the mystic is always to something individual and, in a sense, hidden. He cannot appeal to universal experience. His evidence for conviction or conclusion has no evidential value. It is outside logic.

What the dictionary calls his 'spiritual apprehension' may be regarded by others as mere emotionalism. The contempt with which mystics are often treated is due to the fact that they seem to rely on feeling. Their emotionalism may easily become morbid. Juliana of Norwich, who was born in 1342 and may have lived to be 100 years old, is said to be differentiated from other mystics by the sweetness and sanity of her feelings. A window has been placed in Liverpool Cathedral to commemorate her for the alleged reason that she is not disfigured by morbid emotionalism—'as so many mystics are'.

To escape from this taint or complaint of emotionalism various writers have sought to define mysticism without any reference to μύστης. Florence Nightingale, after proclaiming the necessity of ever-present spiritual ideals, if we are to work on men and women, and her belief that the service of men is the service of God, says that the 'mystical state is the essence of common sense'. William Blake seems to identify mysticism with Imagination. He nowhere says that the mystical state is the essence of Imagination, but that is not far short of his meaning. Imagination is his one reality, the faculty that apprehends both nature and spirit and unites them. It seems to include all that we mean by sympathy, insight, idealism, and vision. He gives to Imagination the name of Saviour or Humanity free from Adam's narrowness and Satan's falseness. Francis Thompson's nearest exponent defined mysticism as 'morality raised to the nth power'. Francis Thompson would seem to have affinities with Florence Nightingale. He once wrote: 'There is something wanting in genius when it does not show a clear and strong vein of common sense. . . . Dante indeed is a perfect rebuke to those who suppose that mystical genius at any rate must be dissociated from common sense. Every such poet should be able to give a clear and logical prose résumé of his teaching, as terse as a page of scholastic philosophy.' Probably 'morality' has reference to law rather than to character. And law is the true embodiment, not of everything that's excellent, but of what has come to be approved by the common sense of humanity.

Akin to the dictionary conception are the following: 'Mysticism is an endeavour to find God at first hand, experimentally in the soul herself independently of all historical and philosophical presuppositions.'

'A saint is necessarily a mystic, but a mystic is not necessarily a saint. A mystic . . . is one who lays stress upon being rather than doing, while a saint holds the balance between the two; he expresses being by

BROWNING'S REPUTATION AS A MYSTIC

doing and regards the one as incomplete without the other.'

To correlate 'common sense' or 'morality' to mysticism is to confuse the issue. A mystic may have common sense or he may be moral to the nth degree, but his mysticism does not consist in his common sense or his morality. If we extend the idea of Imagination far beyond even Samuel Taylor Coleridge's 'esemplastic power' but in the same direction, we may include the mystical state in it. But that does not make for simplicity of description, still less for definition. A great English religious mystic, Brooke Foss Westcott, held that there was no outline in Nature, and deprecated definition. Certainly it seems beyond the ingenuity of man to frame a satisfactory definition of mysticism. If one says that it is an endeavour to find God at first hand, the true mystic will instantly reply that God is always endeavouring to find him. If one says that a mystic spiritually apprehends truths beyond the understanding, the mystic answers that instead of apprehending he seems to be apprehended. The apprehension is an outside arrest. The scientist by his inductive process may arrive at ultimates: he may come upon 'that which is'. 'That which is' comes upon the mystic.

No mystic will ever understand the dictum that he is interested in being rather than in doing. The vision (if we use 'vision' in the unrestricted sense) is the abiding wealth of the mind in contemplation:

> But (when so sad thou canst not sadder)
> Cry;—and upon thy so sore loss
> Shall shine the traffic of Jacob's ladder
> Pitched between Heaven and Charing Cross.

> Yea, in the night, my Soul, my daughter,
> Cry,—plucking Heaven by the hems;
> And lo, Christ walking on the water
> Not of Gennesareth, but Thames!

But, more, the vision is an impelling force to action. Crashaw has expressed this simply:

> She never undertook to know
> What death and love should have to doe;
> Nor has she e'er yet understood
> Why to show love, she should shed blood.
> Yet though she cannot tell you why,
> She can love and she can die.

So in W. B. Yeats's *Countess Cathleen* the woman is moved by love of those who have sold themselves to the devil to sell her own soul in ransom for theirs.

It is comparatively easy to gather out the main convictions of the great mystics. A writer in the *Dublin Review* says that 'to the Poet life is full of visions, to the Mystic it is one vision'. To the mystic life is a 'multitudinous single thing'. All things are brought into one. So Francis Thompson:

> When to the new eyes of thee
> All things by immortal power,
> Near or far,
> Hiddenly
> To each other linkèd are,
> That thou canst not stir a flower
> Without troubling of a star.[1]

And again:

> This is the enchantment, this the exultation,
> The all-compensating wonder,
> Giving to common things wild kindred
> With the gold-tesserate floors of Jove;

[1] *The Mistress of Vision.*

> Linking such heights and such humilities
> Hand in hand in ordinal dances,
> That I do think my tread,
> Stirring the blossoms in the meadow-grass,
> Flickers the unwithering stars.[1]

The characteristic of life is Light or Love. For the mystic this light is not a transient gleam, an ecstatic moment, the memory of which is to be cherished or trusted, but an abiding experience. The Light is the thing, the unchangeable reality in the midst of shows and shadows.

The Light is not essentially inward or self-created; it is essentially outward, Divine, and pervasive. Of course there must be an eye for the light; there must be correspondence. Faith is correspondence. Nor is faith ever 'stricken through with doubt'.[2] Doubt is a condition of death:

> If the Sun and Moon should doubt
> They'd immediately go out.[3]

The pervasive Light seems also to the mystic the pursuing Love. Plotinus and the Middle English author of *Quia amore langueo* and Crashaw have all expressed the idea of the Love Chase. Francis Thompson popularized it in *The Hound of Heaven*. Browning spoke of it in more apprehensible terms:

> For life, with all it yields of joy and woe,
> And hope and fear . . .
> Is just our chance o' the prize of learning love.'

The emphasis is on the word 'learning'. The rest of the poem (*A Death in the Desert*) dwells upon God as the Teacher, the Inspirer. We learn Love because we are apt pupils of the indefatigable Master.

[1] *An Anthem of Earth.*   [2] *In Memoriam.*
[3] William Blake: *Auguries of Innocence.*

I do not know if these convictions have been reached by non-mystics. They may have been. But though these convictions may constitute the philosophy of mysticism they do not define mysticism.

Mysticism refers to the way convictions come rather than to the convictions themselves. Perhaps the safest description (or definition even) of mysticism is Dean Inge's 'personal spiritual experience'. This kind of experience may always be challenged. It proves nothing. It has no evidential value.[1] I will refer for a case in point to an experience of my own. In the summer of 1916 I was in a place called Y wood, and one evening I saw a shell burst on a shallow dug-out, about a hundred yards away from me. I ran to the dug-out. The mess-servants of a battery had been having tea in it, and after tea they had been playing cards. When I looked at the ruin, all I could recognize of humanity was one grey face. And I thought: 'Now I *know* that there is a Resurrection of the dead.' The sudden conviction was forced upon me. It seemed, at the time, to have nothing to do with the logical faculty. It was apparently against reason. For what could be less like life than that ruin? But the conviction was irrefragable.

May I be allowed another example? In the summer of 1926 I was alone in a small room in London. I was troubled in mind and distressingly anxious. I heard a voice. At first it seemed like a child's voice—it was so spontaneous and free, there was a kind of radiance in it. Then it seemed like a woman's voice—it was tender, sympathetic, understanding. Then I knew it for a man's voice—it was strong and bracing, a father calling to his

---

[1] But both St. John and St. Paul proclaim their personal spiritual experiences as evidence.

son across a trench. The words were simple, intimate: 'Can't you trust me?' And I thought, 'I *can*.'

Neither of these personal spiritual experiences proves anything.

Once I was watching a sick woman. She was dying of cancer. I had known her for more than thirty years. She was unconscious. Her wasted face caused me anguish. I looked away to a portrait of her taken thirty years before. I contrasted the loveliness and vitality of that face with the one on the pillow. Then I turned back to the bed. And the face I saw there was the woman's face as God meant it to be, as she essentially was, fresh and eager and yet serene, of an inexpressible youthfulness and beauty.

Could I say that my first experience taught me the survival of those who die? Or that my second experience was evidence of a personal spirit outside men upon whom men may rely? Or that my third experience indicated in a general way something about the glory of bodily life, which must somehow and somewhere be realized? I think not. And for reinforcement of the normal judgement I may confess that these or similar experiences went along with a disqualification for my accustomed activities. Yet I am free to say that they were worth while. They were my own experiences and they convinced me.

I ask pardon for these personal references. My excuse is that personal spiritual experience can best be understood or commented on from a man's own experiences, and that his own experiences help him to understand the conclusions of other men. I give as an example Browning's *Epistle of Karshish*. In that poem he discloses to us that Lazarus, after he was raised again to life, was disqualified for ordinary commonplace life by his revelation of the world to come. I suggest that Browning or possibly Mrs. Browning (I will explain what I mean by this 'possibly' in a few moments) had had some personal spiritual experience, some vision or revelation, that he or she felt as a hindrance to 'carrying on' normally, or as tending to an unbalanced view of ordinary life.

The common conception of a poet is of a mystic. His eye rolls in a fine frenzy and he writes down what comes into his mind. We correct this conception by the cold wisdom of the critic or the professor. We learn that the poet is really a workman who has to acquire the technique of his craft and to exercise his craft with care. Yet one of the most learned and sympathetic of the professors, W. P. Ker, acknowledges that 'the Art of Poetry is much more free than the other arts, in the sense that the right men do not need such steady training'.[1]

The acknowledged mystics, William Blake and William Wordsworth, speak of spontaneity in writing. I have quoted Blake's account of the writing of *Milton*, and also Wordsworth's definition of poetry as the spontaneous overflow of powerful feelings. This seems to be less characteristic of Wordsworth than his other remark about poetry as 'emotion recollected in tranquillity'. Mr. I. A. Williams in his little book called *Poetry To-day* bases his discussion of poetry on Wordsworth's second dictum. But Wordsworth's actual words are: 'I have said that poetry is the spontaneous overflow of powerful feelings: *it takes its origin*[2] from emotion recollected in tranquillity: the emotion is contemplated till, by a species of reaction the tranquillity gradually disappears,

---
[1] *The Art of Poetry*: A Lecture by W. P. Ker (June 6, 1920).
[2] The italics are mine.

and an emotion, kindred to that which was before the subject of contemplation is gradually produced, and does itself actually exist in the mind.'[1]

Another passage is pertinent to this matter of spontaneity. 'Our feelings will be connected with important subjects, till at length, if we be originally possessed of much sensibility, such habits of mind will be produced, that by obeying blindly and mechanically the impulses of those habits, we shall describe objects and utter sentiments of such a nature, and in such connexion with each other, that the understanding of the Reader must necessarily be in some degree enlightened, and his affections strengthened and purified.'

In my first chapter I gave examples of what I ventured to believe was spontaneous writing in Browning.

But Browning is not by any means an acknowledged mystic. His wife, indeed, spoke of him as the 'king of the mystics'. 'It is not a phrase that posterity would use,' says Osbert Burdett,[2] 'but it is worth notice by any curious of the precise causes of the attraction that each found in the writings of the other.' The same discerning critic says: 'The tone in Browning is that of the city and the salon, where the life of art and intelligence, restless and curious, replaces the dreamy content of the fields. . . . As man and artist he was masculine to the core. There was no eccentricity or want of balance in his genius. His life and work prove that the supposed alliance of great wits to madness is not essential. In everything but his magnificent endowment he was an ordinary being, and he used his imagination so plentifully that his works form a literature in themselves.'

[1] *Wordsworth's Prefaces and Essays on Poetry*, ed. A. J. George.
[2] *The Brownings*, by Osbert Burdett (1928), pp. 116, 330, 331.

Dr. Arthur Compton-Rickett[1] speaks to the same effect. In Browning religion is not treated synthetically but analytically. There is 'little mysticism'. Browning is concerned to make religion reasonable.

On the other hand, Dr. Caroline F. E. Spurgeon[2] classes Browning with Shelley, Rossetti, Coventry Patmore, and Keats as one of the 'Love and Beauty Mystics'. 'Browning is a seer, and pre-eminently a mystic; and it is especially interesting, as in the case of Plato and St. Paul, to encounter this latter quality as a dominating characteristic of the mind of so keen and logical a dialectician.' She illustrates his belief in 'unity under diversity at the centre of existence' by quotations from *Prince Hohenstiel-Schwangau* and *Old Pictures in Florence*, and his belief that 'love is the meaning of life' from *Paracelsus* and *Cristina* and *A Death in the Desert*. She compares him with the German mystic, Meister Eckhart, and quotes from Eckhart to show that in several directions Browning's thought is peculiarly mystical. 'He is at one with Eckhart, and with all mystics, in his appeal from the intellect to that which is beyond intellect; in his assertion of the supremacy of feeling, intuition, over knowledge. Browning never wearies of dwelling on the relativity of physical knowledge and its inadequacy to satisfy man.'

If we consider mysticism as 'personal spiritual experience' we are at once emancipated from the prevailing notion that the mystic has a philosophy of life. The mystic need not be a philosopher at all; he need not be educated. Personal spiritual experiences may occur to any man, woman, or child, of any race, age,

---

[1] *Robert Browning: Humanist* (1924).
[2] *Mysticism in English Literature* (1913), pp. 38, 42.

BROWNING'S REPUTATION AS A MYSTIC

or condition. Roughly speaking, the experiences are of two kinds: visionary experiences; and intuitions connected with ordinary appearances and events.[1] Both these kinds of experiences are linked with God, or, at any rate, with some power outside ourselves which influences and guides us. I am ruling out the visions of depraved persons and the morbid impulses that may come to those whose minds are unbalanced. For example, I am not including among visionaries the victim of delirium tremens, or among the intuitional mystics the man to whom the sight of any implement which might be used for an act of violence impels to such an act. The fact that it is necessary to rule them out indicates the slight abnormality of mysticism. The mystic is one who trusts his impulses. He believes in the suggestions that come into his mind. He acts on the assumption that his inspirations are sound. If (to use childish language) God tells him to do anything, he does it. The mystic may be called the Fool of God, because he does not reason about his actions or words—he regards himself as an instrument to be played on by some one else. The pipe does not exist without the piper. Without him, it is a wooden tube pierced at intervals with holes. When Hamlet invited Rosencrantz and Guildenstern to play upon a pipe he emphasized the necessary element for the existence of such instruments.

[1] Intuition is a flash (see *Abt Vogler*, III). But vision has the same quality. The impressions of voices in vision are almost inconceivably swift and yet there is no sense of hurry. This quality is difficult to describe. It inheres in sights as well as in sounds. The non-visionary may understand it by considering the nature of ordinary dreams and the experiences that have proved dreams, apparently long and leisurely, to be of very short duration. Browning believed that 'the truth might be flashed out' even to the vilest of men (see *The Ring and the Book: The Pope*, l. 2127).

They were made by man, and their use—which is their existence—depends upon man. Jesus said the same of all institutions. The lower forms of life also exist in and for the higher. A flower cannot have significance except through the spirit of a man. And when we speak of the significance of a man we are really thinking of his relation with a being higher than himself. At least, the Fool of God regards himself in that light.

The non-mystic, or the ordinary man in his non-mystical moments, is wise—he acts on principle and steadies himself by precedent. He reflects before he acts, and his reflections guide his actions. Nevertheless, wisdom is justified of her children. You can 'get on' without being a Fool of God, and you do not so often have to 'get out'.

A good example of a visionary mystic is Saint Joan of Arc. She had visions of Angels and of the Prince of Angels and she heard voices. She was told what to do and she did what she was told. That was the simple truth of her life, as she herself understood it. Such visionaries are not really uncommon. But the ordinary visionary is not told to walk with kings. He is directed how to walk in peace and equity in his own place.

An unexpected example of the intuitional mystic is George Meredith. He seeks to show in his *Faith on Trial* that he need not divide his soul from his intellect, letting his intellect bear rule alone. He may allow his reason its proper sway, without denying that he may be guided to the ultimate realities by suggestions or intuitions that seem at the moment to be beyond reason. The suggestions or intuitions occur spontaneously. Their spontaneity appears to the mystic to be the guarantee of their soundness. Yet they are not unrelated to the ordinary human experiences of the recipient. Meredith gives an account of a walk in the woodlands of Box Hill on the Monday morning when his wife lay dying. His observation of every detail of Nature comes to him now at his need, because it has long ago become instinctive in him. But the 'young apparition' of a 'wild white cherry in bloom' suddenly compels him not merely to observe but to feel. He is walking by the old Pilgrims' Way that led the march eastward to Canterbury, but their pilgrim banner was not a sign of such 'victorious rays over death' as the white banner of the blossoming wild cherry. That restores his Faith.

The conviction that suddenly came to him was closely related to his previous reasonings. It is a favourite idea of his that the ultimate attainment to God is through the Earth, that 'Earth's Master' is to be reached through his handmaiden Earth. I would refer the reader to the short poem called *Wind on the Lyre* and to the longer and more important poem called *Earth and Man*.

I

Browning may have been a visionary. A vision seems to me to be central in each of the religious poems: *Christmas Eve*, *Easter Day*, *The Epistle of Karshish*, *Cleon*, the second part of *Saul*, and *A Death in the Desert*.

In *Christmas Eve*, when the narrator flings out of the wayside chapel, he decides that this is the real church outside. Here his faith sprang first.

—In youth I looked to these very skies,
And probing their immensities,
I found God there, his visible power;
Yet felt in my heart, amid all its sense
Of that power, an equal evidence
That his love, there too, was the nobler dower.

This Love is the ever-springing fountain. Man cannot multiply or reduce it; he can only enlarge or narrow the channel for the water's play. The love of God meets and satiates the craving of man, just as the sky he is walking under quickens and sublimates the wonder of his spirit. The people of the chapel seek God in their narrow sphere; he will seek God in his way.

Just then the rain and the wind, which had burst out afresh, suddenly ceased, and he had a vision of a double lunar rainbow, and this seemed to be wrapped round the feet of Christ Himself.

> This sight was shown me, there and then,—
> Me, one out of a world of men,
> Singled forth, as the chance might hap
> To another if, in a thunderclap
> Where I heard noise and you saw flame,
> Some one man knew God called his name.

This rainbow that glutted his brain with glory—this, the symbol of hope, the pledge of faithfulness to a purpose of love—is the Garment of the Lord. He sees it dispart and stream down and wind away into the dark, not yet suspecting the disclosure that is to follow. But

> All at once I looked up with terror.
> He was there.
> He himself with his human air,
> On the narrow pathway, just before.
> I saw the back of him, no more—
> He had left the chapel, then, as I.
> I forgot all about the sky.
> No face: only the sight
> Of a sweepy garment, vast and white,
> With a hem that I could recognize.
> I felt terror, no surprise;

>   My mind filled with the cataract,
>   At one bound of the mighty fact.
>   'I remember, He did say,
>   Doubtless that, to this world's end,
>   Where two or three should meet and pray,
>   He would be in the midst, their friend;
>   Certainly He was there with them.'

What makes me sure that this was a genuine experience—though I cannot convey my certainty to others—is the fact that he saw no face.

The vision of *Easter Day* is of the Judgement: It will come suddenly—thus I mused—and we shall wake from our insane dream of life, and find that we have been fools and lost our heaven. No, do not talk of loss. That is merely old wives' talk to frighten one. Take your ancient nurse's advice and pinch yourself awake.

>   And as I said
>   This nonsense, throwing back my head
>   With light complacent laugh, I found
>   Suddenly all the midnight round
>   One fire.

Night was gone and the earth lit up.

>   I felt begin
>   The Judgement-Day: to retrocede
>   Was too late now. 'In very deed,'
>   (I uttered to myself) 'that Day!'
>   The intuition burned away
>   All darkness from my spirit too:
>   There stood I, found and fixed, I knew,
>   Choosing the world.

The very mark of the mystic is that the intuition burns away all darkness from his spirit. The darkness is a veil that he has cloaked his spirit withal, in order to hide himself from the unpleasantness of his own recreancy, and the intuition shrivels up the veil and he is made to see himself as he is, found and fixed.

I am a little more doubtful of the initiating visions in the other poems, but I offer suggestions for what they are worth.

For the *Epistle of Karshish* the vision was of a weary man crossing a ridge of hills—a very strange-looking ridge—and descending into a quiet little town and suddenly meeting another. And at the first glimpse of this other he saw God in his face.

The phrase 'saw God in his face' was given me by a friend of mine who had the following experience: he was just beginning to cross a street in Birmingham when he heard a cry and looking across to the opposite pavement he caught sight of two middle-aged women and he 'saw God in their faces'. The cry was uttered by a little boy whose ball had rolled away and he had run and retrieved it, and the two women were watching him with intensely sympathetic interest, and my friend looked across at them at the moment of the boy's shout of joy.

Here is Karshish's story of the meeting: I apologize for this long and tedious case. After all I do not see anything in what I have written to account for the peculiar awe and interest with which this man has touched me. Perhaps that interest and awe are due to the circumstances of our first meeting. I was at my journey's end and weary.

> I crossed a ridge of short sharp broken hills
> Like an old lion's cheek teeth. Out there came
> A moon made like a face with certain spots
> Multiform, manifold and menacing:

> Then a wind rose behind me. So we met
> In this old sleepy town at unaware,
> The man and I.

The story of the meeting is given at the end of the letter and is followed by the significant postscript:

> The very God! think, Abib; dost thou think?
> So, the All-Great, were the All-loving too—
> So, through the thunder comes a human voice
> Saying, 'O heart I made, a heart beats here!
> Face, my hands fashioned, see it in myself!
> Thou hast no power nor mayst conceive of mine,
> But love I gave thee, with myself to love,
> And thou must love me who have died for thee!'
> The madman saith He said so: it is strange.

But it was the first sight of the 'madman' that led Karshish to make inquiries and to seek an interview with Lazarus, and to learn what he did learn about the man who had been raised up by Christ.

For *Cleon* I suggest that the initiating vision was of a joyous and irresponsible and child-like young man and a fair girl, and that these two seemed to possess a capacity for joy that would go on and on. They would grow not old. Their youthfulness was, in a sense, guaranteed. Change and decay could not touch them. *Cleon* is concerned with the expectation of joy, which life as we know it cannot satisfy. How is it to be satisfied? Has Paulus, a mere Barbarian Jew, access to the secret? Is the youth of the soul the joy of the King's presence? And did Christ guarantee that youth? In the poem the sight of the young man and the fair girl leads Cleon, the Greek philosopher, to imagine

> Some future state revealed to us by Zeus,
> Unlimited in capability
> For joy, as this is in desire for joy,

>   —To seek which, the joy-hunger forces us:
>   That, stung by straitness of our life, made strait
>   On purpose to make prized the life at large—
>   Freed by the throbbing impulse we call death,
>   We burst there as the worm into the fly,
>   Who, while a worm still, wants his wings.

For the second part of *Saul* (published in 1855) the vision may have been of a great strong man laying his hand in tenderness upon the head of a boy, who is so devoted to him that he is ready to give all his love to the limit of life itself to restore the man to happiness. And behind the boy stands the shadowy but ineffably beautiful and familiar figure of the Son of Man. *Saul* is a sublime poem. The first nine sections of it were written before Robert Browning met Elizabeth Barrett, and he afterwards submitted what he had written for her criticism, and adopted the alterations she thought would improve the poem.[1] The second part was written after the poet's marriage. It is the second part that contains David's prophetic vision of the Christ:

> As thy Love is discovered almighty, almighty be proved
> Thy power, that exists with and for it, of being Beloved!
> He who did most, shall bear most; the strongest shall stand
>   the most weak.
> 'Tis the weakness in strength, that I cry for! my flesh, that
>   I seek
> In the Godhead! I seek and I find it. O Saul, it shall be
> A Face like my face that receives thee; a Man like to me,
> Thou shalt love and be loved by, for ever: a Hand like
>   this hand
> Shall throw open the gates of new life to thee! See the
>   Christ stand!

---

[1] See *New Poems*.

BROWNING'S REPUTATION AS A MYSTIC 271

Notice the similarity of this vision to the postscript of *Karshish*.

In the last section David describes how he found his way home in the night after his visit to Saul. The passage is like the coming of sweet sleep, in its caressing loveliness. I refer to it here because of David's reference to the 'Hand' which still impelled him at once and supported, and suppressed all the tumult. This is an echo of Browning's own personal experience. This Hand, he felt, was always above his shoulder, and, as every one knows, it pushed him once towards a booth in Florence where he bought for a lira the old yellow book, which gave him the material for his mightiest work, *The Ring and the Book*.

A Death in the Desert was published after Elizabeth's death. I suggest that the initiating vision was again of a man and a boy. The man was the only surviving disciple of Christ. He was hiding in a cave, with a convert on the watch outside. He was very old, and those who were with him were trying to rouse him from a state of coma. Then the boy rose up and ran and came in again carrying a graven plate of lead. And he searched and found the place he wanted and said (the words were clear and startling), 'I am the Resurrection and the Life.'

These visions may have been Browning's own visions. Or, they may have been told him by his wife. She says in one of her letters to her sister that she was free to tell her dreams and visions to her husband and that she valued this freedom. My own feeling is that Browning was not a visionary[1] in the sense that some of these

---

[1] I am using the word 'visionary' as a name given to those who see, in a waking state, what in the ordinary implication of 'seeing' is not

religious poems would indicate, but that for them all he began, in each case, from a vision of hers.

If it should be answered that he would be unlikely to do so because of his dread of anything occult and his vehement dislike of spiritualism, I would point out that there is no mention of her interest in rapping spirits and whispering voices until 1855, and that on December 19th, 1864 (the year in which *A Death in the Desert* and *Prospice* were published) he had so far modified his dislike as to write: 'The difference between me and the stupid people who have "communications" is probably nothing more than that I don't confound the results of the natural working of what is in my mind with vulgar external appearances.'

About that time, also, he may have been writing the appeal to his dead wife for help in the greatest work he had yet undertaken or was ever to undertake:

O lyric Love, half angel and half bird!

. . . .

Never may I commence my song, my due
To God who best taught song by gift of thee,
Except with bent head and beseeching hand—
That still, despite the distance and the dark,
What was, again may be; some interchange
Of grace, some splendour once thy very thought,
Some benediction anciently thy smile:
—Never conclude, but raising hand and head
Thither where eyes, that cannot reach, yet yearn
For all hope, all sustainment, all reward,
Their utmost up and on,—so blessing back

there. Joan of Arc was a visionary in this sense. Such visions are nearly always accompanied by voices.

In those thy realms of help, that heaven thy home,
Some whiteness which, I judge, thy face makes proud,
Some wanness where, I think, thy foot may fall!

I am glad to quote this passage at this point because it leads on naturally to the consideration of Browning as an intuitional mystic.

II

'L'intuition directe', says Gebhart,[1] 'des choses eternelles, la conversation intime avec Dieu; le mysticisme n'a besoin ni de syllogismes, ni d'expérience.' 'Such a statement', as H. V. Routh says, 'is obviously true as a generalization and undeniably applies to certain well-known characters.' No mystic has need of syllogisms, but many who are usually called mystics have need of experience; or, at any rate, their intuitions are connected with their experience. A scientist, *qua* scientist, may have a keen power of observation of natural appearances and may have a love, as Charles Darwin had, for the objects with which he is experimenting, and yet not derive from them, or associate with them, any intuitions. Nothing 'comes' to him in the way of a feeling for something beyond. He does not converse with God through a flower, nor mount to community with highest truth, as Wordsworth did.

Sir Francis Darwin[2] says of his father: 'Though he took no personal share in the management of the garden, he had great delight in the beauty of flowers. . . . I used to like to hear him admire the beauty of a flower; it was a kind of gratitude to the flower itself and a

[1] Quoted by H. V. Routh in *God, Man and Epic Poetry*, vol. ii, p. 211.
[2] *Reminiscences of My Father's Early Life* in *Autobiography of Charles Darwin*, p. 89.

personal love for its delicate form and colour. I seem to remember him gently touching a flower he delighted in; it was the same simple admiration that a child might have.'

Contrast this with a passage from Wordsworth's *Prelude* (Book III):

> To every natural form, rock, fruit, or flower,
> Even the loose stones that cover the highway,
> I gave a moral life: I saw them feel,
> Or linked them to some feeling: the great mass
> Lay bedded in a quickening soul, and all
> That I beheld respired with inward meaning.

Now take the experience of marriage. To the non-mystic marriage seems to lie within the range of ordinary experiences. He does not reach out beyond it, or see *through* it, to any consummation of life. He is satisfied to remain on the threshold of the house of life or, if he penetrates at all, it is only to an ante-chamber, which he blindly regards as the whole of his abode. To change the metaphor, he inhabits a pleasant garden where the flowers bloom in their season. The flowers are flowers; they appeal to his senses. If they do more, it is only because of some association in his mind. He receives but what he brings. The flowers have no originating power.

But to Browning the house of life somehow enlarged into a mansion of eternity; the garden was a Paradise of God.

If we compare *One Word More*, written when Elizabeth was alive, with 'O Lyric Love', written after her death, we have the same impression of a deep and awful delight. The spiritual experience is of the same kind. It is even of the same kind in *By the Fireside*. His marriage has opened the gates of a new life to him. There is no possibility of ending. Through it he has an intuition of infinity.

This high human passion also delivered up to him the key to the mystery of unity. He felt in his marriage the fusion of flesh and spirit. They were not two elements of life but one. The outward sign and the inward grace coalesced. And this mystery contained its own promise. It not only enlarged and glorified the idea of human intercourse, but it ministered entrance to a Divine fellowship. For unity is fellowship. No one knew better than Browning the intense interest of diversity and difference. In his marriage he realized how diversity and difference may subserve a higher unity.

Worth notice in this connexion is his failure to attain certainty when he makes use of syllogism for arguing about survival, and his tone of confidence when he regards the same subject from the point of view of his marriage. Nothing made him sure of immortality except Her. It was what he calls (in a letter) 'Ba's Baism' that led on to the intuition of a future life.

I have spoken of his personal feeling, expressed in *The Ring and the Book*,[1] of a 'Hand', always above his shoulder. He was ready to gather a hint from any event. A man may walk along a road a hundred times without noticing anything but the road and the loose stones and the trees and a gorse bush or two, and the hundred and first time some change in the tree through the effect of the atmosphere strikes him, or a leaf is whirled in the

[1] *The Ring and the Book:* 'The Ring and the Book' l. 41. See Chapter I. This, at any rate, was a personal spiritual experience of the highest significance and effect. Moreover, if a poet tells us that for his greatest work a Hand 'pushed him', are we to say that the impulse is not a genuine experience?

wind, or he hears a child's voice from a wayside cottage, and the whole face of Christ is turned upon him full.[1] It was often the hundred and first time with Robert Browning. He was walking through Dulwich wood ... well, you know the story. Out of that sprang *Pippa Passes*, one of the immortal poems of the world. Another day—much earlier in his life—he heard the refrain of a folk-song sung by some gipsies. And out of that sprang *The Flight of the Duchess*. Or, to crown all, in the year before Elizabeth died, on a fierce windy summer day ... well, you know that story also. The Hand that day was the Muse in her strength preparing for him her mightiest arrow. As he walked home he mastered the contents of the strange old yellow book. I wonder if when he came to Casa Guidi and saw the woman he loved sitting there awaiting him he had a sudden vision of her as she was before he knew her, as she inevitably was and would be in the purpose of God's shaping, and the vision became one with that rose of all the world, Pompilia.

There is another poem that grew out of a hint, or rather two hints. The first hint was a line in *King Lear*: 'Childe Roland to the Dark Tower came.'[2] The line is spoken by Edgar pretending to be a lunatic. The second hint was a picture of an old horse on a piece of tapestry. From these hints came *Childe Roland*. Browning says he meant nothing by the poem—nothing

---

[1] I am speaking here, of course, metaphorically and not in the strict visionary sense. In vision Jesus is recognized by movement or gesture or by something indefinable. A woman told me: 'It was not so much what He said as His familiarity and the way He sat down. So I said to Him, "Just a few words, Jesus, to clear up the muddle."' Dying people may have a vision of His Face (see Browning's *The Heretic's Tragedy*).

[2] Act III, Sc. iv.

transcendental, nothing mystical. But a poet may write one thing and the reader read another. Housman wrote:

> Too full already is the grave
> Of fellows that were good and brave
> And died because they were.

'Fellows that were good and brave, and died *because they were*' is one of my most comforting convictions. These young men, like some children, had attained to a kind of perfection. They were unimprovable by any farther discipline on the earth. They were good and brave; they had learned in their few years the great realities of life—goodness and courage. The necessity of sojourn was past. They learned quickly, and their death was not a tragedy but a reward.

Childe Roland sees the 'lost' companions on his quest:

> There they stood, ranged along the hill-sides, met
>   To view the last of me, a living frame
>   For one more picture! in a sheet of flame
> I saw them and I knew them all. And yet
> Dauntless the slug-horn to my lips I set,
>   And blew. *Childe Roland to the Dark Tower came.*

This is the end—not failure, but attainment. And all those adventurers, who had been lost in the quest, would find here in their brother's success the fruits of their own strength and boldness, marred as they had been by sensuality or the warped intention. 'There shall never be one lost good.' Though they perished in the long wandering, their brother, their peer, *came* to the Dark Tower; and they who had assembled to see one more failure added to the dread list, witnessed instead the crowning triumph. They heard the trumpet note and saw the sight. Their failure had been

> but a triumph's evidence
> For the fulness of the days.

This closing chapter has had for ambitious object nothing less than the establishment of Browning's reputation as a mystic. It has also shown that a poor poet is always at the mercy of his readers, when he is, at last, fortunate enough, as Browning at last was, to find any.

BIBLIOGRAPHICAL NOTE
OF
BROWNING LITERATURE IN THE TWENTIETH CENTURY

BIOGRAPHY (or containing Biography)

Browning, by G. K. Chesterton. English Men of Letters (Macmillan).	1903
Robert Browning, by E. Dowden. Temple Biographies (Dent).	1904
The Brownings in America, by Elizabeth Gould. Poet Lore Co., Boston, Mass.	1904
Early Environment of Robert Browning, by Fred Rogers (privately printed).	1904
Browning, by Sir F. T. Marzials. Bell's Miniature Series of Great Writers.	1905
Robert Browning, by C. H. Herford. Modern English Writers (Blackwood).	1905
La vita et le opere di Roberto Browning ed Elisabetta Barrett-Browning, by F. Zampini-Salazar.	1907
The Life of Robert Browning, by W. Hall Griffin and H. C. Minchin (Methuen).	1910
The Brownings: Their Life and Art, &c., by Lilian Whiting (U.S.A.).	1911
Early Literary Career of Robert Browning, by T. R. Lounsbury (Univ. of Virginia).	1911
Browning and his Poetry, by Ernest Rhys. Poetry and Life Series.	1914
Robert Browning, by Sir Henry Jones. Cambridge Hist. of Eng. Lit., vol. xiii.	1916
Robert Browning, by Arthur R. Skemp. The People's Books	1916
Robert Browning: His Life and Poetry, by Effie Ryle (National Adult School Union).	1920
The Brownings, by Osbert H. Burdett (Constable).	1928
L'Art et la Pensée de R. Browning, by Paul de Reul (Lamertin, Brussells).	1929

LETTERS

Browning and A. Domett, by F. G. Kenyon.	1906
Letters to T. J. Wise and other Correspondents.	1912
The Death of Elizabeth Barrett Browning: Letter to his Sister, Sarianna.	1916
The Browning Society, Being Letters from Robert Browning to J. D. Campbell (Introd. by Clement Shorter). Privately printed, London.	1917
Letters to my Son (Introd. by Clement Shorter).	1917
Letters to his Son on FitzGerald's Criticism of Elizabeth Barrett Browning (Introd. by T. J. Wise).	1919
Some Records of Walter Savage Landor, in 3 Letters to Isa Blagden. Printed for T. J. Wise.	1919
Letters from Le Croisic (Introd. by Edmund Gosse). Printed for T. J. Wise.	1919
Reflections on Franco-Prussian War—July to Oct. 1870—in 3 letters to Isa Blagden. Printed for T. J. Wise.	1919
Letters to his Son and Daughter-in-law, Fanny. Printed for T. J. Wise.	1920
Opinion on the Writings of Alfred, Lord Tennyson with a statement of his changed views regarding P. B. Shelley, in 5 letters. Printed for T. J. Wise.	1920
Letters to Miss Isa Blagden, ed. by A. Joseph Armstrong (Baylor University Press).	1923
Some Lamb and Browning Letters to Leigh Hunt (ed. by Luther A. Brewer).	1924

ESSAYS

WHICH INCLUDE PRIMERS, A CYCLOPAEDIA, A CONCORDANCE, AND A CATALOGUE

Robert Browning as a Religious Teacher, by A. C. Pigou. Barney Essay (C. J. Clay & Sons).	1901
The Browning Cyclopaedia, by E. Berdoe (Swan Sonnenschein).	1902
The Poetry of Browning, by Stopford A. Brooke (Pitman).	1902
The Bible in Browning, by Minnie G. Machen.	1903
Robert Browning, &c., by James Douglas. Bookman Booklets.	1903
Guidance from Robert Browning in matters of faith, by J. A. Hutton.	1903

BIBLIOGRAPHICAL NOTE

Browning and Tennyson as Teachers, by J. M. Robertson (A. & H. B. Bonner). 1903
A Primer of Browning, by E. Berdoe (Routledge). 1904
Studies in Browning, by J. Flew (C. H. Kelly). 1904
Browning for Beginners, by T. Rain (Swan Sonnenschein). 1904
A Browning Primer, by Defries. 1905
Sermons from Browning, by F. Ealand. 1905
The Immortality of the Soul in the poems of Browning and Tennyson, by Sir Henry Jones (P. Green). 1905
Browning and Dogma, by Ethel M. Naish (Bell). 1906
The Christ of English Poetry, Hulsean Lecture by C. W. Stubbs (Dent) (On Cynewulf, Langland, Shakespeare, and Browning). 1906
Quelques Aspects de la foi moderne dans les poèmes de Robert Browning, by Pierre Berger (Paris). 1907
The Grotesque in the Poetry of Robert Browning, by L. B. Campbell (Univ. of Texas). 1907
Browning's Italy: a Study of Italian Life and Art in Browning, by Helen A. Clarke (New York). 1907
Robert Browning: Optimist, by E. S. Buchanan (Salmon). 1908
Browning's England: a Study of English Influence in Browning, by Helen A. Clarke (New York). 1908
Browning and the Dramatic Monologue, by S. S. Curry (Boston, Mass.). 1908
Robert Browning's Verhältnis zu Frankreich, by Carl Schmidt (Lit. For.). 1909
Robert Browning e il suo capolavoro, by F. di Silvestri-Falconieri (Roma). 1910
Browning, by W. P. Ker (Eng. Assoc. Essays & Studies). 1910
Wordsworth, Tennyson and Browning: a Study in Human Freedom, by S. F. Gingerich (Ann Arbor, Mich.). 1911
Robert Browning, by Emil Koeppel (Lit. For.). 1911
The Bible in Browning, by Helene Meyer-Franck. 1912
Robert Browning, by Pierre Berger (Paris). 1912
The Message of Robert Browning, by A. A. Foster (Hodder & Stoughton). 1912
Browning's Teachings on Faith, Life and Love, by W. A. Hind (George Allen). 1912

Robert Browning Centenary Celebration at Westminster Abbey 1912, by William A. Knight (Smith, Elder). 1912
Studi sulla poesia di Roberto Browning: la filosofia, la psicologia, l'arte, by L. Pellegrini (Napoli).
Robert Browning: The Poet and the Man, by F. M. Sim (St. Catherine Press). 1912
Browning's Heroines, by Ethel C. Mayne (Chatto & Windus). 1913
A Study in Illumination (R. Browning), by Geraldine E. Hodgson (Heath, Cranton & Ouseley). 1914
Browning and Italian Art and Artists, by P. Hogrefe (Kansas University). 1914
Stories from Browning, by Verney C. Turnbull (Harrap). 1914
Studies in Browning, by J. Flew (Every Age Library). 1915
Robert Browning: how to know him, by William L. Phelps (Indianapolis). 1915
Kant and Tennyson and Kant and Browning, by Ânandaşankara Bâpubhâî Dhura. 1917
The Confessions of a Browning Lover, by John Walker (Abingdon Press: New York). 1918
Homage to Robert Browning, collected by Aleph Tanner (Baylor Univ. Bulletin). 1920
On the Poetry of Matthew Arnold, Robert Browning, &c., by Aîkal Amulyachandra. 1921
Browningiana: Baylor University Collection. 1921
Robert Browning: Étude sur sa pensée et sa vie, by Mary Duclaux. 1922
The Seen and Unseen in Browning, by Emma J. Burt (Blackwell). 1923
Concordance to Poems of Robert Browning, by Leslie N. Broughton and B. F. Stelter (Stechert, New York). 1924
The Brownings, by O. Elton. 1924
The Aesthetics of Robert Browning, by Christian N. Wenger (Mich.). 1924
Browning and Calverley: or Poem and Parody, by P. L. Babington (Castle). 1925
Brotherhood in Browning, by Maud A. Price (Cedar Rapids, U.S.A.). 1925
Robert Browning: Poet and Philosopher, by F. M. Sim (Fisher & Unwin). 1925

BIBLIOGRAPHICAL NOTE 283

One Word more on Browning, by Francis T. Russell (Stamford
    Univ. Press). 1927
Browning Essays: Baylor University Collection. 1928
Reinspecting Victorian Religion (with special reference to Browning), by Gaius G. Atkins (Macmillan, New York). 1928
Further Guidance from Robert Browning in Matters of Faith: suggested by 'Ferishtah's Fancies', by John A. Hutton (Hodder & Stoughton). 1928
A Browning Library: Catalogue of printed books, MS. autograph letters, by Thomas J. Wise (privately printed). 1929
Browning: Background and Conflict, by F. R. G. Duckworth (Benn). 1931

ESSAYS ACCOMPANYING SELECTIONS

Robert Browning: Poems (a selection), introd. by Alice Meynell
    (Red Letter Library). 1903
*Studies in Browning (Saul, Karshish, Grammarian's Funeral, Old
    Pictures*, by Susan Cunningham (Swan Sonnenschein). 1906
Poems of Alfred Tennyson and Robert Browning, by F. H. Sykes 1907
Tales from Browning, by Rev. G. Lacey May (Temple Engl.
    Lit. Series). 1907
Selections from Browning, by Aug. Birrell (Golden Poets Series). 1908
Browning: Love Poems, by Hannaford Bennett. 1908
Browning: Pied Piper and other Poems, by A. Guthkelch (Bell). 1908
Browning: Selections, by E. A. Pike (Melrose). 1910
Browning: Selections 1835–1864, by W. T. Young (Pitt Press). 1911
Browning: Selections, by O. J. Stevenson. 1916
Browning: Selections, by W. J. Alexander. 1917
A Browning Anthology, by F. A. Forbes. 1917
A Browning Anthology, by Ada Ambler. 1921
Browning: Selections, by Henry Newbolt. 1923
Robert Browning: Humanist: A Selection from Browning's
    Poetry, with Introduction by A. Compton-Rickett
    (Jenkins). 1924
Tennyson and Browning Contrasted, by G. Boas. 1925
Browning: Selections, ed. by F. W. Robinson (Univ. Press,
    London). 1926

BIBLIOGRAPHICAL NOTE

A Spiritual Anthology from Robert Browning, by H. A. Percival
(Theosophical Publ. House).   1926
Browning: Shorter Selections, by G. D. H. and M. I. Cole
(Douglas).   1928

ESSAYS ON SEPARATE POEMS AND 'THE ESSAY ON SHELLEY'

Classical Elements in Browning's 'Aristophanes' Apology', by
Carl N. Jackson (Boston, U.S.A.).   1909
Gaisford Greek Verse from *Balaustion's Adventure*, by J. B.
Poynton (Blackwell).   1920
Balaustion's Adventure, ed. by Edward A. Parker (Macmillan,
New York).   1928
Christmas Eve, Introd. by T. E. Harvey (Brother Richard's
Bookshelf)   1913
A Death in the Desert, by Rev. G. U. Pope.   1904
Na Balkonie, by J. Kasprowicz.   1912
A Miniature, reprinted from 'The Sibyl'. Note by F. J.
Furnivall.   1904
Paracelsus. Introd. and Notes by M. L. Lee and K. B.
Locock (Methuen).   1909
Parleyings, by W. C. De Vane.   1927
The Pied Piper, ed. by Silvanus P. Thomson (an inquiry into
the sources).   1905
The Pied Piper: easily staged musical play by E. Elliot Stock.   1913
Pippa Passes: by Arthur Symons (Favourite Classics Series).   1906
    by J. Kasprowicz.   1910
    by A. L. Irvine.   1924
    by Ed. A. Parker.   1927
The Return of the Druses, Deutsch von Edmund Rusti (Bremen)   1912
The Ring and the Book: by F. B. Hornbrooke.   1909
    by C. W. Hodell.   1911
    by N. Bogholm.   1918
    by A. K. Cook.   1920
    by J. Cassidy   1924
    (As a connected narrative), by Alexander Haddon.   1924
    (A Paraphrase, published by Blackwell).   1924

BIBLIOGRAPHICAL NOTE

(Plays): Caponsacchi, by A. F. Goodrich.	1927
Pompilia, by David Graham.	1928
The Old Yellow Book: Essay and Notes by C. W. Hodell.	1908
The Old Yellow Book: New Translation and Notes, by J. M. Gest	1927
The Novel in 'The Ring and the Book'	1912
Centenary lecture by Henry James (in *Notes on Novelists*).	1914
The Country of 'The Ring and the Book', by Sir Fred. Treves (Cassell). (Also a cheaper edition).	1913
Sordello: by H. B. Forman.	1902
by David Duff.	1906
by K. M. London.	1906
by Rev. Arthur J. Whyte (Dent).	1913
by E. H. Thomson.	1914
Strafford: Tragic Iambics, Act V, Sc. ii.	1914
Essay on Shelley: ed. with introd. by R. Garnett.	1903
by J. C. Thomson.	1908
by L. Winstanley.	1911
by H. F. B. Brett-Smith.	1921

ILLUSTRATED EDITIONS OF SELECTIONS OR SEPARATE POEMS

The Pied Piper, illustrated by Van Dyck.	1905
Selected Poems, with six illustrations by J. Jellicoe (Melrose).	1906
Christmas Eve, illustrated by Charles Pears (Jack).	1906
Pippa Passes and Men and Women, illustrated by Eleanor Fortescue Brickdale (Chatto & Windus).	1908
Dramatis Personae and Dramatic Romances and Lyrics, illustrated by Eleanor Fortescue Brickdale (Chatto & Windus).	1909
The Pied Piper, illustrated by Ambrose Dudley.	1912
The Pied Piper, illustrated by Margaret W. Tarrant.	1912
Rabbi Ben Ezra and Other Poems from 'Dramatis Personae', illustrated in Colour by Bernard Partridge (Hodder & Stoughton).	1915
The Pied Piper, outline illustrations for colouring (Black).	1927

OTHER EDITIONS

(a) *Comprehensive*

The Poems and Plays of Robert Browning 1833–44, with Introduction by Arthur Waugh (Everyman's Library).	1906
The Works of Robert Browning, with Introductions by F. G. Kenyon (Smith, Elder).	1912
New Poems by Robert Browning and Elizabeth Barrett Browning, ed. by Sir F. G. Kenyon (Smith, Elder).	1914
Also Editions of *Men and Women* in 1903, 1904, 1908, 1909, 1910, 1911.	

(b) *Selections and Separate Poems*

Selected Songs. Oakleaf Press.	1903
Selections: Pragny Press.	1904
Broadway Booklets.	1905
Brochure Series.	1905
Langham Booklets.	1910
Plain Text Poets.	1912
Arden Books.	1912
Christmas Eve. Broadway Booklets.	1903
Heart and Life Booklets.	1905
Astolat Reprints.	1908
Langham Booklets.	1910
Easter Day. Heart and Life Booklets.	1903
Broadway Booklets.	1903
The Flight of the Duchess. Essex House Press (printed on vellum).	1905
In a Balcony. Arden Books.	1912
Pied Piper. Dutton, New York.	1928
Pictor Ignotus, Fra Lippo Lippi and Andrea del Sarto. Golden Cockerel Press.	1925
Pippa Passes. Broadway Booklets.	1905
Arden Books.	1912
King's Treasury Series.	1913
Holerth Library.	1924
Rabbi ben Ezra. Editions in 1901, 1908, 1913.	
Saul. Heart and Life Booklets.	1903

INDEX

Summaries of Chapters are given under the appropriate headings. Poems, of which the authorship is not stated, are by Robert Browning. The titles of single poems or stories are given between inverted commas; the titles of books are italicized.

Abercrombie, Lascelles, 64, 91 n. 1, 104, 155.
'Abt Vogler', 39 n. 1, 47, 54, 182, 203.
'After', 42.
'Afterwards', by Thomas Hardy, 88.
'All Hallows' Eve', by John Davidson, 55.
'Alsace-Lorraine', by George Meredith, 85.
'Andrea del Sarto', 58 n. 2, 129.
Andromeda in Wimpole Street, by Miss Dormer Creston, 2 and n. 1, 228, 229.
'Any Wife to Any Husband', 42.
'Apparition', by W. E. Henley, 146.
Arabel (Mrs. Browning's sister), 235, 241.
Arber, ed. of *English Garner*, 21 n. 1.
Ariel (*The Tempest*), 40, 77.
Armado (*Love's Labour's Lost*), 106.
Armstrong, A. J., 15 n. 3, 244.
Armstrong, Ivor, 25 n. 2.
Arnold, Matthew, 68, 73, 196.
Arnould, Joseph, 113 n. 2.
Art, Browning's, *see under* Browning. Pure, ornate and grotesque (Bagehot), 75, 79.
Asolando, 181.
Asolo, 7, 171.
Asquith, Miss, 161.
Athanasian Creed, 27.
'Aunt Helen', by T. S. Eliot, 110.
Austin, Jane, 140.
Autobiography of a Tramp, by W. H. Davies, 69.
'Autumn', by John Davidson, 53.

Baddeley, V. C. C., 120.
Bagehot, Walter, *Literary Studies*, 76 and n. 1; on the grotesque art, 77; on the ornate art, 79, 98.
Bagni, 250.
Balaustion's Adventure, 50–1.
'Ballad in Blank Verse of the Making of a Poet, A', by John Davidson, 52.
'Ballad of an Artist's Wife, A', by John Davidson, 53.
'Ballad of Heaven, A', by John Davidson, 54.
'Ballad of Hell, A', by John Davidson, 200.
Ballads and Songs, by John Davidson, 52.
Barnes, William, 148.
Barrack Room Ballads, by Rudyard Kipling, 56, 60, 148, 149.
Barrett, Edward (father of Mrs. Browning), 229, 230, 231; his death, 243.
Barretts of Wimpole Street, The, by Rudolf Besier, 228.
Barrhead, 50.
Baylor University Press, 15 n. 3, 244.
Beerbohm, Max, 65.
'Before', 42.
'Before Dawn', by Walter de la Mare, 206.
Bells and Pomegranates, 114, 230.
'Benefactors, The', by Rudyard Kipling, 62.
Benson, Archbishop, 39 n. 1.
Binyon, Laurence, 'The Fallen', 103, 104; philosophy of hope in *The Sirens, The Idols, The Secret*, 'The Death of Adam', 'Sirmione', 207–9.
Biographie Universelle, 38.
'Biography', by John Masefield, 64, 65 and n. 2.

INDEX

Birrell, A., 28 n. 1.
'Bishop Blougram's Apology', 26, 27, 58 and n. 1, 129, 192.
Blagden, Miss Isa, letters of Browning to, 15 n. 3, 20, 32, 33, 57; about Tennyson's art, 80, 111; 113, 229, 244–51.
Blake, William, *Milton*, 2; the writing of *Milton*, 14, 17, 104; mysticism of, 254; *Auguries of Innocence*, 257; 260.
'Blind Child, A', by W. H. Davies, 71, 72.
Bloomsbury, 65.
Bogholm, N., 6 n. 1.
'Boston Evening Transcript, The', by T. S. Eliot, 109.
Boswell, James, *Life of Samuel Johnson*, 1; quoted from, 21–2.
'Boy and the Angel, The', 43, 176.
Boyd, Hugh, 232.
Boyle, Mrs., 236.
Bradley, A. C., on Shakespeare, 95.
'Bredon Hill', by A. E. Housman, 154.
Brickdale, Eleanor Fortescue, 47, 48.
Bridges, Robert, 207; illustrations of optimism in *The Testament of Beauty*, 209–15.
Brini, 248.
'Broadways', by John Masefield, 64.
Brockington, Lieut. C. C., 18.
'Broken Men, The', by Rudyard Kipling, 62.
Brooke, Rupert, 63, 96, 97; conversational method in, 159, 160; on Browning's references to God, 161; change in outlook, 202–5.
  Poems quoted:
  'Fish, The', 97.
  'Grantchester', 160.
  'Great Lover, The', 205.
  'Mary and Gabriel', 204.
  'Soldier, The', 205.
  'Song of the Beasts, The', 96.
  'Voice, The', 160.

'Brother Square-Toes', by Rudyard Kipling, 150 n. 1.
Brown, T. E., and Darwinism, 199.

Browning and his Art, some notes on (Chapter I), 1–34: difficulty of tracing the influence of his poetry, 1; influence of his lovestory, 2–3; writer's chief conviction about Browning. § I, his mysticism: crucial determinations, 3–6; subjects of 'Pippa Passes' and *The Ring and the Book*, 6–9; 'The Flight of the Duchess', 9, 10; Browning's freedom of subject and treatment. § II, his interest in the 'soul', 11 and ff.: spontaneity and study, 14–17. § III, his message or 'central meaning', 17 and ff.: 'meaning' the primary thing, 20. § IV, form of his poetry, 20 and ff.: kept within traditional limits of prosody, 23; his inventions and innovations, 23; effect on 'modernist' poetry, 23–5. § V, the reading of his poetry, 25 and ff.: examples of mis-reading, 26–32; causes of obscurity, 32–4.

  Intention to become a poet, 3; education, 4; dramatized versions of *The Ring and the Book*, 6 n. 1; power of observation, 8 n. 1; Hardy on the *essence* of Browning, 11; Browning's 'testament of hope', 20; and Walt Whitman, 24 (and 109); on his commentators, 28 n. 1; and Tennyson, 36; his reading, 38; his manners, 39 n. 1; *championship of the ordinary*, 40 and ff.; poems on music, 47; 'realist' and 'idealist', 75; *method of curiosity*, 79 and ff.; love of animals, 82 (and 95); and George Meredith, 84–5; possible influence of his poetic achievement on Thomas Hardy, 87.

Browning (*cont.*).
The Psychologist and his Invention of the Dramatic Lyric (Chap. IV), 111-33: description of the soul his object, 111-12; confession of poetic faith, 114-16; drama and dramatic lyric, 116-17; inherent difficulty of dramatic lyric, 117-20. Advantages of dramatic lyric, 120-33: meaning attached to 'lyric', 121-2; 'Cavalier Tunes', 122-3; 'Porphyria's Lover', 123-5; recollections of Pompilia, 126-9; 'conversational' monologues, 129-31; the poet's method scientifically sound, 132-3; how he would have treated Tennyson's subject.

'Galahad' and 'The Statue and the Bust', 112; affection for Domett, 113; possible background of 'Guido', 126; reading of 'Fra Lippo Lippi', 130 n. 1; George Meredith's psychology, 136; use of the letter-form, 142; Tennyson's 'Lazarus', 143-4.

Optimism (Chap. VI), 169-96: Alice Meynell and Bishop Westcott on, 169-70; Francis Paget on, 170-1. § I, his optimism examined: 'Pippa Passes', 171-3; 'Lazarus', 174-5; 'Hervé Riel', 'Pheidippides', 'Echetlos', 'The Boy and the Angel', 'Rabbi Ben Ezra', 'A Death in the Desert', 'Easter Day', 175-7; not wise 'passiveness', see 'The Statue and the Bust', 177-8; 'The Patriot', 'The Guardian Angel', 'Saul', 178-80; conception of heaven in 'The Last Ride Together', 180-1. § II, view of life after death: 'Prospice', Epilogue to *Asolando*, 'Cristina', 'Evelyn Hope', 'A Grammarian's Funeral', 'Abt Vogler', 'Christ-

Browning (*cont.*).
mas Eve', 'Easter Day', 'Cleon', 181-3; compensation in 'Deaf and Dumb', 183; interpretation of suffering in 'Ixion', 183-6; the view in 'La Saisiaz', 187. § III, relation to Christianity: Browning, Saint John, and Saint Paul, 188-94. § IV, general effect of his optimism, 194-6.

probability of a future life, 191; belief in a future life intuitive, 198; Browning a rallying point against Darwinism, 199 n. 1.

Reputation as a Lover (Chap. VIII), 228-52: § I, courtship, from the *Letters of Robert Browning and Elizabeth Barrett*. § II, marriage: her references to him, from *Elizabeth Barrett Browning: Letters to her Sister*. § III, his references to her after her death, from *Letters of Robert Browning to Miss Isa Blagden*.

Reputation as a Mystic (Chap. IX), 253-78: difficulty of definition; various attempts; convictions of the great mystics; modes of apprehension: (1) visionary, (2) intuitional. § I, central visions in 'Christmas Eve', 'Easter Day', 'Karshish', 'Cleon', second part of 'Saul', 'A Death in the Desert'. § II, intuition: Browning's crucial determinations; his experience of marriage and his convictions; the origins of his great poems.

Poems quoted or referred to:
'Abt Vogler', 39 n. 1, 47, 54, 182, 203.
'After', 42.
'Andrea del Sarto', 58 n. 2, 129.
'Any Wife to Any Husband', 42.
Asolando, 181.

INDEX

Browning (cont.).
Balaustion's Adventure, 50–1.
'Before', 42.
Bells and Pomegranates, 114, 230.
'Bishop Blougram's Apology', 26, 27, 58, and n. 1; 129, 192.
'Boy and the Angel, The', 43, 176.
'By the Fireside', 81.
'Caliban upon Setebos', 59 and n. 5; 75, 77.
'Cavalier Tunes', 121–3.
'Childe Roland to the Dark Tower Came', 43, 58 n. 2, 83, 84, 162, 163, 276, 277.
'Christmas Eve', 44, 45, 46, 148, 182, 265, 267.
'Cleon', 46, 47, 58 n. 2, 182, 192, 265, 269, 270.
'Colombe's Birthday', 33, 240.
'Count Guido Franceschini', 121, 125.
'Cristina', 181, 262.
'Deaf and Dumb', 72, 183.
'Death in the Desert, A', 182, 189–91, 192, 257, 262, 265, 271, 272.
Dramatic Romances and Lyrics, 59 n. 3.
Dramatis Personae, 59 n. 5.
'Earth's Immortalities', 118.
'Easter Day', 29, 177, 182, 192, 265.
'Echetlos', 175.
'Epistle containing the strange medical . . . , An' (referred to as 'The Epistle' or 'Karshish' or 'Lazarus'), 142, 144, 164, 174, 175, 192, 242, 259, 265, 268, 269.
'Evelyn Hope', 58 n. 1, 181.
Fifine at the Fair, 87 n. 2.
'Flight of the Duchess, The', 9, 33, 43, 44, 60, 68, 82, 276.
'Fra Lippo Lippi', 129, 130 n. 1, 163.
'Giuseppi Caponsacchi', 6 n. 1, 121, 125.

Browning (cont.).
'Grammarian's Funeral, A', 31, 32 and n. 1, 58 n. 2, 181.
'Guardian Angel, The', 179, 180.
'Guido', 28, 29, 30, 125, 126.
'Half Rome', 125.
'Heretic's Tragedy, The', 276 n. 1.
'Hervé Riel', 175.
'Holy Cross Day', 58 n. 2, 75, 76, 77.
'How they brought the Good News from Ghent to Aix', 82.
Incondita, 4.
'Instans Tyrannus', 43.
'Italian in England, The', 44.
'Ixion', 182, 183–6.
'Johannes Agricola in Meditation', 123.
'La Saisiaz', 67 n. 3, 187, 188, 192.
'Last Ride Together, The', 180, 181.
'Madhouse Cells', 121, 123.
'Master Hugues of Saxe-Gotha', 47, 167.
'Meeting at Night', 119, 120.
'Memorabilia', 43.
Men and Women, 58, 241, 242.
'Muléykeh', 82, 97.
'My Last Duchess', 43, 44, 117, 118 n. 1, 120, 122, 129, 163.
New Poems by Robert and Mrs. Browning, 41 n. 1, 118 n. 1, 270.
'Of Pacchiarotto', 24 n. 1, 169.
'Old Pictures in Florence', 81, 262.
'One Word More', 14, 58 n. 2, 242, 274.
'Other Half Rome, The', 121, 125.
Paracelsus, 171, 262.
'Patriot, The', 178, 179.
'Pheidippides', 175.
'Pippa Passes', 6, 7, 8, 17, 18, 40, 98, 99, 171–3, 176, 276.
'Pisgah Sights', 177.

INDEX

Browning (cont.).
 'Pompilia', 6 n. 1, 125, 126–9, 142, 163.
 'Pope, The', 6 n. 1, 30, 48, 125, 182, 183.
 'Popularity', 82.
 'Porphyria's Lover', 121, 123, 125, 137.
 'Prince Hohenstiel-Schwangau', 262.
 'Prospice', 31, 32 n. 1, 72, 181, 272.
 'Rabbi Ben Ezra', 176, 182, 193.
 'Red Cotton Night-cap Country', 32 n. 2.
 Ring and the Book, The, 6 n. 1, 8, 9, 14, 15, 16, 17, 28–31, 29 n. 2, 48–9, 50, 57 n. 1, 78, 86, 87, 112, 120, 121, 123, 125–9, 131, 132, 134, 139, 142, 182, 183, 263 n. 1, 271, 272, 273, 275 n. 1.
 'Rudel to the Lady of Tripoli', 23 n. 2.
 'Saul', 40–2, 58 n. 2, 180, 265, 270.
 'Serenade at a Villa, A', 82.
 'Sludge the Medium, Mr.', 141, 142, 241.
 'Soliloquy of the Spanish Cloister', 59.
 Sordello, 38, 112, 171.
 'Speculative', 252.
 'Statue and the Bust, The', 112, 178.
 'Tertium Quid', 121, 125.
 'Toccata of Galuppi's, A', 47.
 'Tray', 95.
 'Up at a Villa—Down in the City', 80.
 'Waring', 59, 113.
 'White Witchcraft', 23 n. 2.

Browning as a Philosophical and Religious Teacher, by Sir Henry Jones, 32 n. 1.

Browning, Mrs. (wife of the poet—familiar name, 'Ba'), 5; Pompilia and, 8–9; Sonnets from the Portuguese, 9 and n. 1; her admiration of 'Pippa Passes', 40; her criticism of Browning's poems, 41; 'Wine of Cyprus', 50; 113; background of 'Pompilia', 125; Letters to her Sister, 130 n. 1, 233–43; courtship and marriage, 229–43; her death, 243; Browning's references to her after her death, 244–52; on Browning's mysticism, 261; possible influence by way of vision on Browning's poetry, 270, 271–3; 'Ba's Baism' led Browning on to the intuition of a future life, 275–6.
Browning, Robert (father of the poet), his religious convictions, 37; his character, ib.; his library, 38; his companionship with Pen, 246; his love for 'Ba', 249.
Brownings, The, by Oliver Elton, 26.
 by Osbert Burdett, 2, 199 n. 1, 228, 261.
Buchanan, Robert, on Browning's Christianity, 194.
'Buddha at Kamakura', by Rudyard Kipling, 62.
'Builder, The', by Humbert Wolfe, 162.
'Bull, The', by Ralph Hodgson, 97–8.
Byron, 196.
'By the Fireside', 81.

'Caliban upon Setebos', 59 and n. 5; 75, 77.
Cambridge Browning Society, 28 n. 1.
Cambridge, University of, and religious tests, 37, 38.
'Camp Song of the Baggage Animals, The', by Rudyard Kipling, 62.
Caponsacchi (a play on The Ring and the Book), 6 n. 1.
Carlyle, on The Ring and the Book, 49.

INDEX

'Carnival in Paris', musical episode by Svendsen, 167.
Casa Guidi, 276.
'Catherine', by W. H. Davies, 71.
'Cavalier Tunes', 121-3.
Chance, by Joseph Conrad, 137-8.
'Chant, A', by W. H. Davies, 73.
'Chant Pagan', by Rudyard Kipling, 62.
Chehov, 106.
Chesterton, G. K., 26; quotation from *The Victorian Age in Literature*, 27, 28, 31.
'Childe Roland to the Dark Tower Came', 43, 58 n. 2, 83, 84, 162, 163, 276, 277.
'Christ the Man', by W. H. Davies, 74.
Christianity, the relation of Browning's optimism to, 188-94.
'Christmas Eve', 44, 45, 46, 148, 182, 265, 267.
Civil and Military Gazette, The, of India, 57.
Clark, A. M., *The Realistic Revolt in Modern Poetry*, 63 n. 1.
'Cleon', 46, 47, 58 n. 2, 182, 192, 265, 269, 270.
Cockney Dialect, 148.
Coleridge, S. T., 36, 196, 198, 255.
'College Debate, The', by Robert Graves, 165.
'Colombe', 'the quieter female character', 33; (the play) 240.
Colvin, Sir Sidney, on Browning's obscurity, 32.
Combe Florey, 9, 155.
'Coming of Arthur, The', by Tennyson, 111.
'Common Humanity in Browning and some Twentieth-century Poets' (Chap. II), 35-74.
    The Twentieth-century Poets are: John Davidson, Rudyard Kipling, John Masefield, and W. H. Davies. These poets are content to take men and women on the ground of their common humanity, and they expect to find in the uncultured the great qualities of our nature. This expectation is shown to have connexion with their 'unorthodox' education.
'Common Woman, The', by Humbert Wolfe, 164.
Compton-Rickett, Arthur, 23.
Conrad, Joseph, on *The Dynasts*, 87 n. 3; *Youth*, 137, 138; his method in *Chance*, 139.
'Conversational Method in the Twentieth Century, The', (Chap. V), 134-68.
    Influence of Browning's Dramatic Lyric. § I, prose writers: George Meredith, Joseph Conrad, Rudyard Kipling. § II, poets: W. E. Henley, Rudyard Kipling, John Masefield, W. H. Davies, A. E. Housman, Thomas Hardy, Walter de la Mare, Rupert Brooke, Humbert Wolfe, C. H. Sorley, Robert Graves, and 'Modernists'.
Cook, A. K., 6 n. 1.
'Cooking Egg, A', by T. S. Eliot, 108.
Copperfield, by Charles Dickens, 239.
Cornwall, Barry, 7.
Cotswold Country, 106.
Couch, Sir Arthur Quiller, *Poetry*, 18, 19.
'Countess Cathleen', by W. B. Yeats, 256.
'Count Guido Franceschini', 121, 125.
Country of 'The Ring and the Book', The, by Sir F. Treves, 6 n. 1.
Coup d'état, Napoleon III's, 233.
'Cousin Nancy', by T. S. Eliot.
Crashaw, Richard, 257.
Creative Understanding, by Hermann Keyserling, 19 and n. 1, 20 and n. 1.
Creston, Miss Dormer, *Andromeda in Wimpole Street*, 2 and n. 1, 228, 229.

INDEX

'Cristina', 181, 262.
Cummings, E. E., 23 and n. 3.

Dancing, 19.
'Danny Deever', by Rudyard Kipling, 61.
Darwin, Charles, *Origin of Species*, 197, 198, 222, 273.
Darwin, Sir Francis, 273.
Darwinism, 198, 199 n. 1, 200.
Dauber, by John Masefield, 36, 64, 66, 67.
Davidson, John, 36; common humanity in, 50–6; 57, 93, 94, 99, 146–8, 201.
   Poems quoted:
'Autumn', 53.
'Ballad in Blank Verse of the Making of a Poet, A', 52.
'Ballad of an Artist's Wife, A', 53, 201.
'Ballad of Heaven, A', 54.
Fleet Street Eclogues (Second Series), 55, 99, 146–8.
'Frosty Morning, A', 93, 94.
'Highway Pimpernel, A', 53.
'Northern Suburb, A', 52.
'Piper Play!', 54.
'St. Valentine's Eve', 55.
'Song of the Road, A', 54.
'Spring', 53.
'Testament of a Man Forbid, The', 55.
'Testament of John Davidson', 56, 201.
'Thirty Bob a Week', 52.
'Woman and her Son, A', 94.
Davies, W. H., 36, 47 n. 1, 63; common humanity in, 69–74; 101, 153.
   Poems quoted:
'Australian Bill', 73.
'Beautiful, The', 73, 74.
'Blind Child, A', 71.
'Catherine', 71.
'Chant, A', 73.
'Jenny', 72.
'One Thing Wanting', 72.
'Song of Life, A', 70.

Davies, W. H. (*cont.*).
'Wind, The', 92.
'Wondering Brown', 73.
'Day of Battle, The', by A. E. Housman, 154.
Day's End Club, 117–20.
'Deaf and Dumb', 72, 183.
'Death in the Desert, A', 182, 189–91, 192, 257, 262, 265, 271, 272.
'Death of Adam', by Laurence Binyon, 208.
Debits and Credits, by Rudyard Kipling, 139.
De la Mare, Walter, 91 n. 1, 99, 100, 101, 157, 158, 159, 205, 206.
   Poems quoted:
'Before Dawn', 206.
'Drugged', 100.
'Funeral, The', 158.
'Hospital', 206.
'Imagination's Pride, The', 205.
'In the Dock', 100.
'Listeners, The', 157.
'Miss T.', 158.
'Nicholas Nye', 159.
'Pigs and the Charcoal Burners, The', 159.
'Sam's Three Wishes', 157.
'Wreck, The', 100.
Departmental Ditties, by Rudyard Kipling, 56.
Des Principes de la Guerre, by Marshal Foch, 13.
Devil and the Lady, The, by Tennyson, 51.
Dijon, 11.
Dives, parable of, 184, 185.
Dodsley, 21.
Domett, Alfred, 12, 112, 113, 114.
Don Juan, by J. E. Flecker, 87 nn. 1 and 2.
Dramatic Lyric, 13, 14; Chap. IV, 111–33, *see under* Browning.
Dramatic Romances and Lyrics, 59 n. 3.
Dramatis Personae, 59 n. 5.
'Drugged', by Walter de la Mare, 100, 101.

INDEX

Dryden, *Ode on St. Cecilia's Day*, 21.
Dublin Review, The, 256.
Duclaux, Mary, *Robert Browning: Étude sur sa pensée et sa vie*, 173, 195-6.
Dulwich Wood, 47.
Dureresque, 83.
Durham, University of, 37.
Dynasts, The, by Thomas Hardy, 86, 87 and n. 3, 219, 220, 221, 223, 224.

'Earth and a Wedded Woman', by George Meredith, 83.
'Earth and Man', by George Meredith, 83, 199, 265.
'Earth's Immortalities', 118.
'Earth's Preference', by George Meredith, 83.
'Easter Day', 29, 177, 182, 192, 265.
Ecclesiasticus xxxvii. 14, 10.
'Echetlos', 175.
Eckhart, compared with Browning, 262.
Eddas, 220.
Eddington, Sir Arthur, *Science and the Unseen World*, 216 and n. 1.
Eliot, George, 58.
Eliot, T. S., 'The Hollow Man: A Penny for the Old Guy', 23, 24, 95 ('Rhapsody on a Windy Night'), 107 (*The Waste Land*), 109, 110, 166, 167.
Eliot, T. S., 23, 24, 95, 107, 109, 110, 166, 167.
 Poems quoted:
 'Aunt Helen', 109.
 'Boston Evening Transcript, The', 109.
 'Cooking Egg, A', 108.
 'Cousin Nancy', 108.
 'Hollow Men: A Penny for the Old Guy, The', 23-4.
 'Rhapsody on a Windy Night', 95.
 Waste Land, The, 107-8.
Elizabeth Barrett Browning: Letters to her Sister, 1846-59, 131; and quoted from, 233-43.
Elton, Oliver, *The Brownings*, 26.
England and other Poems, by Laurence Binyon, 209.
English, The, Keyserling's description of, in *Europe*, 3, 17.
'Enoch Arden', by Tennyson, 36, 60; 61, 80.
Epilogue, personal to Browning's last volume, 181.
'Epistle containing the strange medical experience of Karshish, the Arab Physician, An' (referred to as 'The Epistle' or 'Karshish', or, by Mrs. Browning, as 'Lazarus'), 142, 144, 164, 174, 175, 192, 242, 259, 265, 268, 269.
Essay on Masefield, by C. H. Sorley, 67.
Ethick in *The Testament of Beauty*, by Robert Bridges, 213, 216.
Eton, 39.
Euripides, 1, 50.
Europe, by Hermann Keyserling, 3, 17.
'Evelyn Hope', 58 n. 1, 181.
'Evil', by W. H. Davies, 70.
Evolution, 197, 199, 200, 216.

'Facts', by W. H. Davies, 74.
'Faith on Trial, A', by George Meredith, 83, 264, 265.
'Fallen, The', by Laurence Binyon, 103, 104.
Faucit, Helen, 240.
Felippa (or Pippa), 7.
Fifine at the Fair, 87 n. 2.
'Fish, The', by Rupert Brooke, 97.
Five Nations, The, by Rudyard Kipling, 149.
Flecker, James Elroy, 50, 116; *Hassan*, 87 n. 2; 219.
Fleet Street Eclogues (Second Series), by John Davidson, 55, 99, 146-8.
'Flight of the Duchess, The', 9, 33, 43, 44, 60, 68, 82, 276.

INDEX

Florence, 8, 238, 239, 246, 247; the tablet to Mrs. Browning at, 248.
Flotsam and Jetsam, by Alfred Domett, 114.
Foch, Marshal, 13, 17.
Fox, George, 26.
'Fra Lippo Lippi', 129, 130 n. 1, 163.
Freud, *The Psychopathology of Everyday Life*, 132.
'Frosty Morning, A', by John Davidson, 93-4.
'Fuzzy Wuzzy', by Rudyard Kipling, 61.

'Galahad, Sir', by Tennyson, 111.
'G.B.S.', 1.
Gebhart, quoted by H. V. Routh, 273.
George, A. J., 261 n. 1.
Georgian Poetry, 63, 64, 101.
Gerhardi, 106, 112.
'German Rain', by Charles Sorley, 104 n. 1.
Gilbert, W. S., *Pinafore*, 146.
Gissing, 76 n. 3.
'Giuseppe Caponsacchi', 6 n. 1., 121, 125.
Gladstone, Mary, Diaries and Letters of, 39 n. 1, 183 n. 2, 195.
God, Man, and Epic Poetry, by H. V. Routh, 273.
Good Friday, by John Masefield, 68.
Goodrich, Arthur, 6 n. 1.
Gower Street, University of London in, 37, 38.
Graham, David, 6 n. 1.
'Grail, The Holy', by Tennyson, 111.
'Grammarian's Funeral, A', 31, 32 and n. 1, 58 n. 2, 181.
'Grantchester' ('The Old Vicarage'), by Rupert Brooke, 160, 161.
Graves, Robert, 23 n. 3, 103, 104, 109, 165, 166, 167.
    Poems quoted:
    'College Debate, The', 165.

Graves, Robert (*cont.*).
    'Letter to a Friend', 167.
    'Leveller, The', 103, 104.
    'Richard Rolls to his friend, Captain Abel Wright', 166.
Gray, Thomas, 22.
'Great Lover, The', by Rupert Brooke, 160, 205.
Griffin, W. H., *Life of Robert Browning*, 3, 16, 130 n. 1, 194.
'Guardian Angel, The', 179, 180.
Guercino, 179.
'Guido', 28, 29, 30, 125, 126.

Haddon, Alexander, 6 n. 1.
'Half Rome', 125.
Hallam, Arthur, 113.
Hamilton, Clayton, 6 n. 1.
Hamlet, by Shakespeare, 187, 263.
Hampden, Walter, 6 n. 1.
Handbook to the works of Robert Browning, A, by Mrs. Sutherland Orr, 7, 9, 183 n. 2.
Hardy, Thomas, on the *essence* of Browning, 11; 86, 87 n. 3; 'Afterwards' analysed, 88, 89, 90; conversational method in, 156, 178; reaction against optimism, 198; 199, 200; preface to *Winter Words*, 216; 217, 218, 219; preface to *The Dynasts*, 219, 221; philosophy, 222-4.
    Poems quoted:
    'Afterwards', 88.
    Dynasts, The, 221.
    'Reluctant Confession', 156.
    'War-Wife of Catknoll, The', 156.
'Harlot, The', by Humbert Wolfe, 164.
Haworth, Miss, 244, 245.
Haymarket Theatre, 240.
Head, Dr., 26.
Henley, W. E., 144-6.
    Poems quoted:
    'Apparition', 146.
    'In Hospital', 145.
    'Romance', 145.
Henrietta (Mrs. Browning's sister),

229; Letters to, 233-44; her death, 243.
'Heretic's Tragedy, The', 276 n. 1.
Herford, C. H., *Robert Browning*, 33.
'Hervé Riel', 175.
'Highway Pimpernel, A', by John Davidson, 53.
Hodell, C. W., 6 n.
Hodgson, Ralph, 97.
Hodgson, Shadworth, 26.
'Hollow Men, The', by T. S. Eliot, 24.
'Holy Cross Day', 58 n. 2, 75, 76, 77.
Homer, 79.
Hope End House (Edward Barratt's home), 229.
Hopkins, Gerard, 167.
Horace, 164.
Hornbrooke, F. B., 6 n. 1.
'Hospital', by Walter de la Mare, 206.
Hound of Heaven, The, by Francis Thompson, 257.
Housman, A. E., 55; *A Shropshire Lad* and *Last Poems* quoted, 91, 92; conversations in *A Shropshire Lad*, 153, 154; 155; reaction against optimism, 197; 216; *A Shropshire Lad* and *Last Poems* quoted, 225, 226, 277.
'How they brought the Good News from Ghent to Aix', 82.
Hudibras, 22.
Hume, David Dunglass, 240, 241, 242.
Huxley, L., 233.

Iago, compared with Guido, 78.
Idols, The, by Laurence Binyon, 208.
Idylls, The, of the King, by Tennyson, 35, 102, 111, 133 n. 1.
Iliad, The (Homer), 220.
'Imagination's Pride, The', by Walter de la Mare, 205.
Imagists, The, 106, 107.
'Impudence', by W. H. Davies, 74.

Incondita, 4.
Inge, Dean, 168, 258.
Ingelow, Miss, 250.
In Memoriam (xxxi), by Tennyson, 143, 144.
'Instans Tyrannus', 43.
'In the Dock', by Walter de la Mare, 100.
Intuition, 263 and ff., 263 n. 1, 273-7.
'Italian in England, The', 44.
'Ixion', 182, 183-6.

James, Henry, 71; *The Novel in 'The Ring and the Book'*, 143.
Jameson, Mrs. ('Aunt Nina'), 236.
'Janeites, The', by Rudyard Kipling, 139, 140, 141.
Jarvis, Mr., 241.
'Jenny', by W. H. Davies, 72.
'Johannes Agricola in Meditation', 123.
Johnson, Dr. Samuel, Boswell's *Life of*, 1, 2; *Lives of the English Poets*, 21, 22.
Jones, Sir Henry, *Browning as a Philosophical and Religious Teacher*, 32 n. 1.
Juliana of Norwich, 253.
Just So Stories, by Rudyard Kipling, 62.

Kasprowicz, J., 6 n. 1.
Keats, on the poetical nature, 12, 21; 262.
Keeling, F. H., 202.
Kenyon, Sir F. G., ed. of *New Poems by Robert and Mrs. Browning*, 41, 118, 270.
Kenyon, John, 233, 234, 237, 243.
Ker, W. P., *The Art of Poetry*, 260.
Keyserling, Hermann, description of the English in *Europe*, 3, 12, 17, 18; *Creative Understanding*, 19, 20; *The World in the Making*, 222, 223.
King Lear, by Shakespeare, 276.
Kipling, J. Lockwood, 57.
Kipling, Rudyard, 35; common

INDEX

humanity in, 56–62; education, 57; letters from, 58; *Stalky and Co.*, 58, 68; Nature-realism in, 93; animal poems, 95; 104; short story method, 134–41; conversational method in his poetry, 148–53; optimism, 201, 202.
   Poems quoted:
Barrack Room Ballads, 148, 149.
'Chant Pagan', 149.
Dedication to T. A. (*Barrack Room Ballads*), 60.
'If —', 150.
'McAndrew's Hymn', 151, 152.
'Of all the Tribe of Tegumai', 62.
Kirkup, Mr., 240.
'Kitchener's School', by Rudyard Kipling, 62.

'Lark in the Morn, The' (folk-song), 155.
'La Saisiaz', 67 n. 3, 187, 188, 192.
Last Ballad and other Poems, The, by John Davidson, 52.
Last Poems, by A. E. Housman, 90, 92, 154, 226.
'Last Ride Together, The', 180, 181.
Laurence, Miss, 170.
Lawrence, Lady, 195 n. 1.
'Lazarus', *see under* 'An Epistle of Karshish . . .'
Leighton, Lord, 248.
Letters of Robert Browning and Elizabeth Barrett, 5, 37, and *passim*; 229–32.
Letters of Robert Browning to Miss Isa Blagden, 15, 33, 37, 80, 111, 113, 244–51.
Letters of Sir Walter Raleigh, 228, 234.
'Letter to a friend', by Robert Graves, 167.
'Leveller, The', by Robert Graves, 103.
Life and Letters, 96.
Life of Robert Browning, The, by W.

Hall Griffin and H. C. Minchin, 3, 16, 130 n. 1, 194.
Lima, The, 250.
'Listeners, The', by Walter de la Mare, 157.
Literary Studies, by Walter Bagehot, 75.
Liverpool Cathedral, 253.
Llantysilio, 240.
Lodge, Sir Oliver, *Man and the Universe*, 26, 27; 216.
'London Snow', by Robert Bridges, 93.
'London Town', by John Masefield, 64.
London, University of, 4, 37.
Love Chase, The, 257.
'Love in a Valley', by George Meredith, 84, 85.
Love's Labour's Lost, by Shakespeare, 106.

Macbeth, by Shakespeare, 17.
Macdonald, Alice (mother of Rudyard Kipling), 57.
Macready, Charles, 243.
'Madhouse Cells', 121, 123.
Malory, Thomas, 65.
Malvern, 229.
Manchester Guardian, The, 65.
'Mandalay', by Rudyard Kipling, 60, 61.
Mansfield, Katherine, 106.
'Married Man, The', by Rudyard Kipling, 62.
Marsh, Edward, ed. of *Georgian Poetry*, 63.
'Mary and Gabriel', by Rupert Brooke, 204.
'Mary Gloster, The', by Rudyard Kipling, 152.
Masefield, John, *Midsummer Night*, 35; 36; Common humanity in, 63–9; early career, 64, 65; 153; optimism of, 210 n. 1 and reference; poems of the middle period, 66, 67; letter from, 69; 70; nature-realism, 93; animal poems, 95; 104.

INDEX

Masefield, John (cont.).
  Poems quoted:
    'Biography', 64.
    'Fight on the Beech, The', 93.
    Salt Water Ballads (Poem prefaced to), 65.
    'Master Hugues of Saxe-Gotha', 47, 167.
Masterman, Lucy, ed. of *Mary Gladstone: Diaries and Letters*, 39.
Maud, by Tennyson, 130 n. 1, 173.
'Meeting at Night', 119, 120.
'Meeting House Hill', by Amy Lowell, 107.
'Memorabilia', 43.
Men and Women, 58, 241, 242.
Meredith George, 5, 80 n. 2; realistic manner of, 83–5, 104, 109, 110; *The Ordeal of Richard Feverel*, new method in, 135, 136; and Darwinism, 199; 228; mysticism of, 264, 265.
  Poems quoted:
    'Alsace-Lorraine', 85.
    'Love in a Valley', 85.
    'Spirit of Earth in Autumn, The', 85.
Meynell, Mrs. Alice, *Second Person Singular and Other Essays*, 169, 170, 171, 176, 195.
Middleton, Richard, 'On a Dead Child', 62.
Mill, J. S., 21.
Milne, A. A., *Mr. Pim Passes By*, 40.
Milsand, J., letter to, 11, 112, 241.
Milton, by William Blake, 2, 14, 17.
Milton, 69, 220.
Minchin, H. C., part author with W. H. Griffin of *The Life of Robert Browning*, see under Griffin.
Miracles, Browning's view of, and Saint John's view of, 189–91.
Miss Barrett's Elopement, by C. Linlanton, 228.
Modernists, The, 106, 167, 168.
'Money', by W. H. Davies, 74.
Morte d'Arthur, by Malory, 65, 112, 113.

Moulton Barrett, Elizabeth Barrett, *see under* Mrs. Browning.
'Muléykeh', 82, 97.
Murry, J. M., 20, 21.
Music, 18, 19, 20; poems on, 47.
'My Last Duchess', 43, 44, 117, 118 n. 1, 120, 122, 129, 163.
Mystic, 3 n. 1, 8 n. 1, 203; Chap. IX, *see* Browning's Reputation as a Mystic, 253–78.
Mysticism in English Literature, by C. F. E. Spurgeon, 262.

Napoleon, Ode on, by George Meredith, 84; suggested title of Thomas Hardy's drama, 86.
Napoleon III, 233.
Nettleship, J. T., 28 n. 1, 184.
New Ballads, by John Davidson, 52.
Newman, J. H., *The Idea of a University*, 30.
New Poems by Robert and Mrs. Browning, ed. by Sir F. G. Kenyon, 41 n. 1, 118 n. 1, 270.
New Zealand, Alfred Domett in, 113; Alfred Domett's epic of, 114; last letter of Robert Browning to Alfred Domett in (quoted), 114–15.
Nightingale, Florence, 253, 254.
'Northern Farmer, The', by Tennyson, 60.
'Northern Suburb, A', by John Davidson, 52.

Obscurity, 32–4.
'Of all the Tribe of Tegumai', by Rudyard Kipling, 62.
'Of Pacchiarotto', 24 n. 1, 169.
'Old Pictures in Florence', 81, 262.
'Old Vicarage, Grantchester', *see* 'Grantchester'.
Old Yellow Book, The, 48, 49.
Omond, T. S., 25.
'On a Dead Child', by Robert Bridges, 62;
  by Richard Middleton (quoted), 62.

INDEX

'One Thing Wanting', by W. H. Davies, 72.
'One Word More', 14, 58 n. 2, 242, 274.
On Relation of Poetry to Verse, by Sir Philip Hartog, 24 n. 2.
On Some Points in Browning's View of Life, by Bishop B. F. Westcott, 28, 170.
Optimism, Browning's (Chap. VI), see under Browning.
and Reaction against
Optimism in the Twentieth Century (Chap. VII), 197–227: the effect of Darwinism; the attitude of T. E. Brown and George Meredith; reaction in Hardy; remnants of Browning's faith, in John Davidson; Kipling's optimism; the change in Rupert Brooke's poetry; Walter de la Mare; philosophy of hope in Laurence Binyon and Robert Bridges (*The Testament of Beauty*), 197–216; reaction in Hardy and Housman more fully examined, 216–27.
Ordeal of Richard Feverel, The, by George Meredith, 135.
Origin of Species, by Charles Darwin, 197, 198.
'Other Half Rome, The', 121, 125.

Palmer, Miss Rose, 6 n. 1.
Paracelsus, 171, 262.
Paradise Lost, by Milton, 220.
'Parting at Morning', 118, 119 n. 1, 120.
Patmore, Coventry, 262.
'Patriot, The', 178, 179.
Peacock Pie, by Walter de la Mare, 157, 159.
'Pelleas and Ettarre', by Tennyson, 133 n. 1.
Pen (Browning's son), 57 n. 2, 238, 240, 246, 248.
Phaedo, by Plato, 188.
'Pharaoh and the Sergeant', by Rudyard Kipling, 62.

'Pheidippides', 175.
Phelps, William Lyon, 6 n. 1.
'Piet', by Rudyard Kipling, 62.
'Pigs and the Charcoal Burners, The', by Walter de la Mare, 159.
Pinafore, by W. S. Gilbert (and Arthur Sullivan), 146.
Pioneer, The (of India), 57.
'Piper Play!' by John Davidson, 54.
'Pippa Passes', origin of, 6, 7, 8; 17, 18; 40; 98, 99; optimism of, 171–3; 176; 276.
Pisa, 230, 231, 233.
'Pisgah Sights', 177.
Pistoia, 240.
Plato, 188, 262.
Plotinus, 257.
Poems and Lyrics of the Joy of Earth, by George Meredith, 83.
Poetry, by Sir A. Quiller Couch, 18, 19;
Poetry as the highest use of language, 20; what constitutes, 20–25; Keats's definition of, 12, 21; Dr. S. Johnson on, 21, 22; reading and hearing of, 25–34; Robert Browning's view of, and Tennyson's view of, 79–80; use of metaphor, 91 n. 1; Ruskin on realism in, 102; W. P. Ker and Wordsworth on, 260, 261.
Poetry and Contemporary Speech, by Lascelles Abercrombie, 155.
Poetry To-Day, by J. A. Williams, 260.
'Pompilia', 6 n. 1; play by David Graham, 6 n; 125; recollections of childhood in, 126–9; 142, 163.
'Pope, The', 6 n. 1, 30, 48, 125, 182, 183.
'Popularity', 82.
Pornic, 246.
'Porphyria's Lover', 121, 123, 125, 137.
Prato, 240.
Prelude, The, by Wordsworth, 274.
Priestley, J. B., on George Meredith's method, 135, 136.

INDEX

'Prince Hohenstiel-Schwangau', 262.
Principles of Literary Criticism, by Ivor Armstrong, 25 n. 2.
Proctor, Mrs., 7.
'Prospice', 31, 32 n. 1, 72, 181, 272.
'Prothalamion', by Spenser, 108.
Psychologist, Browning the (Chap. IV), *see under* Browning.
Psychology, 'crowd', 129 n. 1.
Psychopathology of Everyday Life, The, and Introductory Lectures on Psycho-Analysis, by S. Freud, 132.
Puck of Pook's Hill, by Rudyard Kipling, 68.
Purtscher, Mr. Alphons, 95.
Pye, Miss Sybil, 96.

'*Quia amore langueo*', 257.

'Rabbi Ben Ezra', 176, 182, 193.
Raleigh, Sir Walter, Letters of, 201, 202, 229 n. 1, 234.
Ranolf and Amohia, by Alfred Domett, 114.
Reading of Earth, A, by George Meredith, 83.
Realistic Manner of Browning and of Twentieth-century Poets, The (Chap. III), 75–110:
    Browning's *grotesque* art; definition of realism. § I, nature realism: examples from Browning, Meredith, Hardy, Housman, Davies, Kipling, Masefield, Davidson, Wolfe, T. S. Eliot, Rupert Brooke, Ralph Hodgson. § II, human realism: examples from Browning, Davidson, Walter de la Mare, Lascelles Abercrombie, Robert Graves (contrasted with Laurence Binyon), Charles Sorley, Amy Lowell, Edith Sitwell, T. S. Eliot.
Realistic Revolt in Modern Poetry, The, by A. M. Clark, 63.
'Recessional, The', by Rudyard Kipling, 61 n. 1.

Red Cotton Night-Cap Country, 32 n. 2.
'Reluctant Confession', by Thomas Hardy, 156.
Reminiscences of My Father's Early Life, by Sir Francis Darwin, 273, 274.
Reputation as a Lover, Browning's (Chap. VIII); as a Mystic (Chap. IX); *see under* Browning.
Requiem, by Humbert Wolfe, 162, 163, 164.
'Respectable Woman, The', by Humbert Wolfe, 163–4.
'Revolution', by A. E. Housman, 266.
Rewards and Fairies, by Rudyard Kipling, 139.
Reynard the Fox, by John Masefield, 68, 95.
'Rhapsody on a Windy Night', by T. S. Eliot, 95.
Riccardi Palace, 8.
'Richard Rolls to his friend, Captain Abel Wright', by Robert Graves, 166.
Riding, Laura, 23 n. 3.
Right Royal, by John Masefield, 68, 95.
Ring and the Book, The, 6 n. 1; origin of, 8, 9; 14, 15; help in writing, 16, 17; G. K. Chesterton and Bishop Westcott on 'Guido', 28–31; 29 n. 2; story of, 48–9; 50; length of, 57 n. 1; 78; effect of Browning's achievement, 86, 87; 112, 120, 121, 122, 123, 125–9, 131, 132, 133, 134, 139, 142, 182, 183, 263 n. 1, 271, 272, 273, 275 n. 1.
Robert Browning, by C. H. Herford, 33.
Robert Browning: Humanist, by A. Compton-Rickett, 23.
Rollin, Ledru, 238.
'Romance', by W. E. Henley, 145.
Rossetti, Dante Gabriel, 130 n. 1, 134, 196.
Routh, H. V., on realism, 76 n. 3; 273.

INDEX

'Rudel to the Lady of Tripoli', 23 n. 2.

St. Aubin-sur-Mer, 251.
Saint Augustine, 224.
'St. George's Day', by John Davidson, 146, 147.
Saint Joan, 264, 271 n. 1.
St. John's, Cambridge, 113.
Saint John's Gospel, view of miracles in, 189–91.
St. Marylebone Parish Church, 232.
Saint Paul, his summary of the Christian Faith, 191–2.
'Saint-She, The', by Humbert Wolfe, 163.
'St. Valentine's Eve', by John Davidson, 55.
'Sale of St. Thomas, The', by Lascelles Abercrombie, 101.
Salt Water Ballads, by John Masefield, 65, 66.
Sarianna (Browning's sister), 246.
Sassoon, Siegfried, 165.
'Saul', 40–42; 58 n. 2, 180, 265, 270.
Savery, Frank, 87.
Second Person Singular and Other Essays, The, by Alice Meynell, 169, 195.
Secret, The, by Laurence Binyon, 208.
'Serenade at a Villa, A', 82.
Seven Seas, The, by Rudyard Kipling, 56.
Shakespeare, 2, 17, 18, 75, 77, 106, 109, 116, 157, 170, 186, 187, 198, 263.
Sharp, Cecil J., 3, 155.
Shelley, 38, 196.
Shropshire Lad, A, by A. E. Housman, 90–2; 153, 154, 225, 277.
Sidney, Sir Philip, *An Apologie for Poetrie*, 21 n. 1.
Sienna, 251.
Sirens, The, by Laurence Binyon, 207–8.

'Sirmione', by Laurence Binyon, 209.
Sitwell, Edith, 107 n. 2, 165.
'Sludge the Medium, Mr.', 141, 142, 241.
Smith, Sydney, 155.
'Soldier, The', by Humbert Wolfe, 164;
  by Rupert Brooke, 205.
Soldiers Three, by Rudyard Kipling, 60.
'Soliloquy of the Spanish Cloister', 59.
'Song of Life, A', by W. H. Davies, 70.
'Song of Love, A', by W. H. Davies, 74.
'Song of the Beasts, The', by Rupert Brooke, 96.
'Song of the Exposition', by Walt Whitman, 24.
'Song of the Road, A', by John Davidson, 54.
Songs of Childhood, by Walter de la Mare, 158.
'Sonnet Reversed', by Rupert Brooke, 161.
Sonnets from the Portuguese, by Elizabeth Barrett Browning, 9 n. 1.
Sordello, 38, 112, 171.
Sorley, Charles, 104, 105, 164, 165.
'Speculative', 252.
Spenser, 108, 109.
'Spirit of Earth in Autumn, The', by George Meredith, 83, 85.
'Spleen, The', in Dodsley's *Collection*, 21.
'Spring', by John Davidson, 53.
Spurgeon, Caroline, F. E., *Mysticism in English Literature*, 262.
Stalky and Co., by Rudyard Kipling, references to Browning in, 58, 59.
'Statue and the Bust, The', 112, 178.
Stephens, James, 101.
Stevenson, R. L., 146.

INDEX

Strauss, Richard, 19.
'Strayed Reveller, The', by Matthew Arnold, 73.
'Sunset', by E. C. Cummings, 23.
Survey of Modernist Poetry, A, by Laura Riding and Robert Graves, 23 n. 3.
Svendsen, 167.
Synge, J. M., 65 n. 3.

Tate Gallery, The, 130 n. 1.
Tempest, The, by Shakespeare, 40, 108.
Tennyson, 60, 61, 71 n. 1, 79, 80, 93, 101; Ruskin's letter to, on realism, 102; letter of Robert Browning about the art of, 111; 112, 131 n. 1, 133, 134, 143, 144, 173, 196, 241.
'Ten Years Ago: A Talk with Marshal Foch', from *The Times*, 13.
'Tertium Quid', 121, 125.
Tess of the D'Urbervilles, by Thomas Hardy, 224.
Testament of an Empire Builder, The, by John Davidson, 51.
Testament of a Man Forbid, The, by John Davidson, 51, 55.
Testament of a Prime Minister, The, by John Davidson, 51.
Testament of a Vivisector, The, by John Davidson, 51.
Testament of Beauty, The, by Robert Bridges, 209-15.
Testament of John Davidson, 51, 56, 201.
'Thirty Bob a Week', by John Davidson, 52.
Thompson, Francis, 254, 255, 256, 257.
'Through Gilded Trellisses', by Edith Sitwell, 107 and n. 2.
Times, The, 5, 13, 195 n. 1.
'Tithonus', by Tennyson, 76.
Titian, 213.
'Toccata of Galuppi's, A', 47.
'Tray', 95.

Twentieth-century Literature, by A. C. Ward, 217.

United Services College, 57, 58.
Unjust Steward, The, parable of, 178.
Unknown Goddess, The, by Humbert Wolfe, 94.
'Up at a Villa—Down in the City', 80.

Veil and Other Poems, The, by Walter de la Mare, 100-1.
Vernon, Prebendary John, 28 n. 1.
Victorian Age in Literature, The, by G. K. Chesterton, 27-8, 31.
'Voice, The', by Rupert Brooke, 160.

'Wage Slaves, The', by Rudyard Kipling, 62.
Wagner, 109.
Wanley, Nathanael, *The Wonders of the Little World*, 38 n. 1.
'Waring', 59; original of Alfred Domett, 113.
Warwick Crescent, No. 19 (Browning's home in London), 247.
'War-Wife of Catknoll, The', by Thomas Hardy, 156.
Waste Land, The, by T. S. Eliot, 107-8.
'West, The', by A. E. Housman, 90.
Westcott, Bishop B. F., 28 n. 1; 29-31, 170 n. 1, 255.
'White Man's Burden, The', by Rudyard Kipling, 61.
'White Witchcraft', 23 n. 2.
Whitman, Walt, 24, 25, 63, 109.
Widow in the Bye-Street, The, by John Masefield, 64, 66.
Wilson (Mrs. Browning's maid), 232, 235, 236.
Wimpole Street, No. 50 (E.B.B.'s home), 229.
'Wind, The', by W. H. Davies, 92.

INDEX

'Wind on the Lyre, The', by George Meredith, 265.
'Wine of Cyprus', by Mrs. Browning, 50.
Winter Words, by Thomas Hardy, 95, 156, 216–17, 222.
'With Scindia to Delhi', by Rudyard Kipling, 61.
Wolfe, Humbert, 94, 162–4.
'Woman and her Son, A', by John Davidson, 21.
'Wondering Brown', by W. H. Davies, 73.
Wonders of the Little World, The, by N. Wanley, 38 n. 1.
'Wood of Westermain', by George Meredith, 83.
Wordsworth, William, his definition of poetry, 13; *Lyrical Ballads*, 36, 196, 198; on poetry, 260–1; *The Prelude*, 274.
World in the Making, The, by Hermann Keyserling, 233.
'Wrong Thing, The', by Rudyard Kipling, 139–40.

Years Between, The, by Rudyard Kipling, 57.
Yeats, W. B., *Countess Cathleen*, 256.
Youth, by Joseph Conrad, story of, 137–9.